THE PSYCHE
OF FEMINISM

Purdue Studies in Romance Literatures

Editorial Board

Floyd Merrell, Series Editor
Jeanette Beer
Paul B. Dixon

Benjamin Lawton
Howard Mancing
Allen G. Wood

Associate Editors

French
Paul Benhamou
Willard Bohn
Gerard J. Brault
Mary Ann Caws
Gérard Defaux
Milorad R. Margitić
Glyn P. Norton
Allan H. Pasco
Gerald Prince
David Lee Rubin
Roseann Runte
Ursula Tidd

Italian
Fiora A. Bassanese
Peter Carravetta
Franco Masciandaro
Anthony Julian Tamburri

Luso-Brazilian
Fred M. Clark
Marta Peixoto
Ricardo da Silveira Lobo Sternberg

Spanish and Spanish American
Maryellen Bieder
Catherine Connor
Ivy A. Corfis
Frederick A. de Armas
Edward Friedman
Charles Ganelin
David T. Gies
Roberto González Echevarría
Patricia Hart
David K. Herzberger
Emily Hicks
Djelal Kadir
Amy Kaminsky
Lucille Kerr
Alberto Moreiras
Randolph D. Pope
Francisco Ruiz Ramón
Elżbieta Skłodowska
Mario Valdés
Howard Young

PSRL volume 28

THE PSYCHE OF FEMINISM

Sand,

Colette,

Sarraute

Catherine M. Peebles

Purdue University Press
West Lafayette, Indiana

Copyright ©2004 by Purdue University. All rights reserved.

08   07   06   05   04   5   4   3   2   1

♾The paper used in this book meets the minimum requirements of
American National Standard for Information Sciences—Permanence of
Paper for Printed Library Materials, ANSI Z39.48-1992.

Printed in the United States of America
Design by Anita Noble

Library of Congress Cataloging-in-Publication Data
Peebles, Catherine M., 1968–
　The psyche of feminism : Sand, Colette, Sarraute / Catherine M.
Peebles.
　　　p.　cm. — (Purdue studies in Romance literatures ; v. 28)
Includes bibliographical references and index.
　ISBN 1-55753-329-6 (pbk.)
1. French fiction—Women authors—History and criticism. 2. French
fiction—20th century—History and criticism. 3. French fiction—19th
century—History and criticism. 4. Feminism and literature—France—
History—20th century. 5. Feminism and literature—France—History—
19th century. 6. Women and literature—France—History—19th century.
7. Psychoanalysis and feminism—France. 8. Sand, George, 1804–1876—
Criticism and interpretation. 9. Colette, 1873–1954—Criticism and
interpretation. 10. Sarraute, Nathalie—Criticism and interpretation.
I. Title. II. Series.

PQ673.P44 2003
843'.91099287—dc22
　　　　　　　　　　　　　　　　　　　　　　　　2003019825

For Petar

Contents

viii **List of Abbreviations**
ix **Preface**
xv **Acknowledgments**
1 **Introduction**
   Psychoanalytic Feminism: Sexual Difference and Another Love
33 **Chapter One**
   George Sand and the Impossible Woman
87 **Chapter Two**
   What Does a Woman Enjoy? Colette's *Le pur et l'impur*
126 **Chapter Three**
   Nathalie Sarraute: After the Feminine Subject
163 **Conclusion**
   The Psyche of Feminism
173 **Appendix**
   English Translations
197 **Notes**
211 **Bibliography**
227 **Index**

List of Abbreviations

To aid those readers who prefer to see excerpts in English, I have provided English translations of French quotations. The longer translations are gathered in the appendix, keyed in the text by the number in brackets that follows the French reference. For the reader's convenience, I have provided page references to published English translations where possible. However, in most cases the translations themselves are my own, as I have preferred to give as literal a rendering as possible of the French. When I have used someone else's translation, I make note of this in the reference.

EDS
 Irigaray, Luce, *Ethique de la différence sexuelle*
ESD
 Irigaray, Luce, *An Ethics of Sexual Difference*
PI
 Colette, *Le pur et l'impur*
SE
 Freud, Sigmund, *The Standard Edition of the Complete Psychological Works of Sigmund Freud*
XX
 Lacan, Jacques, *Le séminaire de Jacques Lacan, Livre XX, "Encore"*

Preface

> Quel lien autre que celui de la force pourra exister désormais entre celui qui a le droit d'exiger et celle qui n'a pas le droit de refuser? [. . .] Quel échange de sentiments, quelle fusion d'intelligences possible entre le maître et l'esclave?
>
> George Sand
> *Lélia* [1]

> Instead of literature being, as is usually the case, submitted to the authority and to the knowledge of psychoanalysis, psychoanalysis itself would then here be submitted to the literary perspective. This reversal of the perspective, however, does not intend to simply reverse the positions of master and slave in such a way that literature would *take over* the place of the master, but rather its intention is to disrupt altogether the position of mastery as such.
>
> Shoshana Felman
> *Literature and Psychoanalysis*

George Sand's heroine Lélia explores, painfully, the impossibility of love between men and women given that their relation is characterized by the domination of the former and the submission of the latter. Shoshana Felman argues that the relation of psychoanalytic thought to literature is fundamentally impoverished when one discourse sets itself up as the master of the other. It is a basic premise of this book that there is a connection between what Jessica Benjamin has called the problem of domination, and the possibility of love, and that this connection may be explored fruitfully via the pursuit of a reading, a way of reading, that does not view the text (literary or psychoanalytical) as a series of questions to be answered or solved via the knowledge of another domain (literature, psychoanalysis).[1] If a text is not a question to be answered, a set of clues to be solved, how then, in what mode, do we read it? Felman suggests, otherwise, noting that the first step toward such reading is the recognition of the otherness of literature, and of psychoanalysis, with respect to each other:

Preface

> [literature] is therefore not simply a body of language to interpret, nor is psychoanalysis simply a body of knowledge with which to interpret, since psychoanalysis is itself equally a body of language, and literature also a body of knowledge, even though the mode of that knowledge may be different from that of psychoanalysis. What the literary critic might thus wish, is to initiate a real exchange, to engage in a real *dialogue* between literature and psychoanalysis, as between two different bodies of language and between two different modes of knowledge. Such a dialogue has to take place outside of the master-slave pattern, which does not allow for true dialogue, being, under the banner of competence, a unilateral monologue of psychoanalysis *about* literature. (Felman, *Literature and Psychoanalysis* 6)

To allow psychoanalytic thought and literature to implicate each other, speak to each other *as different* and related, will be an aim here, one that I hope will be furthered by the fact that it is not psychoanalysis *tout court* with which I am concerned, but psychoanalytic feminism. That is, a mode of psychoanalytic thought that recognizes and problematizes the question of sexual difference as inextricably bound up with both the patterns of individual psyches and lives *and* the foundations of domination, of subjectivity versus objectivity, in short, with the possibility of ethical relation, which includes the question of love, especially between the sexes. In reading psychoanalytic theory, feminist theory, and women's writing keeping in mind the implications of each for the other, I shall be seeking to initiate a discussion in which each discourse enlightens and is enlightened by, questions and is questioned by, the others.

"Women's Writing"

Addressing the status of women authors in the western literary tradition, Monique Wittig argues that the notion of "women writers" (upon which my choice of authors for this book must be seen as predicated, at least in part) is problematic in itself, together with the question of the reception of women authors into the canon. She says:

> To say that writers have been excluded from the canon because they are women not only seems to me inexact, but

Preface

> the very idea proceeds from a trend toward theories of victimization. There are a few great writers in any century. Each time there was one, not only was she welcome within the canon, but she was acclaimed, applauded, and praised in her time—sometimes *especially* because she was a woman. I'm thinking of Sand and Colette. I do not think that real innovators have been passed by. In the university, we ruin the purpose of what we do if we make a special category for women—especially when teaching. When we do that as feminists, we ourselves turn the canon into a male edifice. (Jardine and Menke 193)

Her argument is important for the questions of this book because it emphasizes the role women play in the perpetuation of their own subordination. In crying out for inclusion in the canon of Great Western Literature, for example, Wittig suggests that feminists may not be merely responding to and revolting against its masculinism, but actually propping it up. The question must be put then, whether in framing this book around women writers and women's writing, I unwittingly contribute to ruining the purpose of what we do (suspending, for the moment, the issue of who "we" are). Do I reinforce or (re)constitute the maleness of that edifice called the canon by naming an apparently special category into which certain females fall? One could argue that I do. But such a category may also, and on the contrary, function to transform that category called the "canon" or that category called "great writers." For if what we do in the university is essentially to read literature, then I would argue that "women writers" may refer more to a way of reading than to a group of authors—a way of reading that can ultimately be extended beyond the group of authors that the label "women writers" denotes. If, for example, George Sand or Colette were celebrated *especially* because they were women, this meant, among other things, that their writing could be (and was) read as saying something new, perhaps shocking, about women, and even about "Woman" (that question which historically was debated mainly among men). If, on the other hand, we read such authors as revealing something about *writing* itself, then the potential that their work may change what we understand writing to be cannot be overlooked. Specifically, we may be able to ask questions about the sex of writing, the

Preface

sex in writing, questions that in turn lead us to wonder what we mean by sex in this context, and what sex may have meant/ may mean in the writings of both women and men (cf. Christiane Rochefort's comment that even today, "A man's book is a book. A woman's book is a woman's book"[2]). The works I have chosen to consider in this book inaugurate such questions and insights.

This is not to say that reading women authors brings a new or different apprehension of sex(ual difference) alone. It is on the level of experience, too (so important in the works of such different writers as Sarraute, de Beauvoir, or Cixous, to name a few) that the newness of women's writing has its effects. To start with the most basic point: one of the things we, as women reading, can expect from women is *that they will write* (historically, a new expectation). And that when they write, they will give us a different voice to which to listen. Different (for each person's life is different), but not necessarily "feminine." One need hardly repeat that to be a woman is not necessarily to be either "feminine" or a feminist. But perhaps part of the reason that we scarcely need to emphasize this today is that women have been writing, in significant numbers, for a significant amount of time. And it was found, repeatedly, that their writings did not conform to the "femininity" some of their readers expected to find in them. I think of Rachilde's *Monsieur Vénus*, which Michel Barrès prefaced with the evidently titillating remark: "Ce qui est tout à fait délicat dans la perversité de ce livre, c'est qu'il a été écrit par une jeune fille de 20 ans" ("What is altogether delicate in the perversity of this book is that it was written by a young girl of twenty years"; Rachilde 5–6).[3] *Yes, a woman. . . and a maid at that!* is the general idea here, but just where this idea may lead is another story. If a woman writes this, then:

1. Just what *is* this? (i.e., what is literature?, what is eroticism?, what is desire?, what is love? . . .);

2. Just what is woman if she can write this? (it having been generally supposed that the fact that she could not/would not write this was among the things that distinguished her from us men); and

3. *(with anxiety)* Just what is man, assuming still that he is not that woman who writes?

Preface

And these questions lead to the contemporary situation in reference to which my choice to deal with women's writing has been made. One of the generally agreed upon responses to the second and third questions, from women, has been that whatever women and men may be, we women now refuse to be defined primarily and simply as man's other or negative. For a writer like Simone de Beauvoir, this will mean emphasizing that women *too* are subjects, equal to men if not the same as men. For a writer such as Hélène Cixous, this will mean that women can look for themselves and for their writing beyond what have been posited as their differences from men, in order, ultimately, to get "rid of words like 'feminine' and 'masculine,' 'femininity' and 'masculinity,' even 'man' and 'woman,' which designate that which cannot be classified inside of a signifier except by force and violence and which goes beyond it [the signifier] in any case" (Conley 129). And yet, as Cixous has been the first to insist (and celebrate), writing (which happens in the realm of the signifier) is, if anything, a space where such a transgression of forced categories (masculine/feminine) can take place. The signifier, for Cixous, carries within it the potential for its own rupture; so, I would suggest, with the categories of "women" and "men"; and so with that of "women writers."

The authors I will be reading, George Sand, Colette, and Nathalie Sarraute, write in more or less close relation to the identity crises of our time, and the fact that they are women is closely related to (though not necessarily determinative of) the way in which they pursue and represent these crises. One could say that women have been coming into a new way of being and living (personally, politically, sexually, intellectually, literarily, artistically . . .) just as the very notions of the person, the political, the sexual, etc., have ceased to hold fast to their traditional meanings, and have yet to take on new ones. Thus it should hardly be surprising that women writers participate ardently in the interrogation and re-creation of these concepts. As they do so, they suggest that the dispersal or "death" of the "subject" is at the same time, or on the contrary, the possibility for another life. On this note, I would like to cite a passage from Cixous's *Dedans,* which expresses this pursuit of the new or the unknown:

xiii

Preface

> je compris que la mort était une vie mystérieuse; et que l'horreur des voyages, la peur de l'inconnu, le dégoût du nouveau, la méfiance à l'égard du changement, gonflaient le petit bruit sourd, qui n'était que le bref craquement de l'imagination au bord du noir. "La mort" était l'ogre de ma grand-mère. Dans ma vie il n'y avait pas de place pour la mort; ma vie avait l'immensité de l'imaginable. La mort mourrait dans son propre nom, comme "rien," comme "Dieu," comme "certain," et tout ce qui était inimaginable.
> (Cixous, *Dedans* 21–22 [2])

For the purpose of this book what is "imaginable" (often barely imaginable) includes the subject of writing—in both senses of the word: subject matter, and more crucially, she who writes and subjects herself to writing, thereby reinventing both *herself* (the notion of the "self") and writing itself.

I begin, then, with an exploration of the relationship (actual, possible, and imagined) between feminism and psychoanalysis. The Introduction reviews the history of their entanglement and then argues, through a reading of Lacan's and Irigaray's respective articulations of sexual difference, for the centrality of a radical psychoanalysis to feminist thought, especially to feminist attempts to reconfigure or reimagine, in ethical terms, relations between men and women, masculine and feminine. The first chapter takes up two such attempts in the work of George Sand (an unfinished epistolary work called *Lettres à Marcie* [*Letters to Marcie*], and her genre-exploding "novel," *Lélia*) where the emphasis is on the social and political injustices of women's lot and the impossibility of their desire. Chapter 2 deals with a relatively little-read work of Colette's, *Le pur et l'impur* (*The Pure and the Impure*), in which the narrator speculates on pleasure, especially sensual pleasure, as the key to any understanding of masculinity and femininity. Chapter 3 investigates Nathalie Sarraute's contemporary work *Tu ne t'aimes pas* (You don't love yourself), asking whether it is possible, or perhaps even necessary, for psychoanalytic feminist thought to entertain the question of neutrality put forth in Sarraute's prose. I conclude that, despite the risks, the turn to a Sarrautean neutrality, to the idea that there is someone *after* the feminine subject, is indeed needed because of the room it provides for entirely unpredictable expressions of sexual difference and ethical relations.

Acknowledgments

The Psyche of Feminism began to take shape while I was a graduate student of Comparative Literature at the State University of New York at Binghamton. I thank the professors there who patiently guided and challenged the development of my thinking: Chris Fynsk, Marilyn Gaddis Rose, Tom Keenan, and Steven David Ross. The work could not have been completed without the equally important, sustained encouragement and critique offered by Anne Berger of Cornell University, nor without the generous reading of an early version of a chapter by Joan Copjec of SUNY Buffalo. I wish to thank as well the University of New Hampshire for its support, especially Dean Marilyn Hoskin and the College of Liberal Arts, Provost David Hiley and the Office of the Provost, and the Humanities Program.

The friends and colleagues who shared with me their criticism, conversation, and wit have my cheerful gratitude. I would like to thank, in particular, David Andrew, John Archer, Linda Belau, Rebecca Belfield, Donna and Warren Brown, Ed Cameron, Matt Cory, Bruce and Héloïse Fink, Pamela Genova, Robin Hackett, Brian Jacobs, Aurora Hermida Ruíz, Aida Hozic, Sean Kelly, Kiarina Kordela, Dragan Kujundzic, Mike Monti, Georgeann Murphy, Rosy Nimroodi, David Ost, Patti Palen, Max Pensky, Angelika Rauch-Rapaport, David and Susan Richman, Charlie Shepherdson, Connie Wortman, Emily Zakin, and Ewa Ziarek. In different ways, they each brought questions of the psyche home for me. My family, too, was a dependable source of support. Long before I began to think about this project my late father, Edward Metcalfe Peebles, had given me the loving gift of his confidence, which continues to sustain me. I also thank my mother, Ellen Moloney Peebles, and my siblings John, Mary Ellen, Ted, and Leslie.

Most of all, I am fortunate to be able to thank Petar Ramadanovic, to whom this book and much else besides is dedicated.

Introduction

Psychoanalytic Feminism
Sexual Difference and Another Love

Psychoanalytic feminism is a field that has only begun to emerge over the past three decades, and the question of what constitutes its approach is still being negotiated. Works by Luce Irigaray, Juliet Mitchell, and Sarah Kofman, as well as more recent explorations of the question of femininity in psychoanalytic theory such as Teresa Brennan's *Interpretation of the Flesh* (1992), Jessica Benjamin's *The Bonds of Love: Psychoanalysis, Feminism and the Problem of Domination* (1988), and those gathered in Richard Feldstein and Judith Roof's *Feminism and Psychoanalysis* (1989) have had an important influence, both in their content and in their spurring more scholars to attempt to speak from these two discourses simultaneously. As J. C. Smith and Carla J. Ferstman point out in *The Castration of Oedipus: Feminism, Psychoanalysis, and the Will to Power* (1996), such attempts are still in an early phase. The authors hold that there is as yet no field deserving of the name "psychoanalytic feminism," for the relation between the two fields is a difficult one:

> The paradox of feminism and psychoanalysis is [. . .] that the explanations are in terms of phallic possession or lack, seduction, and castration, all of which seem to privilege the Oedipal structure [. . .].[1] The relationship between traditional psychoanalytic theory and feminism, while important for each, remains ambivalent at best. (Smith and Ferstman 17)

To begin with, then, I should offer a word on why psychoanalytic theory is so important for feminist thought, and vice versa.

Psychoanalysis is fundamentally a discourse that explores sexuality and desire, and feminist theory one that interrogates

Introduction

gender difference and identity. Psychoanalytic theory can offer to feminist thought insights into the psychical workings of gendered sexualities, especially in terms of the role of the unconscious in the formation of an "identity" that can never again (after psychoanalysis) be understood as solid or unified. Feminist theory, for its part, offers psychoanalysis its questions about and insights into difference, particularly sexual and ethico-political differences, leading to what Elizabeth Wright calls "a space for [the] transformations" of both fields (Wright, Introduction xiii).[2] It will be central to my project of reading French women's writing to approach the literary texts having already begun to articulate a dynamic relation between these two bodies of thought that, as I shall argue, are enriched when taken up together, and impoverished when separated. There is thus a need to review some fundamental psychoanalytic and feminist notions and to rethink the most pressing concerns confronting psychoanalytic and feminist discourses, in order to present what may be a crucial intersection for the thinking of the two at once.

In order to approach one such intersection, I will devote a significant part of this Introduction to an examination of the question of sexual difference in the works of Jacques Lacan and Luce Irigaray, works that have been central to debates within both psychoanalytic theory and feminist thought. I will attempt to show the importance for psychoanalytic feminism of what Irigaray calls an ethical sexual difference, and to explore the difficulties involved in thinking such a relation. The last part of this chapter will concern itself with two of the most critical of these difficulties: the question of feminine jouissance and the question of love, as they intersect in both Irigaray's and Lacan's thought. It is from these two questions that I will go on to pursue the writings of Sand, Colette, and Sarraute in the chapters that follow. By way of introduction, I will begin by briefly outlining the background, in feminism and in psychoanalysis, against which these questions have emerged.

Feminism and Psychoanalysis

Luce Irigaray's *Speculum, de l'autre femme* (1974) and *Ce sexe qui n'en est pas un* (1977), and Juliet Mitchell's *Psychoanaly-*

Introduction

sis and Feminism (1974) inaugurated specifically feminist engagements with psychoanalysis that went beyond an understanding of psychoanalysis primarily or solely as a discourse that posits or seeks to reinforce the inferiority of women (for example, Simone de Beauvoir's 1949 *Le deuxième sexe*,[3] and Betty Friedan's 1963 *The Feminine Mystique*). While Irigaray and Mitchell engage in a feminist approach to psychoanalytic theory, they choose to do so from within that theory, believing that psychoanalysis, especially when informed by feminist thought, can offer critical insight into questions surrounding sexual difference. From the 1970s on, then, feminist writers begin to work within psychoanalytic discourse while challenging it.[4] In reading Irigaray's work (including her more recent texts where psychoanalysis plays a much smaller role) as psychoanalytic as well as feminist, I am implicitly arguing for an understanding of psychoanalytic feminism not as a theory nor as a set of common assumptions, but most importantly as a feminist thinking that is not enslaved to (or duped by) the reign of the ego and its claims on unity, identity, equality, complementarity, and so on. In this sense, then, although Irigaray's work since the eighties is not primarily concerned with psychoanalytic theory, it constitutes (or ought to constitute) an important contribution to it. In considering psychoanalytic feminism, I will be concerned with such a double engagement, and with works that perform such an engagement. I will not be treating authors who continue to assert that psychoanalysis deserves the unequivocal censure of feminist thinkers. I would like to take a moment, however, to discuss precisely why I assert the limitations of such a refusal of psychoanalysis from a feminist perspective, for a discussion of these limitations will help to clarify from the outset what is at stake in a psychoanalytic feminism.

Diana Tietjens Meyer's *Subjection and Subjectivity* (1994), for example, takes Freud to task for the answers he comes up with in response to his questions about femininity.[5] She writes:

> Psychoanalysis has long had an ugly reputation among feminists, and this reputation is richly deserved, for Freud's account of femininity is condescending and narrow-minded. He privileges masculine sexuality—a girl's sexuality is masculine until she discovers that her clitoris is much smaller

Introduction

> than a penis, contracts penis envy, and evolves a secondary feminine sexuality. He belittles women's anatomy—they are castrated. He besmirches women's character and intellect—they are jealous, narcissistic, less exacting in matters of morality, and less creative than men. Freud's psychological configurations of gender codify and seek to ratify cultural conventions and expectations regarding maternity and female domesticity [. . .]. Freud supplied some of the most damaging and pervasive imagery working in Western culture to sustain unconscious prejudice against women [. . .]. Still, I believe that some psychoanalytic feminists have successfully modified Freud's rhetoric to redress the relations of domination and subordination between men and women that he used it to reinforce. (62–63)

Let us consider the assumptions at work here. First, "psychoanalysis" equals "Freud" or the "rhetoric" of Freud. Second, psychoanalysis is that thing which Freud somehow finds/founds and then *uses* to his own end, that end being the reinforcement of the subordination of women to men, as well as the sustaining of an unconscious prejudice against women. Third, psychoanalytic feminism is of some worth insofar as it *modifies* Freud in order to *redress* relations of dominance and subordination, as if it could stand somewhere outside of those relations in a corrective mode.

First of all, in reducing psychoanalysis to Freud, Meyers ignores Freud's contemporaries, female and male, and their various and often contradictory contributions to psychoanalytic theory,[6] preferring instead a simplified version of the field, represented by one name, the name of the father of psychoanalysis. She also reads Freud's relation to psychoanalysis as an unproblematic one: psychoanalysis is that doctrine that consists in a certain rhetoric that demeans women, and Freud a thinker who unequivocally asserts this doctrine, not a thinker who, in fact, expresses doubts about both the conclusions he comes to and the questions he asks. In his 1931 essay "Female Sexuality," for example, Freud explicitly notes the insufficiency of penis envy, among other explanatory attempts, to account for infantile female psychical development (specifically, to account for why the girl turns away in hostility from her mother, displacing that object-cathexis onto her father; *SE* 21: 234). Rather than remarking Freud's *exposure* of cultural norms and expectations (precisely *as* normative and cultural, as opposed to natu-

Introduction

rally given), Meyers insists on reading him as an enforcer of these. Only in this picture can psychoanalytically oriented feminists be seen as entering upon the scene simply in order to redress Freud's (read, psychoanalysis's) injustices.

Meyers is of course quite right to note that feminists have modified psychoanalytic theory—that is, that they have brought new questions and perspectives to the fore, and these have in turn affected how sexuality and sexual difference are understood and approached psychoanalytically. What she ignores is that these theorists are grappling with questions—most notably the question of "femininity"—to which Freud did not pretend to have the final answers. Freud did, however, establish certain fundamentals—e.g., the unconscious, repression, fantasy, and infantile sexuality—from and with which he and contemporary thinkers work. These Freudian fundamentals go unacknowledged in such writing as Meyers's even as she makes use of them in order to reveal Freud's "misogyny" (87). What is finally being refused here, although this is never acknowledged, is not so much this purported misogyny as the concept of the unconscious itself, with all the dangers it poses to the primacy of frequently touted feminist goals such as "agency" and "self-empowerment." When such notions are the prime movers of a feminist thought, then the insidious, subversive unconscious (which exposes all sorts of things the empowered agent does not want to hear about) becomes absolute anathema.

This kind of unacknowledged refusal is in evidence in the above citation, where Meyers simultaneously claims that Freud uses psychoanalysis in order to reinforce the domination of women by men, and that he contributes to unconscious prejudice against women. In the first claim, Freud is a (conscious) champion of male domination; in the second, he is (consciously?) helping to sustain an unconscious prejudice. First, if such a prejudice is indeed unconscious, Freud has not much hope of contributing to it in any way but unconsciously. Even allowing that this may be Meyers's meaning, in order for the first claim to have any validity, Freud would have to be the master of his own (not to mention the "West's") unconscious to such a degree as to have created it himself, *consciously* (in order, that is, to make use of it and to shape it). Such a possibility is precisely what Freud's discovery (or, to recall Freud's

5

Introduction

more modest words, his recognition, or inference, or conjecture[7]) of the unconscious would eliminate.

In criticizing Meyer's reading, I do not want to suggest that feminist resistance to Freud is merely or always misguided, for bringing to light phallocentric assumptions in psychoanalytic theory is, among other things, what a feminist approach needs to do in order to analyze them. But this resistance *tout court* does run the risk of misguiding itself, throwing itself off the track, when it takes its main or sole goal to be the unmasking of misogyny or phallocentrism in Freud or in psychoanalytic theory. When such an unmasking becomes an end in itself, one is bound to work on the assumption that to achieve this goal will be synonymous with correcting wrongs, and thus with finding the "right" answers (which, one might incorrectly assume, we now have, whereas Freud did not, prey as he was to prejudices of his historical moment, from which we are free). Furthermore, this assumption precludes from the outset the possibility of coming to an understanding of the very mask it would throw off—what needs this mask serves and how it functions. If instead we take our task to be that of investigating the question of sexual difference (among whose most important aspects are the problem of domination and the understanding of "masculinity" and "femininity") as it is and has been constructed, theorized, and lived, then a feminist critique of psychoanalytic theory is at the same time both a critical and a creative expansion of it. As Irigaray has put it, it is not a matter of claiming that psychoanalysis has exhausted its efficacy: "Il s'agirait plutôt d'en déployer les implications encore inopérantes" ("It would be a matter, rather, of deploying its still inoperative implications"; *Ce sexe* 70, *This Sex* 72).

When Teresa Brennan notes in *The Interpretation of the Flesh* that most feminist readings of Freud have concentrated solely on a certain characterization of "woman" in Freud at the expense of Freud's "specific questions about femininity," she argues for such an expansion:

> The real riddle of femininity is neglected partly because Freud's work on femininity is not known for the precise problems he encountered in its investigation. It is known for a characterology of woman [. . .]. In Freud's own terms,

Introduction

what he has to say about women does not always sound "friendly" [. . .]. [D]espite his denigratory digressions, Freud's riddle of femininity did consist of specific questions about a psychical state that restricts and inhibits both women and men. (6)[8]

To focus entirely on Freud's characterization of woman is necessarily to neglect what psychoanalytic theory might offer for an understanding of sexual difference, an understanding that would take into account its problematic status. Approaching psychoanalysis in this way, far from being tantamount to an uncritical acceptance, involves an interrogation of psychoanalytic assumptions that works to reveal their location within a culture in which women suffer the masculine/feminine binary in specific ways. Furthermore, such an approach has the advantage of situating itself very much within that culture, aware that its own questions and answers are formed always in relation to it, and never simply or wholly outside of it, on the side of some enlightened vision of equality.

A psychoanalytic feminist approach, then, acknowledges first and foremost its own historicity as it explores that of its object (whether that object be "Freud," "psychoanalysis," "femininity," "sexual difference," etc.). This approach opens itself to the ambiguous place it occupies in relation to its object from which it cannot be neatly separate.

* * *

Juliet Mitchell's *Psychoanalysis and Feminism*, published in 1974, was the first English-language work to take up psychoanalytic theory as a viable discourse for feminism. She begins by announcing that she reads psychoanalysis not as "a recommendation *for* patriarchal society, but as an analysis *of* one" and she thus claims that "a rejection of Freud's work is fatal for feminism" (xv; original emphasis). Her book proceeds to resituate Freud's theories of femininity within the context of his work as a whole. When thus situated, she claims, even such concepts as penis envy can be understood as accurate descriptions of the role of the unconscious in female development. Thus Mitchell's book follows an expository trajectory, pointing to the developments in Freud's work with regard to

Introduction

femininity and explaining their significance to a presumably hostile audience. Since Mitchell is convinced that feminist hostility to Freud is based not merely on a refusal of his theories of femininity but on an unacknowledged refusal of his most fundamental insight—the unconscious—hers is a task of arguing for the acceptance of this discovery, and those that go along with it (repression, infantile sexuality, fantasy):

> It is often this notion [infantile sexuality, and more specifically the fæces-penis-baby equation made by the girl in her Œdipal turn away from the mother and toward the father] that gives most offence [. . .]. In the repudiation of the suggestion we have evidence that the strongest opposition to Freud's theories of femininity are made no more solely on the grounds of his male-chauvinist stance than early objections to his work were made solely on the grounds of his scandalous imputation of infantile sexuality: both oppositions have buried within them a strong protest against the fact of an unconscious mind. Here we have an example of how nearly all cases of relentlessly hostile criticism, though paying nominal tribute to Freud's "discovery," deny it in their subsequent analyses. For [. . .] here as elsewhere it is with the manner of the working of the unconscious that we are concerned. (Mitchell, *Psychoanalysis and Feminism* 101)

In Mitchell's opinion, if feminists understand and accept Freud's notion of the unconscious, then they will no longer be engaged in a hostile resistance, but will instead embark on an elaboration of Freud's insights into femininity. Moreover, she suggests that accepting the radical implications of the unconscious could allow feminist thinkers to move beyond the aim of a simple reversal of power, a matriarchal instead of patriarchal order, which would be but "a variation on the theme of the law-of-the-father" (415).

Such an elaboration, I would argue, was beginning simultaneously, in Irigaray's *Speculum, de l'autre femme*, published in the same year, and continued with her *Ce sexe qui n'en est pas un*. And this elaboration, this beginning, showed itself to bear more complexity, and more resistance, than Mitchell predicts when she notes at the end of her book that despite the fact that "specific conditions probably determined some of the formula-

Introduction

tions of particular questions [Freud asked]," psychoanalytic answers, including Freud's preliminary answers to the question of femininity, nevertheless stand on their own merit (Mitchell, *Psychoanalysis and Feminism* 435).

Irigaray will insist on interrogating the conditions of possibility for psychoanalysis's questions. Never arguing for an abandonment of psychoanalysis as a theoretical and clinical approach, at every moment in her analysis she underscores the need for this approach to be turned upon itself in order that new, or other, questions might be uncovered and formulated. This turning of Irigaray's asks not only what a question states or assumes, but more precisely, how a question is gendered. Thus her strategy performs an extra twist, as it were, where the mirror she would offer discloses the hidden gender of a question(er). When she offers a critique of Freud, for example, she does so to explore how the observations Freud makes (about female sexuality, for one) are informed by his sociohistorical context, and further, how this context leads him to formulate his theories without taking account of, or sometimes even perceiving, "internal contradictions" that speak not only to Freud's phallocentric bias, but to the ways in which such a bias is already inscribed in the symptoms he analyzes. She writes:

> Or, Freud décrit un état de fait. Il n'invente pas une sexualité féminine, ni d'ailleurs masculine. Il rend compte, en "homme de science." Le problème, c'est qu'il [. . .] interprète les souffrances, les symptômes, les insatisfactions, des femmes en fonction de leur histoire individuelle, sans questionner le rapport de leur "pathologie" à un certain état de la société, de la culture. (Irigaray, *Ce sexe* 68–69 [3])

It is Irigaray's insistence on bringing historicity to bear on psychoanalytic theory (and on philosophy) that, along with her attempt to think sexual difference anew, marks her critical project in *Speculum* and *Ce sexe*.

Both of these texts functioned to clarify the chief concerns of feminist thought in its relation to psychoanalytic theory. Irigaray's main argument is implicit in her approach to psychoanalytic discourse. As Elizabeth Grosz notes, Irigaray's position is "always ambiguous, always tenuously internal to the discipline or theory she challenges" (Grosz, "The Hetero" 336). In *Speculum*, Irigaray does not place herself unambiguously outside of psychoanalytic (or for that matter "masculine") discourse. Instead, she *analyzes* psychoanalytic discourse, particularly Freud's and Lacan's (and especially the status of femininity [Freud] and Woman [Lacan] therein), using its own insights in order to foreground that within it which remains unsaid, repressed, appearing mainly as symptom(s).

(Later in this introduction, I will address more closely the relation of Irigaray's work to Lacan's. For now, it is enough to point out that her work is heavily indebted to Lacan's, despite and because of the questions she brings to bear upon it, and that Irigaray's analysis of psychoanalysis—as well as of the history of philosophy—calls for its development in or toward a context that would allow for the inclusion/creation of sexual difference, a sexual difference understood as central to the possibility of any ethical relation whatever among speaking beings. These, sexual difference and ethics, are concerns with which Lacan, as I will discuss, is most centrally concerned.)

"What Is Woman?"

Irigaray's emphasis on the question of sexual *difference*, as opposed to sexual *equality*, is a reworking of the question, What is woman? The generally accepted answer to this question, in "first wave" and in much of "second wave" feminism, has been: woman is she who has been excluded from the universal rights of man, from the right to subjectivity and to being; woman is she who now must be included in the enjoyment of those rights, heretofore figured as "human," but in fact limited to men. This reading of the question reached its fullest expression in de Beauvoir's *The Second Sex* (1949), which nevertheless began to suggest the limitations inherent in such an understanding of both woman and the universal category of Being.

Irigaray insists that the question of woman cannot be posed separately from the question of Being;[9] that is, she proposes that the understanding of woman's difference as purely a function of her different political status is insufficient, and ultimately *non-emancipatory*, since such an approach accepts as a given the universal character of the system (the symbolic,

Introduction

Being, the social, the political) from which woman has been excluded.[10]

In effect, she asks whether there might be a fundamental relationship between "universal" and "of man" in a phrase like "the universal rights of man," and her answer is that the universal is sexed, masculine. She thus turns the question "What is woman?" back upon itself, and upon the historically male questioner: this is precisely why she opens *Speculum* by addressing Freud as he addresses an explicitly male audience (in his never actually—orally—delivered lecture "Femininity"). Fundamentally, Irigaray asks, What is this "is," this "to be," of your question? And how is this "to be" determined by its utterance within a discourse that she uncovers, or that uncovers itself, as "among men" (*Speculum* 9/13; English-version pagination follows French)? And what does it hide, what is hidden from it, repressed, in order for this being to be? Moreover, how would being be if it were two, plural?

For, according to Irigaray, the question is not, as we have just said, what woman is or is not, but rather how women suffer within (and might disturb) a "universal" symbolic that cannot/refuses to sex itself or know itself as sexed.

> En réalité, ce qui se veut universel équivaut à un idiolecte des hommes et à un imaginaire masculin, à un monde sexué. Sans neutralité. (Irigaray, *EDS* 117 [4])

In terms of the logic of this symbolic, there is a binary opposition "masculine/feminine," and Irigaray claims that one side of this binary, the feminine, is actually excluded by it. Furthermore, she argues that this exclusion is what allows the (masculine) symbolic order to constitute itself, and she thus sets out to read a given discourse (psychoanalysis or philosophy) for that which it excludes and which at the same time constitutes the condition of its very possibility.[11] The question of how such a reading can proceed will be addressed as I approach the main focus of this chapter.

Lacan and Irigaray: Jouissance and Love

As I proceed to consider the principle questions for a psychoanalytic feminism, moving toward the closely tied questions of

Introduction

feminine jouissance and love, I will first consider the notion of the phallus in Lacan, asking with Irigaray what its ramifications for sexual difference may be. I will then take up Joan Copjec's defense/explanation of Lacan to see whether or not Irigaray's critique might be enriched by Copjec's declaratively Lacanian and feminist perspective. And vice versa, whether or not Copjec's reading might benefit from an Irigarayan disruption.[12] Finally, I will examine closely parts of Lacan's twentieth seminar, starting with "Dieu et la jouissance de La femme" (session 6 of *Séminaire XX*[13]), in order to interrogate Lacan's framing and enacting of the question of sexual difference and the sexual relation, and in order to show that Lacan's understanding of jouissance, when read together with Irigaray's questioning of the negative, in fact calls for a thought of sexual difference in which jouissance as that which is beyond, that which is supplementary (as opposed to the lack alone) is sexed.

In Lacan's understanding of sexual difference, the phallus has the role of the privileged signifier. Lacan insists, in "La signification du phallus," that the phallus is not "the organ" which it symbolizes, but the signifier of desire.[14] It signifies a splitting of, among other things, the appetite for the satisfaction of needs and the demand to be loved. The phenomenon of this split, this difference of need and demand, is desire, of which the phallus is the signifier. And, more broadly, the function of the phallus as signifier of sexual difference, i.e., the structure of the symbolic as based upon a privileged signifier, is that with which Lacan is concerned. Lacan does not attribute this signifier to either man or woman. If there is, in fact, a slippage between Lacan's "phallus" and Freud's "penis," it is precisely insofar as the former will be misrecognized as the latter in the sexual relation. A woman's desire for the phallus will differ from the man's insofar as she is supposed, and supposes herself, not to have it, according to (her) the understanding of the symbolic order. (Even when, in an unresolved and narcissistic identification with the phallic mother, a woman supposes herself to have the phallus, she is doing so in relation to the reign of such an order, whose "punishment," castration, she finds unbearable.) Instead it is understood that she *receives* it from the man, even as, as a function of his desire, she will *become* it (for him). In the case of the man, there is the pre-

Introduction

tense of possession—which says something like, "I am *not* castrated. I have. I am. There is no ambiguity in my case"—and therefore, as Lacan says, his desire for the phallus is always bound up with the sustaining of an imposture (he really doesn't have the phallus) and the anxiety of impotence (fear of castration).

Let us look at Irigaray's repetition of Lacan's description of the sexual relation—or rather the structures that relation is submitted to (I will place only Irigaray's interpolations in italics):

> Si paradoxale que puisse sembler cette formulation, nous disons que c'est pour être le phallus, c'est à dire le signifiant du désir de l'Autre, que la femme va rejeter une part essentielle de sa féminité, nommément tous ses attributs dans la mascarade. C'est pour ce qu'elle n'est pas—*à savoir le phallus*—qu'elle entend être désirée en même temps qu'aimée. Mais son désir à elle, elle en trouve le signifiant dans le corps de celui—*censé l'avoir*—à qui s'adresse sa demande d'amour. (*Ce sexe* 58 [5])

Of which masquerade is it ultimately a question here if not the masquerade of woman's existence in the symbolic? It is a mistaken reading of this passage that would hold that Irigaray is, repetitively, mimetically, accusing Lacan of attributing the phallus to man. Rather, she is pointing up the structure Lacan is describing in order to emphasize, as indeed Lacan will, that within it there is no room for a sexual relation, e.g., between *two* sexes. She is underlining the misrecognition that substitutes for that impossible sexual relation: in this structure, the woman is not, cannot be said to be; she *is* only as missing, and thus takes on the elusive "being" of the phallus, solving the problem of how she could otherwise be desired, how she could otherwise be there as an object of desire. For her part, a parallel misrecognition is required: it must be understood that the body of the man gives her a status that she represents and that she can never be—uncastrated.

Thus Irigaray, with her interpolations, points to the circularity of a system in which the man would not only give the woman what she is, and is not, but would give her *that* she is, and *that* she is not, so to speak (since for her, being is always a function of *his* being). While for the woman's part, this entails

Introduction

accepting the man/penis/phallus/object of desire as a triumph over her castration, for the man's part, it means an anxious avoidance of his own castration: the woman both gives to the man what she hasn't got by embodying the phallus he desires, and also acts as the proof of his non-castration (he gives it to her). In such a relation, the man's existence is confirmed (he has, he gives, he is), while the woman's status vacillates undecidably between existence and nonexistence (she doesn't have/she seems to have, she doesn't give/she seems to give, she is not/she seems to be).

Irigaray's quarrel with Lacan concerns the fact that he does not apparently argue against the crime inherent in this system, or insist on the need for its radical rethinking for the stake of there being two in a (sexual) relation. This is not to say that Irigaray is arguing for a kind of ontological equality politics: let there be woman (as there is man). The question of woman's existence is important here not because she should exist *too*, as man exists, but rather because existence itself is shown to be thought in a way that forecloses difference, and thus the ethical possibility of (any relation to) a woman's living difference. If the thought and possibilities of existence are thus flawed, thus impoverished, thus closed to relation, then another thought of existence is needed. This thought, for Irigaray, would not be that of universal Woman (as Toril Moi suggests[15]), which would result in a repetition of an exclusionary economy (simply reversed), but instead that of "another woman," a woman thought both in her relation to other women and men, and in her singularity, as opposed to her binary difference from man.

Irigaray reads Lacan's understanding of the missed sexual relation and calls for its advent. The following passage, also from Lacan's "The Signification of the Phallus," has to be read, for Irigaray, with the sexual relation's failure, an ethical failure, in mind:

> Si l'homme trouve en effet à satisfaire sa demande d'amour dans la relation à la femme pour autant que le signifiant du phallus la constitue bien comme donnant dans l'amour ce qu'elle n'a pas, —inversement son propre désir du phallus fera surgir son signifiant dans sa divergence rémanante vers "une autre femme" qui peut signifier ce phallus à divers titres, soit comme vierge, soit comme prostituée. (*Ecrits* 695 [6])

14

Introduction

A man desires the phallus. A man's demand for love is satisfied in the relation with the woman, for the woman is giving what she does not possess—but the man . . . is he giving here? He, like she, gives that of which he is deprived, and thus he, too, is split for her, in a different mode. She is split for him inasmuch as she becomes what she is not. Her split is of the order of her existence. His difference is different: he is the other in whom she locates the signifier of her own desire, and then that signifier is replaced (by her) with the being of the "man whose attributes she cherishes" (*Ecrits* 695/290). She replaces by cherishing (and constituting) the being of the very man, precisely because his status as deprived, lacking the phallus, is not perceived. Thus, he is constituted, he exists, so long as he is missed, so long as the woman's desire is mis-placed onto him as always already there, existing and desired, existing as desired in an imposture (of being) guaranteed by the fantasy of desire's satisfaction. And she is constituted, with a similarly necessary missing at play (necessary because there is no being that might be got to and not missed, either in her case or in his), so long as she is (desired as) what she is not. So long as her existence is impossible.

Again, difference as the possibility for an ethical sexual relation thus disappears before it can reveal itself, and is yet traceable in what shows itself as a suffering—not only the passion of the signifier as its singularity eludes it in order for it to signify, but a feminine suffering (suffered by both men and women): hysteria. In *Speculum*, Irigaray writes:

> Le choix qui se propose à elle serait plutôt entre une censure radicale de ses pulsions—qui aboutirait à la mort—et leur traitement, conversion, hystériques. Cette alternative, d'ailleurs, n'en est pas réellement une. Les deux opérations sont conséquentes. (86 [7])

The exclusionary logic of castration leads in this way to an erasure, an annihilation, or a pathologization of the feminine—the feminine *as* pathological.

Thus, to repeat again what is the crucial point for Irigaray, it is not only that Woman does not exist, in accordance with a system that excludes the possibility of her existence, but that women and men suffer the consequences of that nonexistence,

Introduction

of existence thought and constituted around an always missed residue (the *objet a* as the empty kernel of the castrated, masculine subject who disavows his castration) and the conflation of that residue with *La*femme (Woman as nonexistent). A conflation that ultimately destines the sexual relation, and by extension any relation between speaking subjects, to perpetual misrecognition, to an inevitably unethical nonencounter.

Sexual Difference/Not Existing

Doubtless the most well-known statement of Lacan's *Encore* concerns the nonexistence of woman. The assertion comes in various syntaxes: "il n'y a pas de femme qu'exclue par la nature des choses, qui est la nature des mots"; or, "il n'y a pas La femme puisque [. . .] de son essence, elle n'est pas-toute" ("there is no woman except as excluded by the nature of things, which is the nature of words"; "there is no Woman since [. . .] of her essence, she is not-all"; Lacan, *XX* 68). The statements, more than proclaiming woman's nonexistence, proclaim the impossibility of saying anything definitive about her existence at all. In the same seminar, Lacan notes the problematic nature of his statements of nonexistence. Having repeated that there is no sexual relation, he continues:

> Mais que veut dire de le nier? Est-il légitime d'aucune façon de substituer une négation à l'appréhension éprouvée de l'inexistence? (*XX* 132 [8])

One can understand this as a question about the nature of negation, and also, perhaps more importantly, about existence itself and its relation to speech: What is this existence that we might affirm or negate? In her essay "Sex and the Euthanasia of Reason," Copjec emphasizes this question in Lacan, pointing out that "while he does indeed claim, as his readers have often been horrified to observe, that the idea of the woman is a contradiction of reason, and that she therefore does not exist, he also claims, and this has not been as readily observed, that her existence *cannot* be contradicted by reason—nor, obviously, can it be confirmed" (34).

Copjec's analysis will be helpful here because it interrogates explicitly the context in which Lacan is confronting the impos-

Introduction

sibility of *La* femme—the issue to which so much angry criticism has been addressed.[16] Specifically, Copjec (and Slavoj Žižek after her[17]) situates Lacan's discussion of sexual difference in the twentieth seminar in the context of his use of Kant's distinction between two modes of reason's failure. In both *The Critique of Pure Reason* and *The Critique of Judgment*, Copjec writes, Kant "demonstrated that the failure of reason was not simple, but foundered on an antinomic impasse through two separate routes: the first was mathematical, the second dynamical" ("Sex and the Euthanasia" 25). Having established that the sexual relation in Lacan is to be situated at reason's failure, reason's fault, Copjec claims that it functions in much the same way as the difference between Kant's mathematical and dynamical antinomies of reason.

Placing the feminine side of sexual difference in line with the mathematical, and the masculine in line with the dynamical, Copjec then proceeds to examine the antinomies of Lacan's formulae of sexuation as given in "Une lettre d'âmour" (*XX*, session 7). To remind ourselves, then, they are as follows:

$$\exists x \overline{\Phi x} \qquad \overline{\exists x} \Phi x$$
$$\forall x \Phi x \qquad \overline{\forall x} \Phi x$$

which Copjec transcribes as:

There is at least one x which is not submitted to the phallic function.	There is not one x which is not submitted to the phallic function.
All x's are (every x is) submitted to the phallic function.	Not all (not every) x is submitted to the phallic function.

("Sex and the Euthanasia" 26)

The universe of the male, which is a function of the two formulae on the left, can be posited as such because of what is subtracted from it—in strictly psychoanalytic terms, the phallus: castration, therefore man. In other terms, it is a question of something always being excluded from a universe in order for that universe to be posited. On the one hand, all men—that is those that find themselves male without knowing what to do

17

Introduction

about it (*XX* 67)—are subject to the phallic function (the first statement); on the other hand, it is always assumed (or fantasized) that there is at least one man who is not subject to it—an impossible contradiction that nevertheless makes the first, universal statement possible. To put it simply, it is not possible to think, "I am castrated" without supposing that it is possible *not* to be castrated. The result of these two statements taken together is the mode of masculinity, in which man is defined both as always lacking something, and always driven by a desire for the possibility of lacking nothing, of crossing beyond that limit of castration (the first statement) to the second statement's promise of unlimited status, beyond One to an indefinite, infinite series. "Là où est l'être," Lacan writes, "c'est l'exigence de l'infinitude" ("There where being is, there is the demand for infinitude"; *XX* 15). This infinitude does not obtain, of course, because the masculine mode is a function of both of the statements taken together. And thus on the masculine side one is left with the possibility, indeed the demand, to posit a one, a whole, an all, which defines itself in terms of the exclusionary limit.

On the feminine side (on the right above), things at first appear similar: first, there is no woman who is not subject to the phallic function, and second, not all women are subjected to the phallic function. Again, we have an obvious contradiction. But in the former case, that contradiction was the function of a subtraction, a limit (there is one who does not fall under the rule). In the case of the feminine side of sexual difference, on the contrary, it is a function of the lack of a limit. The first statement proclaims the nonexistence of any x that might be excluded from the phallic function, while the second proclaims the impossibility of stating that *all* women, universally, are subject to its reign. So that this second point does not function as a limit to the first point; it does not say that there *is* (using the existential quantifier, ∃) one woman who falls outside, rather it states (using the negated universal quantifier, ∀) that one cannot posit Woman universally. Somehow, it is imagined, not all of Woman is submitted to the rule; a piece of her escapes; she's not all there. Thus on the masculine side we have two positive statements, one of existence and one of universality, which contradict and limit each other, whereas on the femi-

Introduction

nine side we have two negative statements, one of nonexistence and one of nonuniversality, which put each other into question. The masculine is limited and hence lacking, while the feminine is unlimited, hence lacking (still) but in quite another way. Its lack of a limit renders any judgment of Woman's existence impossible.

One can no more state categorically that Woman exists than that she does not: the point is that the question of her existence is entirely undecidable. This impossibility of rendering a judgment of existence is ultimately what leaves open another space within (or beyond) Lacan's figurations of sexual difference, and that space is feminine jouissance, which, as Copjec writes, "cannot be located in experience [. . .] cannot be said to exist in the symbolic order" ("Sex and the Euthanasia" 34), which, in other words, is the very mode of the unspoken, unspeakable, unknowable because unlimited, even as it is produced within a symbolic. When Lacan states that a woman does not "know" what her jouissance is and cannot explain it, cannot speak it, he is referring to jouissance, not to women who don't know enough: jouissance is that which has no relation to knowledge or knowing. It is feminine in that it is unlimited. As Lacan explains it:

> De ce qu'on puisse écrire *pas-tout* χ *ne s'inscrit dans* $\Phi\chi$, il se déduit par voie d'implication qu'il y a un χ qui y contredit. C'est vrai à une seule condition, c'est que, dans le tout ou le pas-tout dont il s'agit, il s'agisse du fini [. . .]. Seulement, nous pouvons avoir à faire au contraire à l'infini [. . .]. Quand je dis que la femme n'est pas-toute et que c'est pour cela que je ne peux pas dire *la* femme, c'est précisément parce que je mets en question une jouissance qui au regard de tout ce qui se sert dans la fonction de $\Phi\chi$ est de l'ordre de l'infini. (Lacan, *XX* 94 [9])

With this, he signals the significance of a jouissance beyond the phallus, a jouissance proper to the Woman as she who does not exist. We might paraphrase: Là où est l'infinitude, c'est l'exigence d'un(e) autre être (There where infinitude is, there is the demand for another being). This is precisely the demand with which George Sand is concerned in the novel we will treat in the next chapter; it is this demand that, quite literally, wracks

Introduction

the soul of her heroine, Lélia, in her quest for another order of being.

As I noted earlier, for Copjec, this jouissance beyond the phallus points to a possibility to think an ethics that could be called proper to the woman in Lacanian terms—an ethics based upon unlimited inclusion, an inclusion that disrupts limits, rather than upon exclusion.[18] Significantly, she makes this observation at the conclusion of her text on sexual difference, gesturing toward a possible path, but not yet articulating how one might start on it. After observing that "the Kantian account of the dynamical antinomies and the Lacanian account of the male antinomies both align themselves with the psychoanalytical concept of the superego" ("Sex and the Euthanasia" 41–42), she further worries:

> Yet once we establish that this logic of the limit, of exception, defines the dynamical antinomies, the male subject, and the superego, we have a problem, or so it seems at first blush. For we now appear to lend support to the notorious argument that presents woman as constitutionally indisposed to developing a superego and thus susceptible to an ethical laxity. In response to this, all we can suggest at this point is that the field of ethics has too long been theorized in terms of this particular superegoistic logic of exception or limit. It is now time to devote some thought to developing an ethics of inclusion or of the unlimited, that is, an ethics proper to the woman. ("Sex and the Euthanasia" 42)

This, of course, is one way of characterizing Irigaray's project for an ethics of sexual difference.

I would suggest that an Irigarayan taking up of the path Copjec points to would involve an initial acceptance of the "notorious" notion that a woman is "constitutionally indisposed to developing a superego and thus susceptible to ethical laxity." This acceptance would involve what Irigaray calls "taking the negative upon ourselves" (*EDS* 116, *ESD* 120).

Lacan opens up the question of the negative, asking, in a passage noted above, about the ramifications of a statement of negation with respect to nonexistence and deferring any precise conclusion:

> Est-il légitime d'aucune façon de substituer une négation à l'appréhension éprouvée de l'inexistence? C'est là aussi une

> question qu'il ne s'agit pour moi que d'amorcer. (Lacan, *XX* 132 [10])

As Elizabeth Weed notes à propos the twentieth seminar, "Again and again, in his readings, Lacan inscribes his discourse as inadequate, where nothing ever meets its mark" (Weed, "Question of Style" 92). This particular inadequacy or deferral is a question to which Irigaray responds by attempting to think toward an ethics that would include, or rather presuppose, both sides of sexual difference; and that calls for an initial assumption, by a would-be (post- or a-patriarchal) feminine subject, of the negative she already embodies as Woman in relation to Man.

How would this taking upon oneself of the negative be understood as an opening toward ethical sexual difference? How is it, in other words, that taking the negative upon oneself amounts, as Irigaray states, to allowing the other his or her liberty and sex? (*EDS* 116, *ESD* 120). In *J'aime à toi*, she elaborates upon the significance of this negative, which I read as closely related to feminine jouissance. An ethical encounter between men and women, she writes, would be characterized by the importance of an absolute silence in order to listen, and by the reversal of the negative—into the possibility of love and of creation—as the limit of one gender with respect to another gender (*J'aime* 28, *I Love* 11). Thus conceived, the negative in sexual difference speaks to the question of feminine jouissance in a silence that is also an appeal to the other, both to speak and to find silence enough to listen, to listen to that which cannot be told or known. This silence is an appeal that presumes and gives the possibility for an unknown creation, in love, between two genders. But how are there two genders in this schema, two limited genders? As Irigaray frames this question, the limit takes place, becomes limit, by means of the reversal of the negative: i.e., the negative, through a listening-toward-possibility, becomes a new creation *between* two. Neither one nor the other contains the limit, *is* as limited. Rather, the limit is rethought, or reimagined, as a potentially fluctuating space that is mutually (re-)created through a love that listens, through a listening that loves.

In the following section, I ask whether Lacan's *Encore*, starting particularly with the session entitled "Dieu et la jouissance

Introduction

de La femme," might be an attempt both to think and to enact such a relation, or its failure, between speaking, sexed subjects named I and you. Where jouissance may come to signify not a beyond, or the limit of a beyond, but an in between, between the relation's "illusory" taking place and its failure.

"Dieu et la jouissance de La femme": Existence in Relation, Relation's Inexistence

In "Dieu et la jouissance de La femme," Lacan situates himself from the outset in the place of a *je* speaking to a *vous*. And furthermore, a *vous* who disappoints him, a *vous* who engages his desire, and lets him down. He begins by speaking of this desire and its disappointment:

> Il y a longtemps que je désirais vous parler en me promenant un petit peu entre vous. Aussi espérais-je, je peux bien vous l'avouer, que les vacances dites scolaires auraient éclairci votre assistance. Puisque cette satisfaction m'est refusée, j'en reviens à ce dont je suis parti la dernière fois, que j'ai appelé *une autre satisfaction,* la satisfaction de la parole. (*XX* 61 [11])

He has wanted, for a long time, to speak to this *vous* in leading himself out a little bit among them ("en me promenant un petit peu entre vous"). The translation here is ambiguous. On the one hand, in the context of an audience, we might expect a sense of *promener* that is along the lines of a turning, even a surveying—one can *promener sa vue* over an audience, for example, turn one's gaze to it, survey it (master it). But Lacan has wanted to *promener* himself, and not on or over his listeners, but among them. He has wanted to be a bit closer. And to this end, he had hoped there would be fewer of them now, during the school holidays. He would have liked to be closer to them, but they are too many. Why this desire for a greater proximity, even union?

A possible response may be found in his discussion of that other satisfaction, which, concretely speaking, was the great, the greatest, satisfaction of reading Jean-Luc Nancy and Philippe Lacoue-Labarthes's reading of his article "L'instance

Introduction

de la lettre." In their text, *Le titre de la lettre,* he finds that he has never been read with so much love. Their text, which he says is a model of good reading, causes him to regret never having obtained anything so good, anything written with so much love ("rien qui soit équivalent") from among those who are close to him (*XX* 62). Thus Lacan has chosen to begin a day's meeting with the evocation of a certain lack—he is not enough among his listeners—a lack that may in part stem from a certain *too much* or *too many,* from a failure of (some of) his audience to withdraw, and that finds its satisfaction, which is not *its* satisfaction, but another satisfaction, and a great one, in another milieu, that of *la parole.* You who come here, and may love me, since in coming here you suppose me to know something, do not read me or hear me with as much love as some others (I won't name them) who de-suppose me of knowledge and who in so doing have allowed me to obtain a loving text, a satisfaction, a word that addresses itself to my word . . . with so much love. Not only this, but perhaps if you read this work, which, though it reads me with so much love was nevertheless written with the worst intentions (it would have been worse had they read me with the best) and declares me to be *quinaud* (confused, at a loss); perhaps if you read this text that for the most part proceeds with the most astonishing clarifying value ("une valeur d'éclaircissement tout à fait saisissante"), then your ranks, so numerous, would themselves be cleared up, thinned out ("éclaircir"). This, for me, would be nothing but advantageous, for then I might be able to be closer to you who, although you are *mes proches,* are evidently not close enough, since you do not read me with so much love even as those who are farther from me. Although in the end I'm not sure that anything would or could rebuff you, make you fewer than you are.

I take the time here to rewrite and refigure part of the introduction to the lecture in order to suggest that this text starts out with something like a "Why don't you love me enough?" or, rather, with an evocation or enactment of such a question. More precisely, the question is about love itself, and the inadequacy of a long-standing historical model for love: two unite and become one. It is an inadequate model because it fails to take into account a withdrawal that must take place in order for such

Introduction

a combination to be effected, or to seem to be effected. Thus his opening remarks go along these lines: you don't love me enough (or I don't love you enough), which may be seen in our lack of proximity; and this lack in our relation is the result of your being too many. A certain relation between us fails to take place due to what I deem to be your quality of *en plus*. Whereas, as a kind of substitute for this missed relation, this apparently unsatisfiable desire that I have in relation to you, I am able to return to another satisfaction, that of *la parole*, wherein I find that I am, or at least my words are, addressed with love.

Things are not, however, so clear in this clarifying realm of *la parole*, for to say that I am loved I must also own that I am hated, by those very lovers, those readers of (and listeners to) my words. And furthermore, the least I can say about their love is already saying too much (*XX* 62). For in saying anything about it, I am evoking them as subjects and/or evoking their feelings[19] and those realms must be closed to me as I consider, nevertheless, their words without so much as naming them, those others who lovingly read me, and who de-suppose me of knowledge.

Lacan is setting himself up in this lecture to speak of the sexual relation in the speaking being that does not take place *as* the domain, or order, of intersubjective relations in general, whatever the sex of the speaking being in question. The "broader" scope of this lecture—intersubjective relations in general—serves not only to frame the more specific question of woman, but is also the question itself. For if these relations can only be spoken in the terms of a language/logic from whose order woman is excluded, then the failures or gaps of that language must be highlighted and questioned. Hence the usefulness of beginning with what seems like a Lacanian contradiction: those who love me not only suppose me to know, but also desuppose me of knowledge, and in fact this desupposition ultimately allows them to write more lovingly of me than would their initial supposition. The introduction to this essay leaves one with the conclusion that "they"—those authors, but also those others?—love me in hating me, leading one to wonder about the nature of the One/Love that Lacan has described as supposing the other to know. Does love rather require, this

Introduction

lecture asks, a de-supposition of knowledge in order to be born? If we consider that what is being questioned is not only the male-female sexual relation, but also intersubjective relations in general, and as sexed, then we might be led to conclude that Lacan is doing something other than continuing Freud's questions about femininity into the domain of language. From the beginning he frames his discussion of God, Man, and the jouissance of Woman, within the impossibility of his finding himself in a (loving) relation with a male "them" and a mostly male "you," both of whose (or rather all of whose, his own included) maleness finds itself undone or not knowing what to do with itself (*XX* 67) in the light of something that it cannot be or have or know; and that something is not the phallus.

It has to do, rather, with a "comfort" (*XX* 63), as well as a certain withdrawal or subtraction that nevertheless produces, and is, a supplement. A withdrawal that may serve to comfort. Let me first discuss particularly this comforting withdrawal that introduces jouissance and cannot be separated from it, and which we have already seen in the guise of Lacan's relation with his audience. In his "Lacan: An Ethics of Speech," Michel de Certeau identifies Lacan's continual withdrawing as the "gesture which constitutes his thought and which gives birth to all its brilliance," and as a way for him to speak to his audience as it "spreads, grows, overflows, increasingly beyond control" (de Certeau 48). As we began to see above, Lacan opens this essay with figures of withdrawal: a wished-for withdrawal of his audience; his own withdrawal both from among them and from a part of the text he recommends to them; and even the withdrawal of the authors of that text from a final accord with Lacan's project (their simultaneously de-supposing him of knowledge and reading him with love).

The next figure of withdrawal or subtraction will come with the metaphor of meiosis. "Withdrawal" and "subtraction" are synonyms here, inasmuch as what is withdrawn or subtracted, for Lacan, is always present, or rather, absent, *as* withdrawn or subtracted. Withdrawal and subtraction both necessitate that one consider relation (self-self, self-other, self-others) in terms of what has taken itself away. Referring to the "fortunate" discovery of the ovum and the spermatozoid, which made it

Introduction

relatively easy for Freud to use the metaphor of Eros as the fusion of two made one, Lacan speaks of that biological fusion that engenders

> un nouvel être. A ceci près que la chose ne va pas sans une méiose, sans une soustraction tout à fait manifeste, au moins pour l'un des deux, juste d'avant le moment même où la conjonction se produit, une soustraction de certains éléments qui ne sont pas pour rien dans l'opération finale. (*XX* 63 [12])

He proceeds to link this metaphorical mode of thinking to the subtraction or withdrawal it designates: he notes that here, where jouissance is in question, the biological metaphor will not be enough to "comfort us" (*XX* 63), precisely because the withdrawal implicit in it is unacknowledged when it is used (by Freud, for example) to figure the sexual relation. Thus, in order to pursue that comfort involved in jouissance, what is needed is a turning away from biology toward language *(langue)*.

As Weed notes, Lacan's use of the biological metaphor here allows him to point to that which "blocks the thinking of other possible relationalities" (other, that is, than as a function of "the fetishistic nature of the production of the subject in discourse [. . .] the anxious formation of subjectivity within our cultural order"; 97). In other words, by seeming to invoke and then renounce the usefulness of biology for thinking human subjectivity and relationality, he figures the impossibility of a discourse to wholly contain that which it seeks to account for. In the very turn to language (specifically the One/Love of/in language, which not even the course of centuries has managed to reduce or lessen, but which psychoanalytic experience manages to renew, to increase; *XX* 63), Lacan is then pointing up a certain inadequacy or failure. The book without the subtraction of its last thirty pages, and the fusion of egg and sperm without the subtracting action of meiosis, might seem at first comforting enough in themselves. But neither the biological metaphor nor the clarifying text can take into account also what escapes them. And what escapes them is what makes it impossible for Lacan to claim that they are adequate, equivalent to that which they, the biological metaphor and the book that reads him, and

Introduction

finally language, mark or refer to, namely, love, that which would be One, that in which the subject(s) would be One. In this way, Lacan finds himself not far from what Irigaray will begin to say in *Ethique de la différence sexuelle*:

> Vous ne ferez qu'un, édicte la loi. Elle ne dit pas comment cela est possible. Elle oblige sans indiquer le chemin.
> La découverte serait de faire *deux* pour pouvoir peut-être un jour faire *un* dans ce tiers qu'est l'amour, par exemple.
> Actuellement, il y aurait du *un* [. . .] qui n'est qu'une complémentarité asservissante [. . .]. Pour que le *un* de l'amour puisse peut-être un jour s'accomplir, il faut découvrir le *deux*. (*EDS* 69; Irigaray's emphasis [13])

Love, as a traditional figure for wholeness (One/Love), underscores instead the excess or surplus—Irigaray's *feminine*, Lacan's *La*femme—which always accompanies/escapes any relation between speaking beings. The law of the symbolic itself is grounded in its own fault. In order for the symbolic to emerge, as the order in which the subject relates to others (where the subject assumes his/her own desire in the splitting of need and demand—or in other terms, the recognition of maternal desire beyond the child and the answer "father"— paternal metaphor—to the question, "What does she want?"), it must also contain its own surplus effect or fault. And this fault is precisely the place of sexual difference, that difference whose origin or meaning can never be finally named or known, but that nevertheless structures relations such that they are always more than they are, *en plus*. If woman is confounded with this fault, this excess, this confusion always takes place with respect to the phallic function, or more precisely, to man's relation to the phallic function, which, as Lacan notes, is a relation of imposture. This imposture involves the covering over of a symbolic gap, namely, castration. As Lacan writes in his essay "The Subversion of the Subject and the Dialectic of Desire in the Freudian Unconscious,"

> C'est en imposteur que se présente le Législateur pour y suppléer, le Législateur (celui qui prétend ériger la Loi [in this context, the Father as opposed to the Mother]). (*Ecrits* 813 [14])

Introduction

Thus this imposture of being involves the pretense of wholeness, a pretense that finds a parallel in the story of (and wish for) the One/Love. Lacan identifies feminine jouissance as that which is beyond this (desire for) One, "au-delà du phallus":

> elle [la femme] a, par rapport à ce que je désigne de jouissance la fonction phallique, une jouissance supplémentaire.
> Vous remarquerez que j'ai dit *supplémentaire*. Si j'avais dit *complémentaire*, où en serions-nous! On retomberait dans le tout. (*XX* 68 [15])

And rather than falling back into the whole, Lacan insists that we consider instead this *en plus*. In order to do so, he will focus on the question of knowledge (*savoir*)—feminine jouissance being that which one may or may not experience, but about which one cannot know—and introduce the "concept" of *lalangue*. First, he makes two claims: (a) that for the speaking being, knowledge is that which is articulated, and (b) *lalangue* is that which structures the unconscious, and has nothing to do with language as communication (*XX* 125–26). Thus, we have a schema with articulated knowledge (knowledge as articulated) on the one hand, and *lalangue* on the other. But the two are intertwined in a complex relation. For although *lalangue* is not communicated, neither is it silent. On the contrary, in the speaking being, *lalangue's* effects are perceived in *affects*, which in turn are due to the function of *lalangue*, as it articulates pieces of knowledge that are much beyond what the speaking being can bear to know enunciated, knowledge much beyond anything the speaking being is likely to enunciate (consciously, knowingly) (*XX* 127). Thus, Lacan explains, the unconscious is a *savoir-faire avec lalangue*, the important point here being that *lalangue* signals the *en plus* of the subject (the subject is more than s/he knows), and structures the unconscious like a language, a language that cannot be said to exist, that is always hypothetical, and that is posited based on the perceived effects of *lalangue* (*XX* 127).

What then, is the relation of *lalangue* to feminine jouissance, to the jouissance proper to the Woman as she who does not exist? Might we draw a kind of parallel, and say that the jouissance of the Woman as she who does not exist—she whose existence can only be hypothetically posited—is structured on

Introduction

the basis of a superegoistic logic of the limit and exclusion, just as language as that which does not exist is structured on the basis of *lalangue*? Thus, language is "made of" *lalangue* (*XX* 127), and feminine jouissance is made of the logic of castration (in terms of which the woman cannot be supposed *to be* and feminine jouissance cannot be *known*)? This parallel, while it may not be adequate, may be helpful, for in it we can see a particular inadequacy, namely, that the jouissance of the Woman cannot be seen simply as a corollary to language as an effect of *lalangue*. For feminine jouissance also has a particular relation to *lalangue*—both can never finally be known, though they are experienced and leave their traces (in language, in Woman who does not exist by virtue of feminine jouissance being located always beyond the phallus, beyond castration, beyond the limit). Finally then, Woman herself is also situated beyond, and any possibility of relation between two sexed subjects is foreclosed. This may seem an insufficient conclusion, and yet Lacan insists on it just as much, as we have seen, as Irigaray insists on reading this conclusion in Lacan. The important point now becomes *how* to read this conclusion.

As I suggested at the end of the previous section, Irigaray chooses to speak (from this conclusion) toward the possibility of reading (universal) Woman's nonexistence (she is only as excluded, beyond) toward its own undoing, toward the undoing of its underlying structure, by way of what she calls taking the negative upon oneself, a self disappropriation, in relation with another, that would engender new (sexual, ethical) limits that would be neither the limit of one nor the limit of the other, but that of a continually creative third, a third Irigaray names love. Within such a gesture, it is no longer solely feminine jouissance that occupies the beyond of a (phallic) sexual-but-not-sexed nonrelation. Instead, sexual difference itself—and as embodied and lived in two nontotalized and untotalizeable subjects, two subjects who subject themselves to each other's irreducibility—becomes that which allows for the advent of another love where feminine jouissance is now but one (sexed) expression of this irreducibility, and no longer its only possible expression. Irigaray writes:

> Je te reconnais signifie que je reconnais que tu es, que tu existes, que tu deviens. Dans cette reconnaissance, je te

Introduction

> marque, je me marque de l'incomplétude, du négatif. Tu n'es ni je suis le tout, le même, principe de totalisation [. . .]. Le *mien* du sujet est toujours déjà marqué par une désappropriation: le genre. Etre homme ou femme revient déjà à ne pas être le tout du sujet [. . .] mais aussi à ne pas être tout à fait soi [. . .]. *Je* n'est jamais simplement *mien* en tant qu'il appartient à un genre. Donc, je ne suis pas tout: je suis homme ou femme. (*J'aime* 164–66 [16])

The fantasy of wholeness, the (masculine) desire to deny castration, or the (feminine) desire to be its cure, is here rejected in favor of a mutual acknowledgment of incompleteness.

We can further add that Lacan need hardly be read as excluding this Irigarayan ethics where sexual difference is the locus, or better, the non-place (never finally determined) of two subjects' difference, despite the fact that he does not pursue his "there is no sexual relation" in this direction. For he states quite clearly that Woman's situation beyond existence, and her jouissance as always excessive, leads to a fundamentally unethical sexual relation:

> De sorte qu'on pourrait dire que plus l'homme peut prêter à la femme à confusion avec Dieu, c'est-à-dire ce dont elle jouit, moins il hait, moins il est—les deux orthographes—et, puisqu' après tout il n'y a pas d'amour sans haine, moins il aime.[20] (*XX* 82 [17])

In this light, we can read Lacan's demand that his audience desuppose him of knowledge (as his good, loving, and also hating, readers do) as a demand for, or at least a gesture toward, another love, a love that does not situate a subject (supposed or desupposed of knowledge) as all versus not-all, a love that would allow something else to come between subjects. A jouissance, perhaps, that while not known or mastered, would be mutually created and lived between subjects who listen without supposing finally to know what is heard and said, thereby forging a tenuous, always shifting and shared, limit. (And this limit defined by jouissance situates the questions that Colette's work will bring to bear on the being of Woman and her desire. For Colette, the question of Woman's desire can only be approached via the more dangerous terrain of enjoyment, as we shall see in chapter 2.)

Introduction

Further Questions

Finally, I would note that this Irigarayan, other, limit points to what may be the most important difference in Lacan's and Irigaray's thinking yet to be given in-depth consideration, a difference that is also of the utmost importance for a psychoanalytic feminism, namely, the difference between this shared-limit-in-creation and the limit of/as the death drive. What, as Peggy Kamuf asks in her essay "Woman before Death," is the relation between the limit(s) of sexual difference and the limit of our mortal finitude? In order to approach this difference, we would first need to ask how the death drive is related to the phallic limit Lacan elaborates in his thinking of sexual difference. On the one hand, Irigaray clearly sees an ethical, loving limit in sexual difference as opposing what she calls "the reign of death" in philosophy and psychoanalysis (*J'aime à toi*). But on the other hand, there is the need to consider just how the death drive figures for Lacan, in his rethinking of Freud's concept. The death drive is arguably of central importance for Lacan, as Richard Boothby suggests in his *Death and Desire* (1991). And it may not be necessary to read it as a solely destructive drive. Boothby writes:

> it would not be wholly inappropriate to speak of the death drive [. . .] as a self-mutative or self-transformative drive. Lacan's insistence on retaining the Freudian term "death drive" [. . .] stems from a polemical intention, calculated to oppose the claims of ego psychology and its normative tendencies [. . .]. The place of death in analysis is to be located in the orientation to *jouissance*. (219)

Might it be that we can find here a formulation that speaks to this other (Irigarayan) limit? To give a little more shape to what this question might entail, I would point to the possibility of a relation between, on the one hand, Irigaray's emphasis on the irreducibility of the other to the self (which includes also the self's irreducibility to itself: *I* am not *mine*), and on the other hand, Lacan's notion that the subject is only "born posthumously," after access to its desire has demanded a death with respect to the ego (the ego as all-powerful and undivided).[21]

In short: is there, in the Lacanian understanding of the death drive, the possibility for (even the demand for) Irigaray's

Introduction

engendering limits? My reading of both so far would indicate that there is, although, paradoxically, we will only be able to pursue this question to its farthest reaches with Nathalie Sarraute and her insistence on the "neutral" with respect to sexual difference. In what follows, I shall be concerned with pursuing these questions in the writing of women who have explicitly taken up the impossibility of Woman's existence in relation to a "whole" masculine subject, as well as the question of love between, among, and within subjects for whom mortality constitutes a limit still to be thought.

Chapter One

George Sand and the Impossible Woman

It would be difficult to think of an author as important to the development of women's writing and feminism in France as George Sand, the more so because her relation to both of these categories is ambiguous. If she wrote "as a woman," then she also wrote "as a man." If she was a feminist, arguing for the right of women to divorce and for an end to their social and political oppression, she also dissociated herself from feminist groups, and rejected the idea that women should take up positions in the "virile public functions" of the state[1] (*Lettres à Marcie* 231). In short (as has been pointed out by Naomi Schor and Isabelle Hoog Naginski[2]), Sand's feminism is complicated and shot through with dilemmas and debates, as is the history of French feminism itself.

In taking up George Sand's writing, I am first of all seconding Schor's suggestion that "[i]t is time to read Sand as a theoretician of sexual difference" (*Sand and Idealism* 76). To attempt to rethink sexual difference is inevitably also to ask about the nature of love and of ethical human relations. As I will show, this is what Sand does in *Lettres à Marcie* (1837) and *Lélia* (a novel that was first published in 1833, and then substantially revised and republished in 1839), both of which I will discuss here. I will introduce my discussion of *Lélia* by outlining some of Sand's principal questions through a reading of her never-completed text *Lettres à Marcie*.

Lettres à Marcie and the Desire for the Impossible

Written in between the publications of the first and second versions of *Lélia* as "a sort of novel without events" (*Marcie* 165),

Chapter One

Lettres à Marcie is an epistolary work that contains some of Sand's most extended discussions of the relations between the sexes, the question of their difference versus their equality, and the possibilities available (and not) for the improvement of women's lot. This work has, however, seldom been addressed by Sand's readers.[3] This could be for any number of reasons. Sand's corpus is enormous, of course, and this incomplete epistolary work (originally published serially in *Le Monde*) has perhaps been eclipsed by other major texts. Also, there is no contemporary or even relatively recent edition of *Lettres à Marcie:* the latest is the 1869 edition (referred to here), where it appears together with a grouping of other shorter works.

In addition, the text was written under a kind of censorship, and the project was abandoned when Sand's editor refused to allow the frank discussions Sand wanted to include. While Sand wanted complete freedom to include considerations of divorce, for example, her editor at *Le Monde,* the religious writer Félicité Robert de Lamennais (known as l'Abbé Lamennais), was opposed to this "audacity" (Sand's word).[4] In her preface, Sand insists that her leaving the work in mid-stream was a function of pure chance, but she also acknowledges the challenge that the work represented for her (as well as the reason for which we may wish to take it up again):

> Je n'avais accepté l'honneur de concourir à la collaboration du journal *le Monde* que pour faire acte de dévouement envers M. Lamennais, qui l'avait créé et qui en avait la direction. Dès qu'il l'abandonna, je me retirai, sans même m'enquérir des causes de cet abandon; je n'avais pas de goût et je manquais de facilité pour ce genre de travail interrompu, et pour ainsi dire haché [demanded when writing for serial publication in a daily paper]. N'ayant pas eu l'occasion de continuer en temps et lieu les *Lettres à Marcie,* j'ai eu bientôt oublié l'espèce de plan que j'avais conçu. On m'a reproché, dans quelques journaux d'*émancipation,* de reculer devant les difficultés de l'entreprise. Le hasard seul m'a forcé de m'arrêter. (*Marcie* 166 [18])

Sand contextualizes the difficulty of the enterprise she had undertaken in writing the *Lettres* in terms of the response she received in newspapers devoted to the emancipation of women, and not only the resistance of her editor. She reflects, also in the preface, that to write the novel she intended was perhaps "une entreprise impossible" ("an impossible undertaking"). It was to have been a work that would take for its subject matter the inner life "d'un seul être, d'une femme qu'on n'eût même pas vu, qui n'eût jamais écrit, et qu'on n'eût connue que par les lettres et les réflexions de son ami" ("of one sole being, of a woman whom one would not even have seen, who would never have written, and whom one would know only through the letters and reflections of her friend"; *Marcie* 165). Of her male friend, to be precise. Significantly, the difficulty for Sand lies not in embodying a male writer writing to a woman, but that woman herself. As if in order to evoke Marcie, this essentially invisible woman, she has first to confront every nuance of the differences between the sexes. To "represent" Marcie precisely in, or by way of, her absence, Sand says, was her intention from the beginning, implying that whatever truth she would get to in this work would begin from the truth of the woman's invisibility.

Having elected such a starting point, Sand finds herself in deeper waters than she had anticipated, feeling it necessary to establish the truth of the difference between the sexes as she sees it. Taking on a male voice, speaking to a woman, she is, as she writes, pushed by her thoughts to come to some final conclusions that would provide a framework adequate to her epistolary novel. In her letter to Lamennais, she further underscores her doubts. She finds herself, "poussée par l'invincible *vouloir* de mes pauvres réflexions" ("pushed by the invincible *will* of my poor reflections"), in the midst of writing upon serious matters regarding the fate of women, "sans savoir le moins du monde si je me trompe ou non, sans pouvoir m'empêcher de conclure comme je fais et trouvant en moi je ne sais quelle certitude, qui est peut-être une voix de la vérité, et peut-être une voix impertinente de l'orgueil" ("without knowing in the least if I am mistaken or not, without being able to prevent myself from concluding as I do, and finding in myself I know not what certitude, which is perhaps a voice of truth, and perhaps an impertinent voice of pride"; *Correspondance* 3: 712).

On several topics, Sand finds a certitude that nevertheless remains less than certain. They include: the place and role of women and men in marriage; the history, present, and future of relations between the sexes; the changing face of Christianity

Chapter One

and its dogma throughout history versus its eternal truths; and women's position with respect to philosophy. In fact, all of these considerations are subsumed under the first, the problem of marriage. The *Lettres* begin with the very likely possibility that Marcie will never be able to marry because of her poverty and isolation, a situation that leads her and her correspondent to reflect on other prospects available to a woman.

Sand, then, is trying to think through questions about the nature and roles of women. As she grapples with these questions, along with Lamennais's censorship and the complexity of the project, she faces another one, closely related: the fundamental question of the representation of woman. It is a problem precisely because this woman is *unseen, unlettered, unknown*. And it is this attempt to represent the invisible woman that, as Schor has noted, situates Sand's work very much in the context of contemporary feminist thought in France, where the notion of impossibility informs feminism's utopian dimension (Schor, *Sand and Idealism* 80–81). For Sand (as well as others, especially Irigaray), utopian thought is aimed at a certain "not yet" rather than at the traditionally utopian "nowhere," and thus her utopian vision depends upon radical changes in the here and now between men and women.

As Marcie and her correspondent address the possibility of her future as a woman, that future is presented as somehow intimately bound up with that of her friend, despite his manifestly different situation (he is male, married, and has a child). Throughout the narrative, he repeats that he shares her doubts, and that "quand je vous exhorte au courage, c'est à nous deux que je parle" ("when I exhort you to courage, it is to both of us that I speak"; *Marcie* 203). His partaking of her plight makes it impossible, he says, to advise her; but after confessing his own position with regard to hers, he will present what he believes is her only alternative.

> [Vos] inquiétudes m'affligent et ne me retracent que trop celles qui dévorent souvent mon propre cœur. Je ne suis pas plus héroïque que vous, Marcie [. . .]. Marcie, notre esprit est malade [. . .] je suis si triste et abattu aujourd'hui, je confonds tellement dans mon angoisse ma misère et la vôtre, qu'il m'est impossible de vous donner des conseils. (*Marcie* 179, 180–81 [19])

He goes on to suggest that Marcie has two options. First, he holds to the hope that she may well find a soul to match her own, and thus fulfillment as a wife and mother. But, even if this turns out to be impossible, he argues that by virtue of her unique spirit and strength, she will forge a "path of exception" that will enable her to use her philosophical and poetic brilliance to the fullest (*Marcie* 203). This second option entails the creation of something absolutely new, namely, a future path for a woman that would be neither melancholy solitude and isolation nor marriage and maternity.

Was the task of representing such a path ultimately the most intransigent of the "difficulties" that kept Sand from completing this work? While the letter writer insists that marriage need not be seen as the only available positive fate for Marcie, his evocations of the alternative are always drawn in terms of its sublimity and rarity, leading us to wonder how Marcie will be able to attain it in her everyday life. Lacan might have included such an alternative in the "nouvel ordre," to which he referred in order to underline that it does not exist, at least not yet, and that therefore nothing concrete can be said of it. But, Sand asks, can it not be forged, created?

While it is certain that the third path Marcie might take involves a philosophy, a philosophy that would be *hers*, it is by no means certain that any currently existing philosophy is appropriate. Although the future as that which is not yet is to be struggled for and created, there is a distinction to be made between this not-yet, on the one hand, and the impossible on the other.[5] If a particular philosophy's aims amount, for Sand's letter writer (and Sand herself), to impossible desires, then that philosophy must be rejected. For to wish the impossible is inevitably to turn away from the concrete challenges, opportunities, and limitations that face one here and now. At one point, Marcie favors Saint-Simonism, the philosophico-political movement of mostly proletarian women who called, among other things, for the participation of women in government and for the abolition of marriage.[6] But in a turn crucial for the understanding of Sand's feminine philosophy, the friend discourages this alliance. In no uncertain terms, he sees its aims (as did Sand) as entirely incompatible with the goals that women should set for themselves; as, in short, an illusory project.

Chapter One

> Vous vous croyez propre à un rôle d'homme dans la société, et vous trouvez la société fort injuste de vous le refuser. Je crains, Marcie, que les promesses impuissantes d'une philosophie nouvelle ne vous aient fait du mal. Soit que vous ayez mal compris la véritable pensée du saint-simonisme, soit que, dans ses hésitations et ses recherches, le saint-simonisme n'ait pas trouvé le mot de vos destinées, vous y avez puisé le désir de l'impossible. (*Marcie* 193 [20])

And this "desire for the impossible" is to be suppressed at all costs, even at the cost of Marcie's life, because it implies a kind of irresponsibility that puts individual claims and dissatisfactions before those of the community, the "human race." "[G]rande âme cachée," her friend counsels, "sachez vous anéantir plutôt que de désirer, pour satisfaire un besoin personnel, que le genre humain fasse un acte de démence [namely, the act of admitting women into parliament]" ("[G]reat, hidden soul [. . .] know how to annihilate yourself rather than desire, in order to satisfy a personal need, that the human race commit an act of lunacy"; *Marcie* 197). There is a clear division here between what are called personal desires and what can be considered valid hopes for a future in which the sexes would no longer live in a master-slave relation. When a woman expresses the desire to take on public and "virile" roles, the desire is characterized as personal; whereas her desire for marriage and maternity is lauded as in conformity with that which a woman justly wants: the fulfillment of her proper (private) role in society. It is the fact that this latter wish should be so difficult to fulfill because of the tyranny of man (which turns marriage into servitude and even strips her of authority over her children) that constitutes the grave injustice to which women are subject and which must be changed. To attempt to redress this injustice by introducing women into the public sphere is seen as at once perverse and criminal:

> Mais quelle confiance pourraient inspirer à des juges intègres des femmes qui, se présentant pour réclamer la part de dignité qu'on leur refuse dans la maison conjugale, et surtout la part sacrée d'autorité qu'on leur refuse sur leurs enfants, demanderaient pour dédommagement, non pas la paix de leur ménage, non pas la liberté de leurs affections

maternelles, mais la parole au forum, mais le casque et
l'épée, mais le droit de condamner à mort? (*Marcie* 202 [21])

What, then, remains for Marcie if not marriage and maternity? It is certainly not the alternative of occupying a public, i.e., male, role in society. How is the other alternative characterized, beyond adjectives like "exceptional" and "sublime"? Finally, and without ever completely giving up on the possibility of marriage, what her friend suggests is that Marcie become an artist (*Marcie* 106). It has been argued that this answer to woman's fate and to her relation to man constitutes Sand's successful resolution to the problem of sexual difference, understood as the domination of one sex over the other. Apropos of *Consuelo, La Comtesse de Rudolstadt,* for example, Lucy MacCallum-Schwartz writes:

> C'est à cause de sa vocation d'artiste-créateur que Consuelo réussit à assumer sa sensualité et à devenir femme complète. Lélia et Blanche [of Sand's *Rose et Blanche*] sont transformées en statues—donc en objets passifs—par la sensualité. Consuelo nie cette qualité statique et refuse d'être un objet pour l'homme qu'elle aime. Elle choisit d'être un sujet agissant en créant des œuvres d'art. Dans *La Comtesse de Rudolstadt* Sand nous présente une vision positive de la sexualité féminine et une trêve dans la guerre des sexes. (177 [22])

Certainly the vocation of the artist is an attractive one for Sand; however, I would point out that if it helps Sand to present a "positive vision of feminine sexuality," this vision is nevertheless entirely dependent upon the existence of an ideal *masculine* sexuality, and can be realized only on condition that the ideal man be found, and a truce (albeit an extremely local one, between one exceptional woman and one exceptional man) thereby declared. Indeed, as MacCallum-Schwartz notes, "Elle [Consuelo] peut accepter sa sensualité et se satisfaire sans perdre sa volonté *parce qu'elle a trouvé l'homme que Lélia cherchait en vain—l'homme supérieur* qui la traite comme une égale" (177 [23]; emphasis added).

Now for Marcie the situation is quite the opposite. *Because she will not have found the man,* she might—she ought to—

Chapter One

become an artist, an exceptional being who would exist outside of the wife-and-mother/miserable-old-maid dilemma and claim a unique place for herself, almost *faute de mieux*. As her friend puts it:

> il me paraît très probable que vous serez appelée par de meilleures circonstances, par la rencontre imprévue de ces bonheurs [which life *en famille* brings] dont l'ange de notre destinée nous murmure quelquefois le secret à l'oreille, à réaliser votre premier vœu. Si la fortune continue à vous maltraiter, vous serez plus forte qu'elle; vous tournerez vos aspirations vers des hauteurs sublimes, vous chercherez entre le mysticisme et la philosophie un rôle d'exception, une mission de vierge et d'ange; si votre âme n'y atteint pas, vous souffrirez longtemps avant de vous résoudre à risquer votre sagesse sur des promesses incertaines, sur des espérances trompeuses. Vous mourrez plutôt que d'accepter la fortune et le plaisir de quelque source impure. (*Marcie* 202–03 [24])

In Marcie's case, the destiny of the woman artist entails the complete renunciation of any erotic relations whatsoever, in favor of a newly assumed identity (virgin-angel) utterly free from (because far above) the risks of sexuality. One cannot help noticing, however, the fact that this "rôle d'exception" is exceptional not only in that it would be a difficult, challenging, and sublimely rewarding one for Marcie, but because it is literally the *one exception* to the general rule that there is nothing (acceptable) for a woman to do outside of marriage. In fact, the possibility that Marcie could become an artist is mentioned in the midst of a catalogue of the options that must remain closed to her (among which: orator, priest, soldier, parliamentarian, professor, all of which Marcie expresses a desire to pursue). "Cherchez dans la hiérarchie sociale, dans tous les rangs du pouvoir ou de l'industrie, quelque position où la pensée de vous installer ne vous fasse pas sourire. Vous ne pouvez être qu'artiste, et cela, rien ne vous en empêchera" (*Marcie* 196 [25]). Achieving this unique position (or dying in the attempt), she will not only be outside, but above her sex (173). For, "Toutes les fois que nous faisons des actes de force, nous nous élevons au-dessus de la nature humaine vulgaire. Vous savez que de grandes destinées morales sont condamnées à une sorte d'isolement, et que l'esprit de sagesse [...] a amplement dédommagé ceux qui se retirent de la route commune pour entrer volontairement dans la vie intérieure" (173–74 [26]). Finding a new, future place for this exceptional woman, then, entails her raising herself above her sex, which is to say above a vulgar human nature. And as we have seen, this means, specifically, human nature as sexual. Art, then, would be not so much the solution to sexual difference as it would be the transcendence of it altogether. It is marked out as the one domain which is not, so to speak, sexed in advance; it exists in sublime altitudes where the virility demanded by public roles and the femininity essential to marriage and maternity cancel each other out once and for all. In the world of artistic creation, then, it is possible for an exceptional woman to unleash her soul and produce cultural works that may even have an impact on the world in which she lives. Politics, however, the all too human realm of sex and power, sex as power, ensures the exclusion of women, who can only be taken for what they are in that domain: the legal dependents of men.

The Political Future

> Il ne faut pas qu'un homme obéisse à une femme, c'est monstrueux. Il ne faut pas qu'un homme commande à une femme, c'est lâche.
> George Sand
> *Correspondance* [27]

Sand's central argument concerning possibilities for the future revolves around how society will change with respect to women: if both society and women themselves are to change, which change comes first? According to Marcie's correspondent, it would be a grave error for women to assume radically different roles before society itself has been sufficiently altered. The question, still echoed in today's utopian discourses, of where "society" ends and "women" begin poses itself as Sand attempts to lay out the requirements for real change. She addresses this same question at greater length in a letter she wrote eleven years after the appearance of the *Lettres à Marcie* in *Le Monde*. Writing in April 1848 to the members of the

Chapter One

"central committee" (a committee of the left that gave its backing to electoral candidates[7]), Sand gives the clearest expression of her position vis-à-vis the admission of women to political life.

She begins by declaring her agreement on two points: (1) that women should "participer un jour à la vie politique" ("participate one day in political life"), and (2) that "pour que la condition des femmes soit ainsi transformée, il faut que la société soit transformée radicalement" ("in order for the condition of women to be thus transformed, society must be radically transformed").[8] But she goes on to address a third point:

> Quelques femmes ont soulevé cette question: Pour que la société soit transformée, ne faut-il pas que la femme intervienne politiquement dès aujourd'hui dans les affaires publiques?—J'ose répondre qu'il ne faut pas, parce que les conditions sociales sont telles que les femmes ne pourraient pas remplir honorablement et loyalement un mandat publique. (*Correspondance* 8: 401 [28])

She argues that as long as women are, by law, completely disenfranchised once they marry, there is no possibility for them to contribute publicly to the life of the polis: how could they represent others, runs Sand's argument, when they are not permitted even to represent themselves?[9] Constantly bringing the argument back to marriage and divorce laws (under which wives were the wards of their husbands, had no property rights, no legal authority over their children, and were subject to the caprice of their husbands' mercy or cruelty when it came to the question of adultery: murdering—or privately imprisoning, beating, etc.—an unfaithful wife was the right of the wronged husband), Sand insists that there is not yet any place for women to speak from when it comes to *making laws* of whatever sort, since under the current civil laws of the Napoleonic Code they are but slaves, or at best "half-men" (*Correspondance* 8: 407).

Sand's argument may strike us as counterintuitive today: if the laws are flawed with respect to the rights they fail to accord to women, would not a crucial remedy be the admittance of women into the law-making body? To understand why her answer is in the negative, it is necessary to focus precisely on her utopian ideal of what relations between the sexes should be. In Irigarayan terms, we could say that she is attempting to ward off the danger of a "repetition of the same" that would be the result of a more or less revenge-driven struggle for equality. If the order of human relations is to be altered truly for the better, then, Sand insists, this alteration must begin in the hearts and minds of the women who work for change. If there is to be an eradication of men's dominance over women, there must be an eradication of the wish for dominance over the men who have kept women in a state of subjugated minors. If you want to be men's equals, Sand urges, then

> Veuillez être leurs égales afin de renoncer à ce lâche plaisir de les dominer par la ruse. Veuillez être leurs égales afin de tenir avec joie ce serment de fidélité qui est l'idéal de l'amour et le besoin de la conscience dans un pacte d'égalité [. . .]. Veuillez être leurs égales, au nom même de ce sentiment chrétien de l'humilité qui ne signifie pas autre chose que le respect du droit des autres à l'égalité [. . .]. Il ne faut pas qu'un homme obéisse à une femme, c'est monstrueux. Il ne faut pas qu'un homme commande à une femme, c'est lâche. Il faut que l'homme et la femme obéissent à leurs serments, à l'honneur, à la raison, à leur amour pour leurs enfants. Ce sont là des liens sacrés, des lois supérieures aux conseils de notre orgueil et aux entraînements des passions humaines. (*Correspondance* 8: 406 [29])

The same concern for changes that, in Sand's terms, would be affected not only on the level of laws but on the level of mores, occupies Irigaray's thought. For although we can point to some concrete advances in the realm of politics, Irigaray stresses that political overtures to the world of women,

> elles s'opèrent comme concessions de la part des pouvoirs existants et non comme mis en place de nouvelles valeurs. Trop peu pensées et affirmées par les femmes elles-mêmes, qui en restent souvent à *une revendication critique*. Ce qui permet un reflux mondial des points obtenus dans leurs luttes, faute d'en assurer des fondements autres que ceux sur lesquels s'érige le monde des hommes? (*EDS* 14 [30]; emphasis added)

We can hear Sand responding with an unequivocal "Yes!" Her crucial point, that women cannot represent others until they

Chapter One

become, literally, "representations of themselves" is one that continues to assert itself keenly, and the idea that women will never get beyond a politics of revenge, rancor, and concessions, of "critical demands," until the foundations underlying what Irigaray calls "the world of men" are transformed is precisely what Sand wishes to foreground in her arguments against "equal" political participation for women.

For such participation, before any radical change in relations between the sexes, would inevitably amount to women's participation in, as opposed to transformation of, the moral corruption that already reigns. Thus Sand sees the Saint-Simoniennes' call for equality in love, under the banner of a sort of free love in which both men and women (rather than men alone) would be completely at liberty with respect to their liaisons and in which marriage would be abolished, as a too hasty sacrifice—and to a reigning degeneracy, at that—of the possible difference that women could offer to notions and practices of love itself. When her imagined and invisible woman, Marcie, has apparently begun to yield to such a temptation, such an ill-advised concession, her correspondent reminds her of the exceptional nature of her soul in order to discourage this falling away. The emphasis placed on her virtuous character may be especially important for him (or Sand) here, since Marcie fits precisely the description of the typical Saint-Simonienne: young, unmarried, and poor.

> Et, quant à ces dangereuses tentatives qu'ont faites quelques femmes dans le saint-simonisme pour goûter le plaisir dans la liberté, pensez-en ce que vous voudrez, mais ne vous y hasardez pas, cela n'est pas fait pour vous. Vous ne sauriez aimer à demi, et, si vous aimez un jour, vous aimerez à jamais. Vous aurez accepté un hommage libre, et bientôt vous aurez horreur de ce droit d'infidélité [. . .]. Que serait donc une société nouvelle où les belles âmes n'auraient pas le droit d'étendre leurs ailes et de se développer dans toute leur étendue, où le fort [i.e., the morally strong, who love strongly] serait de *par la loi* le jouet et la dupe du faible? Et comment cela n'arriverait-il pas sans cesse sous un régime qui l'autoriserait, puisque cela arrive si souvent sous un régime qui le prohibe? Etrange remède à la corruption d'une société que de lui ouvrir toutes grandes les portes de la licence! (*Marcie* 176–77 [31])

One can compare with some legitimacy the strategies of the Saint-Simoniennes with those of some of today's radical feminists. In arguing for the abolition of any legislation whatever over anything pertaining to sexual relations between men and women, both would work toward a new equality through a sort of legislative *fait accompli* that would inevitably accomplish other goals further down the road. In Sand's time, a Saint-Simonienne might have responded to her that while beginning from absolutely free relations between the sexes (free from economic dependence as well as from other legal conjugal bonds) might seem at first blush like license, this would in fact lead to the ideal and true relations Sand envisions: there would be no material, legal trappings between women and men, hence their unions would ultimately come to be based on love, respect, and the truth of the desires of each, rather than on dominance. Indeed, such was precisely the argument of one Joséphine-Félicité, a Saint-Simonienne who wrote for the *Apostolât des Femmes*. "How would we be false," she asks, "when we are no longer held criminal for being that which GOD has made us, loving women?"[10] Similarly today, when certain feminists (for example Monique Wittig and members of the *psych et po* group) argue that in order to abolish patriarchy what is needed is the establishment of communities of women that would (at least at first) exclude men, the logic goes thus: if women can first come to love themselves and each other, and thus newly discover their being *in their difference as women,* and the kind of values that both Sand and Irigaray intimate they might offer to disrupt and displace those that currently hold sway, then and only then might relations of mutual love between men and women be possible, for only then will men also have had to challenge their own masculine identities, in the face of women's difference, especially their difference from the traditional identities ascribed to them, or legislated for them, in patriarchal culture.

What is more, we find today at least one contemporary argument, from a psychoanalytic perspective, against this line of thought that almost perfectly parallels Sand's against the Saint-Simoniennes. In his *Clinical Introduction to Lacanian Psychoanalysis,* Bruce Fink addresses the solution offered to the violence and injustice of patriarchal Law proposed among

Chapter One

some feminist thinkers, who suggest that nontraditional familial structures will make this Law a thing of the past just as they do the traditional, male-headed nuclear family in which the father lays down the law. Fink counters that this is not only too optimistic a prediction, but that if new structures do take hold and begin to change the Law, this will in fact entail a change for the worse. His argument recalls Sand's above:

> If we are to preserve some notion of a just Law above and beyond the particular laws of the land—given the current legitimation crisis of the legal, juridical, and executive branches of government—a just Law that is equitably and uniformly enforced, we must have an experience at home which at least approaches that ideal to some degree. As rare as this experience may be in the stereotypical nuclear family, practices currently being advocated seem likely to make it rarer still. (Fink 254n71)

By way of comparison, we might recapitulate thus:

> Sand: It is rare now—under a regime which officially prohibits infidelity and hence upholds, theoretically at least, the ideal under which men and women should live—that men and women (but especially men) are faithful. It would be still rarer (infidelity would happen still more often, the law of fidelity would be broken more frequently) under a regime which authorized it.

> Fink: The experience of an ideal justice and its workings is rare already in the stereotypical nuclear family (where the father should lay down the Law as justly as possible). It would be rarer still under practices offered up as alternatives to the nuclear family, practices that would attempt to overcome the injustice of the Law by getting rid of the Legislator.[11]

Both of the alternatives Sand and Fink consider and argue against are offered in the interest of a more just, equitable, and ethical distribution of power for the two sexes. The Saint-Simoniennes argue that complete sexual freedom for both women and men would mean that each sex approaches intimate relations on the same footing, women no longer depending on men (and themselves) to live up to an ideal of romantic love that so frequently in practice results in women's victimized, jilted status and men's victimizing independent status (men are free to come and go; women wait and hope). The feminists Fink addresses argue that the nuclear family (set up to ensure just relations, just as an ideal love should ensure them in Sand's scenario) in fact ensures the opposite: domination, victimization, the universal instantiation of patriarchal Law; and so they conclude that breaking out of its laws and conventions may be the only way to realize truly ethical relations. Like Marcie's friend (and Sand herself), Fink cautions that this utopian approach (for example, the idea that women raising children without men can in fact avoid instating an unjust, patriarchal law) in fact constitutes a danger to the possibility of justice. Getting rid of the father and his Law, Fink argues, will only carry us further away from the ideal of a just law equally applied to all.

We might be surprised here that Fink does not emphasize more what is the virtual impossibility, from a Lacanian perspective, of doing away with the paternal metaphor and triangulation that constitute the instantiation of the Father's law. Whatever the answer to the question "What does she (Mother) want?" (i.e., whether it is "Daddy" or someone/something else), the mere fact that the question can be posed is enough for what Lacan refers to as the paternal metaphor to be instated, for triangulation to occur (and hence, the entry into language, the fundamental alienation of the subject). The question might then be about *what if anything* would be changed about the law of the Father if triangulation, the entrance of a third term, were generally represented by a female rather than a male being. Instead, Fink concentrates on the danger of its not happening at all, which is fitting in part, given that (1) his note comes at the end of a chapter dealing with psychosis (and thus precisely with the failure of triangulation to take hold), and that (2) his interlocutors are suggesting that a subject can come into being *without* triangulation. But even with respect to the feminist objections he counters, this is nonetheless a misleading track, for it can all too easily be misconstrued to imply that without the (male) father, psychosis will ensue, while in fact the emphasis should be on the fact that, father or no father, the "paternal" metaphor most often does indeed *get itself instated,* so that the questions Fink might put to the feminists he responds to would concern the nature of the relation to the Law. For example: (1) How can the paternal metaphor possibly be got rid of?, and (2) Assuming that it cannot be avoided, assuming that its avoidance leads to psychosis, what will be the difference of its instantiation being differently represented?

Sand, in turn, concentrates on the risks of license: if those doors are opened—if the sacred and just law of fidelity is done away with—then how could relations between men and women be based on anything but deceit and even violence? The option here would be to ask about the nature of the law of fidelity itself, and men and women's relation to that law (as, in the above case, one could ask about the nature of the law of triangulation with respect to men and women's relation to it). Why is it, for example, that fidelity is so often breached in the present, by both men and women? (In the Lacanian/feminist debate above: Why or how is it that the paternal metaphor does sometimes manage *not* to be instated?) Instead for Sand, the assumption holds: infidelity would be more rampant (the incidence of psychosis would increase) if the law were done away with. Marcie, then, must not hazard the "dangerous efforts" of the Saint-Simoniennes, for she would be crushed under the lack of a law.

Whether or not the transformation of the law, by forging and occupying a unique space with respect to it, will be possible for Marcie (or whether she would be able finally to find *the right man* in order to enter into the way of maternal love, perhaps supplemented by artistic creation) is left open. Is the woman, Marcie in this case, of whom Sand would write "impossible" to write because of her invisibility before a law that cannot conceive of her? In this sense, it would be a question of the difficulty of representing a woman who is, besides invisible, also cultivated and deeply thoughtful. A question, that is, of the poverty of language with respect to a yet-to-be-written (but currently existing) feminine subjectivity. Or is Marcie for Sand a yet-to-be-woman, a vision she would like to develop of what a woman might be, might become, in some future that would allow women to overcome the impasse between dependence on men, a longing for romantic union and maternity, and a desire to create their own destinies? Had the *Lettres* been completed, would Marcie have foundered (or thrived?) in her poverty and isolation, or would Sand have found a way for Marcie to find "between mysticism and philosophy an exceptional role" (203), and would such an exceptional role require that Marcie follow her correspondent's advice: that she learn to annihilate herself, to die, rather than satisfy her personal desires, rather than take pleasure from any impure source? In short, will the woman of the future require the annihilation of the woman of the present, along with her desires? The literally open-ended status of the *Lettres* leaves all of these questions in suspense.

The contemporary example I have provided here—of Fink's brief Lacanian response to a feminist argument—is instructive, I want to argue, *not* because it demonstrates the rigidity of a so-called masculine theory (psychoanalysis, or even Lacanian psychoanalysis) with respect to feminism, but because it suggests the mutual need of each for the other. A feminist claim that getting rid of the men will automatically change the psychic structure of subjects and their relation to the Law is facile, not to mention essentialist, resting as it does on the assumption that women together somehow transcend the need for law, authority, the imposition of one rule versus another, etc. None of these go away when women come together, although they may be differently manifested or repressed. A woman, in short, is as liable as any man to impose her will on another while pretending (to herself) that it is the will of the other to which she is responding. But a feminist engagement with the question of triangulation, of the Law, has to confront these questions, acknowledging as it does, at the very least, the facts of repression and unconscious desire. The question of a child's link with and separation from its mother cannot be avoided, and thus neither can the issue of the imposition of a law that says "No" (the Lacanian "nom" or "non" du père[12]) to the child's fusion with the mother, a no that comes down as a law that ultimately requires the assumption of a more or less separate identity. The real question around which all of these arguments—Saint-Simonian sexual freedom, Sand's ideal of an exceptional woman, a contemporary feminist escape from the father, and Fink's cautioning against his absence—dance is perhaps ultimately the apparent superfluity of the father, the man, and the

Chapter One

anxiety it provokes. On almost all sides, what is clear is that the masculine element seems unnecessary. The Saint-Simoniennes say as much (or are understood to say in their day, at least) by asserting the financial and sexual independence of women. Those who argue for the father's exit clearly see no necessary role for him. From a Lacanian psychoanalytic perspective, one can maintain that it's not the father who lays down the law so much as it is the mother's desire (for him or anyone/anything other than the child), which is why Lacan refers to the paternal *metaphor*. Even Sand envisions a future of fulfillment for Marcie that would not require her to find the right man and define/find her being primarily in her relation to him. The following question inevitably asserts itself (again): in reaching toward an ideal of equality (for women), do we necessarily end up excluding the now dominant side of sexual difference, and thus repeat the logic of domination? Psychoanalysis without feminism might miss this question, since it could tend to explain away too quickly the problem of the father's superfluity. A psychoanalytically inflected feminism cannot fail to see and then to address the point, pregnant as it is with the question of unconscious desire (the desire to kill the father?). Is it the intimation of such a desire that keeps Sand from arguing with the Saint-Simoniennes? Is it more than her historical moment (and what we might write off as her conservatism) that prevents her from giving up completely on the unlikely possibility that Marcie will find the ideal man? Is it perhaps that she feels within her own feminism and that of others the insidious risk of the refusal or fear of difference (a masculine difference) in the quest for equality? Why is it, after all, that she writes not letters *from* Marcie, but *to* Marcie, from a masculine instance figured as a friend, a fellow sufferer, a man who is as confused and fearful of the future as Marcie herself?

The incompleteness of the *Lettres à Marcie* adds to its force when we take into account not merely that it is unfinished, but that it is by definition only one part of a drama: by providing only the friend's letters, Sand has perhaps not so much rendered her woman invisible as she has effectively placed her readers in Marcie's position. Ultimately this may be more significant even than the impossibility of representing her. Embodying already (and in anticipation?) her reasonable, pious male friend, she also gives body to the woman, in the shape of her (male and female) readers who, willy-nilly, find themselves "on her side" of the discussions and debates, the side of the invisible, impossible woman. To "finish" such a work may have meant risking the end of the heroine as opposed to her tentative invention. Furthermore, in *Lélia*, which was twice finished, the path taken is precisely Marcie's unknown "path of exception," and it indeed leads the heroine to risk both sublime heights and her own annihilation, the question for Lélia being whether the former necessarily entails the latter.

Lélia

In *Lélia*,[13] contrary to what we might have expected, we find that a woman's choice of an exceptional path destines her to become "une exception maudite" (accursed). Unable to combine the brilliance of her intellect and the strength of her desire with any of the objects available to her, she instead progresses gradually to a complete isolation from a society she can only reject. *Lélia* is a novel (or as Sand also called it, "a poetic essay"; 1: xx) that, with its persistent interrogations of what constitutes the difference between the sexes, its unconventional narrative structure and generic status, its preoccupation with fundamental ethical questions, and its central representation of a woman struggling with (against, for, because of) her own desire, cannot fail to interest those of us today who are so much engaged with these issues in feminist literary and psychoanalytic thinking.

Lélia is a novel without a plot, or with a plot pared down to a minimal presence, the better to make room for the philosophical reflections Sand pursues throughout the book. The intelligent and extraordinary Lélia restlessly seeks some fulfillment that always escapes her; the young poet, Sténio, loves her to the point of worship but is always rebuffed as a sexual lover, and eventually kills himself; her wise friend Trenmor does what he can to help her, but is alarmed by the excesses of her ambition and pride; and the mad priest, Magnus, lusts after, and thus conceives a murderous hatred for Lélia. At the end of the final (1839) version of the novel, Lélia dies in the environs of the convent where she has exiled herself from the world. (In the first version, Lélia is murdered by Magnus, who kills her in order to end the temptation she represents for him.)

The novel, which can also be read as a sustained meditation on traditional notions of love, and possible alternatives, begins with a question that will never be finally answered: "Qui es-tu?" (1: 61). The impossibility of answering this question, put to Lélia by her would-be lover, Sténio (who Eileen Boyd Sivert claims "comes closest to the description given by Cixous of a bisexual man"; Sivert 55), is for Lélia tied up with her apparently conflicting desires to love and be loved in a heterosexual relationship on the one hand, and not to find herself in a relation based on domination, on the other. It is not until part 3 of the novel that Lélia is able to express the root of her frustration, which, broadly described, consists in what she sees as the impossibility of love in the world of humans, *ici-bas*. As Schor has summed it up, "*Lélia* is the story of its female protagonist whose graphic confessions of frigidity and bleak howl of metaphysical despair constitute the central scandal of this work" ("*Lélia* and the Failures of Allegory" 77).

This world of humanity, this *ici-bas,* associated in *Lettres à Marcie* with a rotting and "vulgar human nature" that must be overcome, is more particularly and emphatically linked to the corrupt and corrupting world of men in *Lélia,* whose heroine is especially disdainful of what passes for love among them. In their love, she sees nothing but the satisfaction of sexual desires, a satisfaction that, moreover, is directly proportional to their violent enslavement of women. The all-pervasiveness of this masculine order steels Lélia's resolve and scorn, and leads her to despair of any love between men and women other than an ideal characterized by a disembodied communion of intellects. Physical love, she claims, is always the debasement of such an ideal, for in it, women are reduced to the property of their would-be lovers, and their own desires are discounted as either unsatisfiable or demonic in their excess. When Irigaray writes of the difficulty of an ethical (love) relation between the sexes here and now, she points to the exclusion of any imaginary other than the masculine, an exclusion that, in terms of the sexual relation, amounts to normativizing jouissance according to the masculine experience and figuration of erection and detumescence. Any idea of another kind of jouissance is absent from this conception, and indeed, rejected by it. Irigaray writes,

> Elle [Woman] en voudrait toujours *encore,* écrivent certains psychanalystes (notamment Jacques Lacan), assimilant ce *toujours plus* à une pathologie [*sic*]. En fait, ce toujours plus n'est que le statut du désir sexué féminin. Inassouvissable, sans doute, dans la vie quotidienne. Pas pathologique pour autant. [. . .] Elle jouit du *toucher* en quelque sorte indéfiniment. (*EDS* 67 [32])

And when Lélia is approached by her suitor at the opening of the novel, her difference is characterized immediately as frightening and unknowable. "Il doit y avoir en toi," Sténio writes to her, "quelque affreux mystère inconnu aux hommes" ("There must be in you some terrible mystery unknown to men"; 1: 61). If she is not an angel in her mystery, then she must be a demon, for there is something "infernal" about her, upon which Milton may have looked when he created the visage of Satan (1: 64). Lélia wastes no time in giving the lie to Sténio's hyperbolic and dehumanizing rhetoric. Her first words in the novel are a protest against his insistence upon making of her something more or less than human:

> Que t'importe cela, jeune poète? Pourquoi veux-tu savoir qui je suis et d'où je viens?. . . Je suis née comme toi dans la vallée des larmes, et tous les malheureux qui rampent sur la terre sont mes frères [. . .]. Que peut-il y avoir d'étrange et de mystérieux dans une existence humaine? [. . .]
> Vous demandez si je suis un être d'une autre nature que vous! Croyez-vous que je ne souffre pas? [. . .]
> Vous demandez si j'adore l'esprit du mal! L'esprit du mal et l'esprit du bien, c'est un seul esprit, c'est Dieu [. . .]. Le bien et le mal, ce sont des distinctions que nous avons créées. Dieu ne les connaît pas plus que le bonheur et l'infortune. Ne demandez donc ni au ciel ni à l'enfer le secret de ma destinée. C'est à vous que je pourrais reprocher de me jeter sans cesse au-dessus et au-dessous de moi-même. (1: 65 [33])

In his response, Sténio fails to take in the import of this reproach, even as he acknowledges having done Lélia a certain violence. "L'âpreté de mes sollicitudes pour vous, je l'ai trop

Chapter One

franchement exprimée, Lélia; j'ai blessé la sublime pudeur de votre âme" (1: 66 [34]). Lélia remains (and will remain throughout the novel) for Sténio a sublime being, not wholly of this world, while Lélia herself will constantly struggle with her inability to enter the world wholly, as a fully human woman who can accept the satisfaction of her desires, instead of being "blessés par toutes nos jouissances" ("wounded by all our jouissances"; 1: 65).

She explains to her sister when they meet for the first time since early adolescence, "Plus sage et plus heureuse que moi, vous ne viviez que pour jouir; plus ambitieuse et moins soumise à Dieu peut-être, je ne vivais que pour désirer" (1: 160 [35]). And when her desire is faced with the possibility or demand for its specifically sexual fulfillment, Lélia flees, quite literally, to the divine ideal of Love. Her desire, she says, keeps her from any possibility of enjoyment.

> Toute créature, si médiocre qu'elle soit, peut inspirer ou ressentir ce délire d'un instant et le prendre pour l'amour. L'intelligence et l'aspiration du grand nombre ne vont pas au-delà. L'être qui aspire à des joies toujours nobles, à des plaisirs toujours vivement et saintement sentis, à une continuelle association de l'amour moral à l'amour physique, est un ambitieux destiné à un bonheur immense ou à une éternelle douleur. [...] D'où vient donc qu'on refuse aux femmes pures la faculté de sentir le dégoût et le droit de le manifester aux hommes impurs qui les trompent? [...] une femme fière ne peut connaître le plaisir sans l'amour: c'est pourquoi elle ne trouvera ni l'un ni l'autre dans les bras de la plupart des hommes. Quant à ceux-ci, il leur est bien moins facile de répondre à nos instincts nobles et d'alimenter nos généreux désirs que de nous accuser de froideur. (2: 13–14 [36])

Lélia frequently expresses this "generous" nature of her desires, refusing the idea that she should have to curb them in order to submit to an enjoyment that can in no way match their scope. Irigaray's characterization of feminine desire (its *always more* character—unsatisfiable, but not pathological) cannot fail to come to mind, as well as Lacan's exposure of the fundamental misrecognition at the core of the sexual relation between men and women. For Lélia, it would first be a question of doing away with one of the first effects of this misrecognition: the conviction that women are either frigid stones or whores.[14] These are indeed the two women we have in the novel, the statuesque Lélia and her courtesan sister, Pulchérie, both of them exposing the masculine fear that dictates their relegation to one or the other role, but nowhere in between. Lélia details her own critique of what they would call her "frigidity," while Pulchérie, as we shall see, knows only too well that she has a strictly delimited choice between being one among "their" women, a possession, or taking upon herself the life of a paid courtesan who would be mistress at least of when, how, of whom, with what measure of enjoyment (and for how much) she will be a temporarily possessed good.

In much of the recent scholarship on *Lélia*, there has been an alternative set up between reading Lélia's "impotence" either as a bodily expression of her refusal of phallocentric sexuality (Lélia as a kind of *jeune née* disturber of patriarchy), or as a symptom of what would ultimately come to a psychotic denial of sexual difference (Lélia as victim of patriarchy).[15] I would suggest that even as both of these factors may be at work, Lélia's problem (her "sexual impotence" is but one manifestation of an all-consuming existential misery) and Sand's thinking of sexual difference might be better understood if the focus were brought more specifically to bear on the question of Lélia's desire. This is at the same time to insist on the importance of the ethics put forward in *Lélia*. From the outset of the narrative, Sand explicitly links the problem of sexual difference (and it is always a problem in this work) to the possibility of ethical relation as well as to the heroine's seemingly boundless, and binding, desires.

As Lélia struggles with the impossibility of any heterosexual love relation, she finds herself constantly reaching toward a something else, a something more, usually conceived as divine, that can never be attained *ici-bas*. At the same time, although Lélia seems to despair of the possibility of an intimate, embodied love between men and women in this world, she nevertheless struggles throughout the novel to forge just such a possibility, and is always thwarted when she finds herself the object of masculine, sexual desire. In her apparently objectless quest, she figures what anthropologist Michel Tournier has described as the nonexistent destiny of women in societies that offer them no place, no destination toward which to progress.

Chapter One

Writing on initiation rites in "primitive societies," Tournier notes that for girls who would become women,

> Il s'agit d'une sorte d'initiation inversée, centrifuge au lieu d'être centripète [...]. Un adolescent quitte le groupe féminin pour s'intégrer au groupe masculin. L'initiation a pour lui valeur de revendication d'un statut. Que peut faire une fille? Prisonnière du gynécée, elle peut chercher à en sortir. Pour aller où? C'est tout le problème de la libération des femmes. Entre le gynécée et la société des hommes, il n'existe pas encore la société unisexe pour l'accueillir [as we saw so plainly explained in *Lettres à Marcie*]. Il lui reste donc l'initiation-révolte [...]. Pour l'adolescente, l'initiation ne peut être qu'une fugue permanente. (Michel Tournier 340, qtd. in Penrod 86 [37])[16]

What Lélia would embark upon as a journey, then, can only be for her an endless wandering. It is as if Marcie had left her home and her correspondence and attempted to stray into the world and assert therein her own purpose—only to find that there is no purpose for her to assert, no site for her to stray to, and even, or especially, no proper relation for her to establish with either men or women, since she herself has refused to inhabit the place of either kind. In order, then, to ask how it is that Sand's narrative may offer an alternative thinking of traditional, phallocentric relationships, I shall attempt to see how, with *Lélia*, she understands and negotiates sexual difference as the *ici-bas* relations to which Lélia cannot reconcile herself. And I will insist upon the importance of the relation between Lélia and Pulchérie, for it is in this woman-to-woman, and twin sister-to-twin sister, relation that there may open up the possibility for something more, something other, that is nevertheless *ici-bas*.

Lélia and Pulchérie

Confronted with the sister she has not seen since early adolescence, Lélia is asked to explain her situation, to explain why it is that, filled with the desire to love, she nevertheless finds it impossible to do so. Significantly, it is not until this conversation with her *sister*, Pulchérie, that Lélia is able to articulate her thoughts and feelings about the until now vague but consuming malaise that has overtaken her life. "Les bruits de la fête se sont éloignés," says Pulchérie, "j'entends l'orchestre qui reprend l'air interrompu; on vous oublie; on renonce à me chercher: nous pouvons être libres quelque temps. Parlez" (Sand, *Lélia* 1: 162 [38]). Pulchérie's presence in the narrative introduces a new circumstance into the novel: a freedom that stems from the fact that Lélia is *forgotten,* that the crowd at the ball, society in general, has *given up looking for* Pulchérie. Nothing remains in this space but the two women together, forgotten and unsought, outside of the larger world, able to attempt a discourse about the *ici-bas* from a temporarily removed position. Until now, in her encounters and dialogues with others, Lélia's mysterious identity has always been in question: who is she, and what is her nature? What sense can be made of her in terms of her relation to society? Only when society has forgotten her, forgotten its stubborn interrogation, its demand for an answer to the question "What is Lélia?" does she become capable of a speech that she qualifies as her own, and as utterly at odds with what is normally, normatively, required. Only, in other words, when she is not required to respond to questions concerning her origin and identity (here, she is simply her sister's sister; they share an origin and a genus, as it were) does she embark on a kind of speech that is not (solely) a protest, but an exploration.

She begins, then, by stating that hers will not be a linear, logical narrative, but rather her own peculiar history, related in a mode she does not quite control. In order to tell her story, Lélia claims, it is absolutely necessary for her to leave the domain of the conventional narrative, and to attempt another one that will enable her to speak precisely of that which renders such a conventional mode impossible for her.

As their conversation progresses, Pulchérie will try to talk Lélia out of her angst by urging her to enjoy the exploitative nature of the male-female sexual relation, instead of constantly desiring to transcend it. And Lélia reiterates that she is a slave to her desire as much as she would be to a man were she to be able to submit herself to his jouissance. As Béatrice Didier has noted, "Le drame de Lélia ne consiste pas exactement à ne pas savoir jouir, mais à avoir désiré intensément et à souffrir d'un décalage entre l'immensité du désir et les limites de la

Chapter One

jouissance" (in Sand, *Lélia* 2: 197 [39]). Jouissance, in a word, means the death of desire, and so does the sexual relation between men and women—indeed, *any* sexual relation where the body of a woman is involved, for inevitably the woman's body, together with her desire, will be not only missed but annihilated, which is in fact Lélia's fate in the first version of the novel. But here with Pulchérie, she at least approaches the ability to express how it is that jouissance is impossible for her, how an unquenchable desire, at odds with the world in which she finds herself, would either shatter that world or be buried by it. For the first time, in other words, Lélia speaks her desire without silencing that in it which, lacking any proper representation *ici-bas*, must normally remain unsaid, and describes herself as one who "ne savais jouir de rien à force de vouloir jouir splendidement de toutes choses" (1: 165), who above all is "tourmentée d'un insatiable désir *d'être* quelque chose" (1: 166 [40]; emphasis added).

This desire to be—to distill something that *is* out of her infinite desire—is, as we saw in the Introduction, the ultimate burden of the woman (who is always the Woman) in patriarchy, where being is not for her, and she is not to be. How then, if at all, will Sand evoke another kind of being for Lélia, a being that will include its own impossibility? She begins simply by stating the impossible nature of woman's lack of being, most strongly in this passage with the twin sisters, the one sublimely nonexistent and the other vulgarly so. And she will proceed by a way that is neither wholly of this world nor outside of it: Lélia's desperate love of the future. At the end of her life, she will be attached only to that, unable to bear that the old world should finish without a new world emerging (2: 156). But first she will have to confront the impossible status of her desire, and in order for her to do this, Sand provides not a lover but a sister, a twin to whom she can both speak and listen.

We hear a contemporary echo of Lélia and Pulchérie's unfettered conversation in the speech of two other *parleuses:* Marguerite Duras and Xavière Gauthier, whose dialogues are presented in *Les parleuses,* in a mode that sheds light on the Lélia-Pulchérie exchange. In the preface to this collection of their transcribed dialogues, Gauthier remarks on their unconventional and uncorrected character, noting the risk involved

George Sand

in publishing their speaking exactly as it occurred, without straightening out the digressions, pauses, and ellipses into a conventionally structured, familiar mode of thought. She goes on to explain that the refusal to censor themselves is especially significant,

> parce que nous sommes toutes les deux des femmes. Il n'est pas impossible que si les mots pleins et bien assis ont de tout temps été utilisés, alignés, entassés par les hommes, le féminin pourrait apparaître comme cette herbe un peu folle, un peu maigrichonne au début, qui provient à pousser entre les interstices des vieilles pierres et—pourquoi pas?—finit par desceller les plaques de ciments. (Duras and Gauthier 8 [41])

These reflections serve well as a way to think about Sand's writing, particularly in *Lélia,* the more so as it is a novel that many have pronounced "unreadable," and that even favorable critics of Sand's time, notably Sainte-Beuve, faulted for its lack of structure. With Gauthier's words in mind, then, let us turn to that conversation between Lélia and Pulchérie.

Free to speak, Lélia announces that her narrative will not be based on "de faits circonstanciés et précis" ("detailed and precise facts"), but instead on "l'histoire d'un cœur malheureux" ("the history of an unhappy heart"; 1: 163). The rejection of traditional narration puts into relief the unconventional form of the novel as a whole, which led the contemporary critic Gustave Planche to declare it a "revolution in literature" that would signal a new writing of the invisible (or ideal) as opposed to the visible (or real) (qtd. in Van Rossum-Guyon 9).[17] As Naginski notes, "*Lélia,* the most poetic of Sand's novels [. . .] is also one of the most theoretical in its efforts to articulate a new kind of prose" (107). Schor calls *Lélia* "Sand's most iconoclastic work, a narratologist's nightmare" (*Sand and Idealism* 57). And writing in the *Revue des Deux Mondes* in August of 1833, Planche warned his readers that *Lélia* is not an "account of an adventure [. . .]. It is therefore not any ordinary novel or poem, and one must not seek episodes in it which excite an idle imagination, or traits of exterior reality which anyone can locate in one's personal life" (qtd. in Naginski 113). Sand herself, in the preface to her novel, declares:

Chapter One

> j'écrivis *Lélia* sans suite, sans plan, à bâtons rompus, et avec l'intention, dans le principe, de l'écrire pour moi seule. Je n'avais aucun système, je n'appartenais à aucune école, je ne songeais presque pas au public; je ne me faisais pas encore une idée nette de ce qu'est la publicité [. . .]. Était-ce modestie? Je puis affirmer que oui, bien qu'il ne paraisse guère modeste de s'attribuer une vertu si rare. Mais comme, chez moi, ce n'était pas vertu, je dis la chose comme elle est. *Ce n'était pas un effort de ma raison*, un triomphe remporté sur la vanité naturelle à notre espèce, *mais bien une insouciance du fait*, une imprévoyance innée, une tendance à m'absorber dans une occupation de l'esprit, sans me souvenir qu'au-delà du monde de mes rêves, il existait un monde de réalités sur lequel ma pensée, sereine ou sombre, pouvait avoir une action quelconque. (1: 53 [42]; emphasis added)

The language of this declaration in the preface is echoed in the Pulchérie-Lélia scene, where the two women speak only for themselves/each other, where they forget about the world of realities from which they are temporarily released through their mutual absorption, and where Lélia will narrate a story "sans plan," obeying not the laws of reason, but those of her own heart, as if for herself alone. In light of all this, the last part of the passage cited above indicates something more about the Lélia-Pulchérie encounter and the nature of the telling this encounter engenders: it points to the chance that Lélia's narration, which is somehow not one, and Lélia's intimacy with her sister, may have an effect on the world of realities, the *ici-bas* to which each woman will return from their mutually created, temporary haven. Does the brief exile, which allows Lélia to speak, ensure, despite its remove, that her speech will have taken on the force of some transformation when she returns? In order to answer this question, we will look more closely at that "histoire d'un cœur malheureux" that Lélia relates.

Her story soon reveals that her suffering is intimately related to the situation of the two sexes, which she describes as prohibiting any love, indeed any relation whatsoever between them.

> Quel œil paternel était donc ouvert sur la race humaine le jour où elle imagina de se scinder elle-même en plaçant un

sexe sous la domination de l'autre? N'est-ce pas un appétit farouche qui a fait de la femme l'esclave et la propriété de l'homme? Quels instincts d'amour pur, quelles notions de sainte fidélité ont pu résister à ce coup mortel? Quel lien autre que celui de la force pourra exister désormais entre celui qui a le droit d'exiger et celle qui n'a pas le droit de refuser? [. . .] Quel échange de sentiments, quelle fusion d'intelligences possible entre le maître et l'esclave? (1: 170 [43])

It is the very nature of the relation between the sexes—or rather, the nonrelation between the sexes—to which Lélia points as the undoing of any possibility of love between them, and as the misfortune under which she labors. Ultimately, this problem, which is such an important one in feminist thought today,[18] will not be resolved in the novel. As Sivert points out, the two options that seem most hopeful in terms of attacking the problem of femininity versus masculinity in patriarchal society—Pulchérie and Sténio—both disappear from the novel. Indeed, at the end of the 1833 version, Lélia herself literally falls victim to the violent nonrelation between the sexes, murdered by Magnus, the priest who desires and therefore despises her. Nevertheless, the character of Pulchérie, Lélia's double, deserves more careful consideration. While Sténio is both hoped for and rejected from the beginning of the novel (as a kind of last hope for any male-female relation), Pulchérie appears literally out of nowhere, and disappears just as inexplicably. And what occurs between the two women is striking in its singularity: it is the only woman-to-woman relation in the entire novel, and the only discourse that approaches frankly issues of sexuality and desire. This interlude represents a window Sand opens from within the patriarchal, phallocentric discourse *ici-bas*—that slavery Lélia feels so keenly—onto the imagination, if not the possibility, of another kind of thought and existence.

The scene of recognition between the two sisters begins with a touch: Pulchérie reaches out and surprises Lélia by placing her hand on Lélia's bare arm, after which the two women embrace each other and "se touchaient avec des mains étonnées. Elles ne revenaient pas de se trouver encore belles, de s'admirer, de s'aimer, et, différentes comme elles étaient, de se

Chapter One

reconnaître" (1: 156 [44]). Thus the first contact between two women in the novel comprises at once the sensual, the ability to love mutually, and the ability to recognize each other in their *difference*. In a word, the very conditions Lélia finds impossible to fulfill between men and women in patriarchal society where one sex is subordinate to the other. I underline the notion of difference here because Sand, even as she uses each character as the double of the other, repeatedly stresses the difference between them, especially during this scene in which the two are together, speaking.

This difference becomes particularly significant in light of the lesbian overtones Sand includes in the Lélia-Pulchérie relation. Although, in the 1839 edition, Sand suppressed part of the passage hinting at lesbianism, she left enough intact to indicate a sexual tension between the two characters. It was from Lélia, Pulchérie explains, that she received her "première leçon d'amour, [sa] première sensation de désir" ("first lesson in love, [her] first sensation of desire"; 1: 162). When Pulchérie confides to her sister that it was Lélia who first awakened sexual desire in her, Pulchérie notes not only that Lélia was beautiful in their girlhood, but that she was beautiful in a different way from herself. "Oh! vous étiez belle, Lélia! mais belle autrement que moi" ("Oh! you were beautiful, Lélia! but beautiful in another way than I"; 1: 161). In this way, what Irigaray would call falling into a repetition, in a woman-to-woman relation, of the (patriarchal) economy of love of same without love of other seems not at all to be the issue here, even when we are clearly dealing with a set of doubles. These two, so similar to others' eyes that they will be confused even by Sténio when he makes love to Pulchérie-cum-Lélia, these two love and recognize in each other what is most other from themselves. Whereas Lélia is unable to love and be loved by a man *as a woman,* distinct and different in a difference that would not entail subservience or domination, the love that she and Pulchérie share is described in terms of a mutual recognition that transcends not merely difference, but even the uncanny resemblance of the two that otherwise might threaten to efface both.

Pulchérie's erotic career began with the perception of her sister's different beauty in adolescence: for the first time, as the two lay dozing on the banks of an idyllic stream, she saw in her twin something "fière et froide de votre visage endormi, il y avait je ne sais quoi de masculin et de fort qui m'empêchait presque de vous reconnaître. Je trouvais que vous ressembliez à ce bel enfant aux cheveux noirs dont je venais de rêver, et je baisai votre bras en tremblant" (1: 161–62 [45]). Lélia awoke and responded with a mocking, severe look to Pulchérie's innocent "première leçon d'amour, [. . .] première sensation de désir." Now, Lélia says, she remembers that moment:

> —Je me souviens même d'un mot que je ne pus m'expliquer, répondit Lélia. Vous me fîtes pencher sur l'eau, et vous me dîtes: —Regarde-toi, ma sœur: ne te trouves-tu pas belle? Je vous répondis que je l'étais moins que vous. —Oh! tu l'es bien davantage, reprîtes-vous: tu ressembles à un homme.
> —Et cela vous fit hausser les épaules de mépris, reprit Pulchérie.
> —Et je ne devinai pas, répondit Lélia, qu'une destinée venait de s'accomplir pour vous, tandis que pour moi aucune destinée ne devait jamais s'accomplir. (1: 162 [46])

Pulchérie's initiation into her sexual destiny arrives with the perception of "something male" in her twin sister: Pulchérie will remain in the world of women, a sort of secondary or temporally extended gynaeceum, choosing to let men enter there on her terms, rather than leaving to become one of "their" women. Pulchérie's perception of difference, however, coincides with Lélia's refusal of that difference, and with being condemned to live out a life without a destiny, or destination, of her own. She will be eternally outside of both the gynaeceum and the world of men, in a permanent exile. In this scene of adolescent coming into sexuality, Lélia shrugs off the masculinity attributed to her just as she will refuse the femininity available to her, always searching for another route—neither that of one of their women nor of the "cold, strong" male. But though she may escape a confining femininity, the attributes of masculinity—her coldness, distance, and strength—remain with Lélia until the end of her life, notwithstanding this early refusal. Her task, as she sees it, is to transform these attributes into another, new definition of self that would surpass the duality of the feminine and the masculine. Her quest is to become a

Chapter One

woman without becoming the other of man, without, in other words, accepting a femininity that amounts to a shutting down of her desire. The dilemma in which she must exist, then, consists in the fact that the insistent assumption of her desire (as neither properly masculine nor feminine desire) leaves her with nothing but an errant desire, with no possibility for its fulfillment. Her question is constantly whether there is not something beyond the feminine/masculine choice. "Il est temps," she declares toward the end of the novel, "que je me repose, et que je cherche Dieu dans ses mystiques sanctuaires pour lui demander s'il n'a fait pour les femmes rien de plus que les hommes" (2: 22 [47]). Nothing more, in other words, than a complementarity that offers her subservience or, at best, the role of an idealized object destined to be possessed.

Her rejection of femininity, then, is more complicated than her refusal of masculinity in that she is determined to find in the former more options than the latter provides. In condemning man, in general, because of his condemnation of woman, she will not surrender the hope that she has more choices than he has left to her: "Malheur! malheur à cette farouche moitié du genre humain, qui, pour s'approprier de l'autre, ne lui a laissé que le choix de l'esclavage ou du suicide!" (2: 25 [48])

It has been argued that Lélia's chosen alternative to this deadening feminine position is a maternal femininity,[19] and if this is so, then what sort of maternity is this? What version of maternity might we find in her choice of a retreat into a community of women? It is first of all a maternity that denies the erotic male-female relationship. In her attempts at an intimacy with Sténio, for example, she is content to be embraced by him so long as the embrace is that of mother and child. And when she renounces Sténio for good, after his seduction by Pulchérie (posing as Lélia, with Lélia's knowledge), she describes the loss of him in the following terms:

> Perdre un enfant qu'on a nourri de son lait et porté tout un an attaché à son sein, n'est pas plus cruel au cœur d'une mère que ne me l'a été le détachement soudain et terrible qui s'est opéré à ce moment entre Sténio et moi [. . .]. Trouvez-vous que j'aie montré [. . .] un instant de dépit à Pulchérie ou à Sténio? N'ai-je pas essayé de consoler celui-

ci de sa honte, et d'ennoblir celle-là aux yeux du poète? N'ai-je pas offert à l'enfant mon éternelle amitié, mes sollicitudes et ma direction maternelle? (2: 12 [49])

The loss of Sténio is the loss of her child, precisely to the realm of sexuality into which she cannot follow him. But what was it that could exist in this maternal relationship, and that cannot in a sexual one? What, in short, is the loss that coincides with the change from maternal erotism to sexual erotism? For Lélia, maternity allows for something of the divine to survive in woman, whereas the moment she submits to a sexual relation, she is at once a possession and a prostitute, "Prêtresse de la matière [qui a] étouffé tout ce qu'il y avait dans la femme de divinement humain" ("A priestess of matter [who has] snuffed out all that there was of the divinely human in woman"; 2: 14). She refuses to give up this feminine divinity, the one femininity she has accepted, even if it is an impossible one, and proceeds toward the realization that absolute solitude is also not the answer for her. What she must have, she decides, is life in a community of women. Only there, in the Camaldules convent to which she retreats at the novel's end, can she feel sure of another sort of existence, one not predicated upon the kind of sexual difference that is synonymous with enslavement. Upon first hearing the voices of the women and children in the convent,

> Lélia, frappée d'admiration, s'agenouilla instinctivement comme aux jours de son enfance.
> Des voix de femmes pures et harmonieuses montaient vers Dieu comme une prière fervente et pleine d'espoir, et des voix d'enfants pénétrantes et argentines répondaient à celle-ci comme les promesses lointaines du ciel exprimées par l'organe des anges. (2: 18 [50])

A world of women and children, pure and harmonious, is the last and best place to which Lélia can flee. It is the only one, more importantly, that can reassure her as to the future possibility of the impossible love and mode of being she desires. "Chaque instant que je passe ici," she explains, "me fait pressentir une existence nouvelle" ("Every instant that I spend here makes me foresee a new existence"; 2: 24). Thus, although

Chapter One

the Pulchérie-Lélia window onto women-to-women relations as a kind of alternative to the traditional relations between the sexes is not itself kept open for long in the plot (the two part, and Pulchérie soon disappears from the narrative), it is perhaps more telling to see this window instead as a kind of impetus that leads Lélia to further feminine association. The specifically spiritual nature of that association is something I will discuss more further on, especially as it speaks to Irigaray's essay "La mystérique," in which a feminine access to the divine is in question.

Rethinking Women's Slavery

Even during the encounter between the two sisters, Sand gestures toward the idea that a change in patriarchal tradition is possible. When Lélia, encouraged by the open ears of her sister, rails against the status of slavery, to which, it seems, God has relegated women, it may appear that she is describing an unalterable human condition from which there is no escape. She describes the relation as that of a slave to a master, and contrasts women's situation to that of (male) children, who are also under paternal authority. The difference, she explains, is that those male children eventually grow up and assume for themselves the right of the patriarch, whereas women are never permitted to escape from their role as ruled-over minors. It is worth noting here that Sand, although she stresses she does not belong to any particular philosophical school, was well-read in philosophy. In this section dealing with female slavery/infancy, she is almost certainly reading and responding to Aristotle's *Politics,* where he holds forth on the natures of masters, slaves, and women. In his discussion of the household in Book I of the *Politics,*[20] Aristotle emphasizes two points from the outset. The first is that some humans are born naturally to rule while others are born to be ruled; hence, that there are masters and slaves is both natural and right. The second is that women do not belong to the category of slaves. How does he maintain their difference, given the fact that he defines both in terms of their obedience and their status as ruled-over? He does so in two ways: first, by stating unequivocally that the slave "has no deliberative faculty at all; the woman has" (*Politics* 1260^{a}12–13); and second, by emphasizing that the master's rule over his slave is of a different nature from the husband's rule over his wife, a point that demands some examination.

According to Aristotle, the master rules over the slave with a royal, or monarchical rule (a rule over those who are not the ruler's equals) (1255^b16-21), but over the woman he rules with a "constitutional rule" ($1259^a36-1259^b5$), which Aristotle defines as obtaining between "freemen and equals" (1255^b20). Woman and slave are ruled over differently due to their different natures, for women are credited with the ability to make judgments, as opposed to slaves, who cannot. We might then wonder how it is that Aristotle can describe the rule of husband over wife as constitutional, equal to equal, when he also maintains that "the male is by nature superior, and the female inferior, the one rules, and the other is ruled" (1254^b12-13). In order to answer this question, we need to take note of another of Aristotle's distinctions, one that he does not comment on, and that is the distinction between constitutional rule and the rule of husband over wife. For, although he says that the latter *is* the former, he goes on to specify a difference between them:

> But in most constitutional states the citizens rule and are ruled by turns, for the idea of a constitutional state implies that the natures of the citizens are equal, and do not differ at all. Nevertheless, when one rules and the other is ruled we endeavor to create a difference of outward forms and names and titles of respect [...]. The relation of the male to the female is of this kind, but there the inequality is permanent. (1259^b5-10)

So the rule of the male over the female is like a constitutional rule, in that each is a fully-grown "free" person, but it is unlike it in that the difference between ruler and ruled in a constitutional state is merely external, conventional, and transient, an outward form, whereas the difference, the inequality between men and women is permanent, not merely a passing name or title, but a natural difference.

Here we have arrived at what we could call the in-between space of Aristotle's binary opposition: on the one hand woman is like a slave (she is ruled, she obeys), on the other hand like a master (she makes judgments); on the one hand she is ruled

Chapter One

constitutionally, as an equal, on the other hand she is less fit to rule than man and is permanently *unequal* to him. Thus she occupies a political space that is always between two realms; she is always able, but not quite able, to occupy both or either. In fact, woman fits into none of Aristotle's categories (slave, freeman, master, child) because she lacks, unlike the others, an unambiguous ontological relation to the master. This difference sets her apart, outside, and, as it were, leaves her there. She cannot *be* a citizen, or a slave. This permanent inequality or difference (her existing without being) is what marks the difference between the sexes in Aristotle.

Never interrogated or defined, but always assumed a priori, Aristotle's sexual difference situates women outside the realm of those who rule and are ruled in a constitutional state. Furthermore, this sexual difference is always the difference of *her* from *him*, and never the other way around. There is no possibility of saying "women are not men," or "women are unlike men," and then going about showing why this is so; it is instead a question of stating that the difference, the inequality that *there is* between them, is a permanent one. And since women cannot be included in a discussion pertaining to those who are equal, who rule and agree to be ruled, it follows that they will make up part of the discourse on those who are unequal, who do not rule or agree to be ruled, who obey.

In Aristotle's version of society, women are unlike slaves in that they lack a ground, a "nature." The slave is born into his own particular nature ($1254^b21-1255^a2$), and it is this that makes him a slave. Woman, however, has no nature except as a function of the already-established nature of man. A slave can be said to exist as such, although he would perish were it not for the union formed with his master. Woman does not have this quality of *as such*. She begins when man begins to articulate what he is not. Aristotle's "natural" sexual difference results in the following descriptions of woman: she is silent, she is obedient, she has no authority, she stays primarily indoors, she is sedentary, she is prone to fear, she is the sole nurturer of the children (cf. $1343^b29-1344^a8$). In short, "woman" is what "man" is not, or does not wish to be. We can say, perhaps calling to mind Wittig's famous statement that "lesbians are not women" (because they have run away from the heterosexual order that imposes the binary opposition man/ woman), that in Aristotle, woman *is not,* and that one of the prerequisites subtending Aristotle's community or state, the male-female relation, is in fact the prerequisite that woman *not be.*

That we should reach such a conclusion by following Aristotle's argument with a different question in mind is not surprising, given the nature of his consideration of community. Aristotle claims to explain and describe those things or relations that are natural and necessary, and this includes the heterosexual relationship, which he stresses is a matter of necessity and nature: "this is a union which is formed, not out of choice, but because, in common with other animals and with plants, mankind have a natural desire to leave behind them an image of themselves" (1252^a27–29). In light of the above discussion, we may ask directly who mankind is. It certainly cannot include women, who insofar as they *are,* are only in relation to men. They have, then, no "natural desires" of their own. Aristotle's notion that heterosexuality is necessary and natural is indeed a picture of *man*kind's, *master*kind's desire. While Aristotle defines the respective natures of master and slave, he fails to do so for woman, who is always somewhere between the two, yet never wholly one or the other—like the slave in that her highest virtue is obedience, but like the master in that she is possessed of the faculty of judgment. Sand's frenzied representation of Lélia's insatiable desire *to be something* is best understood as a struggle within this philosophico-political context.

But in Lélia's protest, Sand does not limit herself to classical philosophical treatments of women; she also includes Judeo-Christian myths, especially that of the Fall. Lélia concludes her remarks to her sister in the following manner:

> Il n'y a donc pas de véritable association dans l'amour des sexes; car la femme y joue le rôle de l'enfant, et l'heure de l'émancipation ne sonne jamais pour elle. Quel est donc ce crime contre nature de tenir une moitié du genre humain dans une éternelle enfance? La tache du premier péché pèse, selon la légende judaïque, sur la tête de la femme, et de là son esclavage. (1: 171 [51])

First, Lélia qualifies her statement with the comment "selon la légende," emphasizing the fictional nature of this particular authority on matters between the sexes. It is only according to a certain legend that women are doomed to be enslaved. Secondly, Lélia goes on to insist on the need for the condition of slavery to end, even within the terms of the same biblical story. She continues her reflection, saying, "Mais il lui a été promis qu'elle écraserait la tête du serpent. Quand donc cette promesse sera-t-elle accomplie?" ("But it was promised to her that she would crush the head of the serpent. When, then, will this promise be fulfilled?"; 1: 171). With this, Sand emphasizes that slavery is not necessarily an immutable condition for women, suggests that there is another destiny yet to be realized, and implies that it is women themselves who need to struggle to put an end to it, by accomplishing for themselves the promise that they will crush the tradition of their enslavement.

Thinking toward a Divine, Thinking toward the Feminine

To attempt to change that tradition would entail an entirely different way of thinking and being for woman and women (and, therefore, for men as well). Any hope for a change lies in what Lélia names "la flamme immortelle" (1: 171) in women, a flame that she says burns intensely in women while it has gone out in men because of their will to possess, and hence erase, women. When Pulchérie, sparked by Lélia's simultaneous condemnation and rereading of the biblical legend, declares, "And yet we are worth more than they," Lélia responds,

> Nous valons mieux dans un sens [. . .]. Ils ont laissé sommeiller notre intelligence; mais ils n'ont pas aperçu qu'en s'efforçant d'éteindre en nous le flambeau divin, ils concentraient au fond de nos cœurs la flamme immortelle, tandis qu'elle s'éteignait en eux. Ils se sont assuré la possession du côté le moins noble de notre amour, et ils ne s'aperçoivent pas qu'ils ne nous possèdent plus. En affectant de nous croire incapables de garder nos promesses, ils se sont tout au plus assuré des héritiers légitimes. Ils ont des enfants, mais ils n'ont pas de femmes. (1: 171 [52])

In this very dense passage, Sand covers much ground: from the notion of a difference crucial to what constitutes being a woman, to what we might call the patriarchal economy of the proper, and property, to woman's nonexistence *as such, in herself.*

The first issue this passage speaks to, the notion of a central or constitutive male-female difference, is of course still today a difficult and contested question (as evidenced in the essentialist/constructionist debates within feminist theories). Is sexual difference always and only a ploy perpetuated by patriarchy for the purpose of the domination of women, as in Wittig's thought? ("For the category of sex is the product of a heterosexual society which imposes on women the rigid obligation of the reproduction of the 'species,' that is, the reproduction of heterosexual society"; Wittig 6). Or is a female (*féminine*) difference that which has scarcely begun to be thought, to the detriment of women who, if and when they are declared to be outside of or supplemental to what Irigaray calls "hom(m)osexuality," are simply silenced altogether, relegated to "la béance de l'Autre" ("the hollowness of the Other"; *Ce sexe* 101, *This Sex* 104)? It is hardly my intention, I should say, to label Wittig as a "constructionist," or Irigaray as an "essentialist," but instead to frame my discussion of Sand's discourse here where these two thoughts (might) meet. Thinkers such as Wittig and Irigaray are addressing fundamental questions around the problem of what I would call, with Irigaray, "sexual difference." It will require a brief detour to elucidate a certain closeness in their thinking, to read Wittig (a warrior against, refugee from, sexual difference) and Irigaray (a champion of the advent of a different sexual difference) *together.* What I hope to be able to show, as a result of the possibilities such a reading may yield, is how Sand is dealing with similar problems of difference on the one hand, and the limitations of binary differences on the other, in a way that is only beginning to receive the theoretical attention it deserves. As Schor has argued in *George Sand and Idealism,* it is time that Sand be theorized, not only read, or, in other words, it is time that she be read as a thinker of sexual difference (216).

Women "entre elles" and Difference

Wittig and Irigaray differ, of course, in their understandings both of women and of sexual difference. For Wittig, women

Chapter One

are slaves to men, whereas lesbians are "runaway slaves," not women, beyond the categories of men and women; and sexual difference is that ploy, operative in the heterosexual order, that guarantees the subordination of women to men. Nevertheless, if we were to try to read them together concerning the question of what Irigaray calls the erasure of one side of sexual difference and what Wittig calls the slavery of women, we could note that each turns to the position of women, or lesbians, *outside* the order of heterosexuality as a locus for the possible transformation of that order. What might we discover, by dwelling on this particular point, that these two thinkers share?

For Wittig, the *entre elles* of lesbianism offers women a way out of their position as subject to men in that it situates this other, lesbian subject outside heterosexuality. It is, she writes, "the only concept I know which is beyond the categories of sex (woman and man), because the designated subject (lesbian) is *not* a woman, either economically, or politically, or ideologically" (Wittig 20). The subject in lesbianism is not a woman because her relationship to man is not one of servitude, and furthermore, she is called on to fight for "the destruction of heterosexuality as a social system which is based on the oppression of women and which produces the doctrine of the difference between the sexes to justify this oppression" (Wittig 20).

In her essay "The Trojan Horse" (68–75), Wittig is concerned with lesbian strategies for overturning the heterosexual order. Although she recognizes that such subversive work is performed in a "hostile territory" (69), Wittig does not emphasize or dwell on the writer/lesbian's ambiguous relation to that territory. Her basic notion is that the work of the "Trojan Horse" needs to be done by and among those who have escaped the class of "women" (and thereby heterosexuality), and that eventually, such work will radically change the domain in which it is received (or not received). She writes:

> And the stranger it appears, nonconforming, unassimilable, the longer it will take for the Trojan Horse to be accepted. Eventually it is adopted, and, even if slowly, it will eventually work like a mine. It will sap and blast out the ground where it was planted. The old [. . .] forms, which everybody was used to, will eventually appear to be outdated, inefficient, incapable of transformation. (69)

The lesbian, in her subversive practice, is planting mines in the ground of heterosexuality, mines that will eventually be adopted, take root, and, again eventually, blast that ground. The repercussions of such mining on heterosexual society "are still unenvisionable," Wittig writes (32), and ultimately, it is less important for her that they be envisioned or planned than that they begin to be enacted. From the "outside" then, lesbians slowly disable or destroy the "inside," until that inside cannot but yield to, indeed become, a new order, mined and shaped by those who have gradually, insidiously, destroyed it until something altogether different emerges from its ruins.

For Irigaray, the outside/inside distinction is not so clear-cut as it is for Wittig. Irigaray emphasizes that women are outside the hom(m)osexual social order *because* they are imprisoned within it. Keeping this ambiguous relation of women to the social order (or "enemy territory") in mind, Irigaray intimates a possible site of transformation, suggesting that women use their situation as outside/imprisoned as a space from which to bring about the transformation of hom(m)osexuality. Unlike Wittig's lesbians, Irigaray's women are not engaged in destroying that social order, but in turning that order in on the abyss that it has created for itself, an abyss that, in hom(m)osexuality, woman marks. For Irigaray, making hom(m)osexuality turn (within itself) and face this abyss may be a way to force it (help it?) to discover that which it has erased, and a way for woman to become that which she has never been, namely, a subject.

This Irigarayan abyss is the erasure of women, their exclusion from the social order, or on the ontological level, woman's exclusion from being. (As we saw in the Introduction, Irigaray maintains that there is an intimate relation between the two.) But this is not only *women's* darkness, for it is not, could not, be the case that such an exclusion affects only those who are directly its object. It taints both sides of sexual difference. As an example of this, Irigaray takes up Antigone as a representative for woman as imprisoned/excluded. She begins by insisting that Antigone "doit être sortie de la nuit, de l'ombre, de la pierre, de la totale paralysse par un ordre social qui se condamne en la condamnant" (*EDS* 115 [53]). Irigaray points to patriarchal society's self-condemnation with the following interpretation of Creon's law:

Chapter One

> Créon, qui a interdit la sépulture de Polynice, qui a suggéré à Antigone de se taire à jamais sur ses rapports aux dieux, qui l'a fait enfermer dans une excavation de rocher, ne lui laissant qu'un peu de nourriture pour ne pas être coupable de sa mort, Créon a condamné la société à une schize dans l'ordre d'une raison qui laisse la nature sans dieux, sans grâce; la famille sans autre avenir que le travail pour l'Etat; la procréation sans joie, l'amour sans éthique. (*EDS* 115 [54])

For how can love be ethical if it loves no other? Creon says, "she is the man if I let her live" because what she cannot *be* is a woman. If he allows her *to be*—*to be* as anything other than as object—there is nothing in the hom(m)osexual order *for* her to be, except a man. In this way, as we have seen, Sand also evokes the poverty of any relation in the (her) present order: *there is no veritable association between the sexes,* Lélia argues, because the immortal flame in women has been forgotten, to the extent that even women are ignorant of their own relation to divinity, of their potential to be, as she puts it, *divinely human.*

It is man, then, who has something to risk, Irigaray would add. If he lets her live, then he is sacrificing his values, his order, for something that, as far as he knows, does not exist. And yet, in punishing her, he also risks the possibility of others taking up her cause, and thereby asserting the existence of other values, the possibility of another order. Creon's mistake, the wound he inflicts, the wound hom(m)osexuality, or the heterosexual order, inflicts, is not to recognize the other, not to recognize that he is also an other. The recognition of this error would mean, for women, the importance not so much of *destroying,* or *only* destroying the heterosexual order, but of bringing it into a different realm, one in which man and woman face an other who is not merely an inverted reflection.

In calling for women to move toward the transformation of hom(m)osexuality as *the unerasable embodiment of the chasm or abyss inscribed in the very heart of society,* Irigaray is signaling that which must not be forgotten in such a transformation of both sexual difference and community, i.e., the *ethical,* or, an ethical that is in need of creation. The self that is lost through giving is not the self that has yet to be created, but that very self that, in the case of woman, does not exist, and that, in the case of man, can be said to exist only by virtue of the impossibility of woman's existence. The ethical act of "taking the negative upon ourselves" (*EDS* and *J'aime*) is thus the act of disturbing that social order from within its own exclusionary and encircling logic, from within the limits of its inability to think beyond the "split in the order of reason"—this split that is inhabited by Sophocles's Antigone, by Wittig's woman-as-slave, by Lacan's *Lafemme*, and by Sand's Lélia. Wittig's lesbian would escape this split by refusing it, by attempting to free herself by an act of will from the order that necessitates it (thereby also running the risk of repeating it). Irigaray's Other: woman[21] would take on her occupation of this split, this impossible in-between, as a way toward the recognition that what makes this no-place of nonexistence possible is the failure, the refusal, to recognize or (re)think an ethics of sexual difference. Taking the negative upon oneself is ethical for Irigaray because, essentially, it amounts to the recognition and assumption of alterity. *Not* the quasi-alterity woman has traditionally occupied and that has gone hand in hand with her ontological and political erasure; that is, not woman-as-other-to-man. In order for what Irigaray calls a female generic, or another sex, to become, the work of the negative must take place for both women and men. For men, in order that they might recognize their own alterity, their own limited (as opposed to universal) status, the fact that they are not the whole of the human subject. For women, in order that there might come into being a "female generic as such" (*J'aime* 110, *I Love* 64), and not in terms of woman as complement to, other of (but not other in herself), less than, more than, equal to, etc. . . . always in terms of man, without any other terms available. Irigaray's negative would entail a new understanding and a new mode of being, wherein the state of being limited, finite, is never covered over by recourse to a neutral transcendence, be it God, Reason, or even Love (which is born, for Irigaray, precisely out of differences encountering each other, and can thus never be neutral). "Être homme ou femme revient déjà a ne pas être le tout du sujet ni de la communauté ni de l'esprit," she writes, underscoring the negative work of sexual difference

Chapter One

that would redefine the nature of human being, being human, as complex as opposed to simple, plural as opposed to singular (*J'aime* 166 [55]).

Certainly, Wittig's lesbian materialist project and Irigaray's ethics are at odds with each other when it comes to the political and ontological status of sexual difference, but it is also true that reading them together (if only temporarily, experimentally together) brings into relief the fundamental effort that to a large extent defines the various projects of feminist theory and politics today. Namely, the attempt at a creation and assumption of a self, which is to say of an alterity, whose difference is not a function of hom(m)osexuality, not a function of a woman's ontological and political status as man's complement, implement, tool, or slave in heterosexuality. This, as both Irigaray and Wittig emphasize, is at once the most essential and the most difficult goal that contemporary feminisms pursue. And no feminist thought or practice of community—community always relating to the coming together of different subjects—can have any meaning without this accompanying assumption of alterity. For Wittig this difficult assumption, which has to be made in the midst of a society whose *modus operandi* is the domination of women by men, ought to be, or will be, sexless. Since the territory one would escape to has yet to be created, for now "the only thing to do is to stand on one's own feet as an escapee, a fugitive slave, a lesbian" and hope by one's practice to effect radical change (Wittig xiii). For Irigaray, as we have seen, the emphasis is on the "escapee's" situation inside the community she refuses and would remake, for it is there, on a ground that is both inside and outside, that she must stand on her own feet. For both, I would underline, the possibility of a different community, of different, plural thoughts and practices of human being and citizenship, is concomitant with the creative labor of forging new identities, and a new universal. In the case of Irigaray this is more or less immediately clear. But Wittig, too, who roundly rejects the "ideology" of sexual difference, also argues for the creation of a universal that would no longer be the property of Man. "It is part of our fight to unmask them [the dominators], to say that one out of two men is a woman, that the universal belongs to us although we have been robbed and despoiled at this level as well as at the political and economic ones" (Wittig 56).

Rather than focus on Irigaray's and Wittig's different understandings of sexual difference, we can find what this similarity of their emphasizing women-outside points to. For Irigaray, women are outside, excluded, in terms of the present order of sexual (in)difference. But for Wittig, as I have said, this order is precisely that inside which women are trapped. What they (as lesbians) are outside of, for Wittig, is the social contract called "heterosexuality." Neither thinker, though, suggests that we should be content with simply ridding ourselves of either of these respective categories, sexual difference on the one hand, the social contract on the other. On the contrary, Irigaray claims that sexual difference, thought differently and in its utopian dimensions (its being not-yet) represents the possibility for a future. And for Wittig, the social contract, inasmuch as "it has not yet been fulfilled by history [as an achievement "for the good of all and of everyone". . .] retains its utopian dimension." Wittig continues, in a way that reads harmoniously with Irigaray's thought:

> Now when I say let us break off the heterosexual social contract per se, I designate the group "women." But I did not mean that we must break off the social contract per se, because that would be absurd. For we must break it off as heterosexual [. . .]. I want to confront the historical conditions and conflicts that can lead us to end the obligations that bind us without our consent while we are not enjoying a reciprocal commitment that would be the necessary condition for our freedom [. . .] (35)

It seems to me that such a reciprocal commitment and such freedom go very much along the lines of what Irigaray calls granting the other her/his liberty and sex. In both visions, the other as owned, as property, as *mine*, dissolves in the face of the recognition of her difference, which calls for the recognition of oneself as other—to another, and also to oneself.

Wittig and Irigaray share a concern with the future, a future that would be effected starting from that which is not the future, those who are not yet the future, that which and those who are "outside" the future in *our time*. And the awaiting that women undertake among themselves is perhaps an intimation of the birth, the birth as a different "salvation," that such a future would be. Not a passive waiting, which is the age-old

Chapter One

position of women, but an awaiting that is a mode of creation, an expectancy that produces a future (being).

Irigaray's woman, at once imprisoned within and thrown out of hom(m)osexuality, also recalls Lélia's argument that men, by possessing "our least noble part," do not in fact have anything of women. Not only do they not possess them, they cannot even encounter them: women, for the appropriating men of Lélia's universe, are quite simply unreachable inasmuch as they have been erased/imprisoned. Lélia desires some sort of *other love,* a love that seems impossible, and she protests that the so-called love between men and women is a travesty, based solely on possession. She explains that in her experience she has never found the co-presence of physical and spiritual desire, and that, being unable to accept the former without the latter, she has rejected even Sténio's attempts at loving her. As Irigaray writes, "Et la cour d'amour n'est pas réellement une réponse car la femme y est désirée corporellement et non spirituellement, énergétiquement," and in the respect for her different being (*J'aime* 153 [56]).

Sand's Difference

Lélia responds to Pulchérie's declaration that women are worth more than men, are better than men, by simultaneously agreeing with and qualifying her remark. We are better than them *in one sense,* she says, and goes on to elaborate. The two important terms in her elaborations, as we began to see, are "le flambeau divin" and "la flamme immortelle," a masculine (divine torch) and a feminine (eternal flame) noun. How analogous are these terms? Do they mirror each other, or are they marking a particular difference? While striving to snuff out the divine torch in women, men have unwittingly concentrated in the depths of women's hearts the immortal flame, while that same (feminine) flame has gone out in men. First of all, how is it that men have been trying to extinguish the divine torch? By an effort of negligence, a pretending not to see: the phrase "Ils ont laissé sommeiller notre intelligence" (1: 171) is in fact a description of men's effort with respect to women. Thus, in beginning to speak of a difference between men and women, Sand immediately deals with the man-woman *relation,* from which, it would seem in this passage, she argues differences stem. Or perhaps not so much *stem* as *are perceived*. Sand will locate the difference she describes from within the relation, never attempting to pronounce a prior difference, anterior to that relation. In attempting to identify in what sense women are better than men, she speaks of the nature of their relation as it exists, and as it affects both sexes. Women's status in that relation as barred from the realm of intelligence has led them to a stronger, more passionate (the word *flamme* has much more ardent connotations than does *flambeau*) engagement with the "immortal," unhelped, *and unhindered,* by the more stable light of the "flambeau" whose light is that of intelligence or reason. Speaking in terms of the (limiting) essentialist/constructionist division, we can say that Sand has her cake and eats it too: on the one hand she frames women's difference within the context of an always already obtaining relation, and on the other hand she is able to create a figure for sexual difference (*flambeau/flamme*) in order to suggest a feminine alternative to the current state of relations between the sexes (which is to say, after, and much earlier than, Lacan, their nonrelation).

Which leads us to the second issue in Lélia's response to Pulchérie: the critique of the masculine economy of possession (the term *masculine* now understood to refer to men's ways within the male-female relation, and not to any prior masculine essence). Let us compare Lélia's words, "Ils se sont assuré la possession du côté le moins noble de notre amour [. . .] ils se sont tout au plus assuré des héritiers légitimes" (1: 171), to some of Irigaray's:

> C'est que les corps des femmes assurent—de leur usage, de leur consommation, de leur circulation—la condition de possibilité de la socialité et de la culture mais qu'ils restent une "infrastructure" méconnue de leur élaboration. L'exploitation de la matière sexuée femme est si constitutive de notre horizon socio-culturel qu'elle ne peut trouver son interprétation à l'intérieur de celui-ci. (*Ce sexe* 167–68 [57])

In investigating male-female difference, Sand—not unlike Irigaray in her investigation of society as the "marketplace" of women—links the male lust to own or possess women to their obsession with legitimacy, another sort of ownership. This

Chapter One

understanding of (masculine) society as based upon possession is further emphasized in Pulchérie's response, when she declares, "voilà pourquoi je n'ai pas voulu prendre une place dans leur société. N'aurai-je pas pu m'asseoir parmi *leurs* femmes [. . .]?" (1: 171 [58]; emphasis added). With Pulchérie's response, Sand points out again that to be a woman/wife in society is not to take up one's own place, but is rather to take up a place as an owned thing, and to perpetuate, through that status, a society of, to borrow Irigaray's words again,

> la valorisation exclusive des besoins-désirs des hommes, et des échanges entre eux [. . .] où l'homme engendre l'homme comme son semblable, la femme, la fille, la sœur ne [valant] que de servir de possibilité et d'enjeu de relations entre hommes. (*Ce sexe* 168 [59])

For Sand, women's reduction to the "côté le moins noble de notre amour" ("least noble part of our love"), their material, useful bodies, amounts to their being utterly lost for men and for society in general ("ils ne s'aperçoivent pas qu'ils ne nous possèdent plus" ["they do not perceive that they no longer possess us"; 1: 171]). In the masculine quest for possession, children are had, owned, and women's bodies ("woman-sexed matter") are possessed, but women in themselves are never had, owned, possessed, since women *in themselves* are not, and since an acknowledgment of another, female being would undermine the whole economy of possession. Which brings us to the third point we wanted to discuss in light of this passage: woman's existence as such, in herself.

While Sand exposes the nonrelation between the sexes in light of her complaint that woman is not able to enter that so-called relation except as a slave to man's desire, especially the desire to possess legitimate heirs, she nevertheless does not come to the same radical conclusion of a Wittig or a Lacan that woman does not exist. Or, to put this another way, she *does* reach this radical conclusion, inasmuch as she points out that there is no place for woman (for what woman might be) in society, but she refuses to end her discourse there. Rather, she chooses to accentuate what there is of woman. The situation of women as nonexistent does not mean for Sand that she does not or cannot exist, but that this situation of nonexistence must change. In this light, it is telling that in the passage we have been considering, Lélia says, "*En affectant* de nous croire incapable de garder nos promesses" ("*By affecting* to believe us incapable of keeping our promises"; 1: 171; emphasis added). This forgetting of women, this enslavement of women, needs affectation, ruse, in order to persist, needs a falsehood. And it is for woman, as a different kind of possessor of a different kind of light, a blazing flame instead of a burning torch, to give the lie to that falsehood, to consume it as a flame consumes that which it touches, transforming it into a different matter.

As Françoise van Rossum-Guyon has pointed out,

> avec *Lélia* George Sand introduisait, et de manière radicalement nouvelle, la philosophie dans le roman. Aux interrogations sur les modalités et les déviations du lien social, succédait une interrogation sur le fondement même de la Société. (82 [60])

But in *Lélia*, we see not only this interrogation of the foundations of society, as we have discussed, but also a, perhaps tentative, attempt to approach another thought on which society, a new society, might begin to base itself, and this new thought is tied up with the "mise à nue d'une sexualité féminine telle que personne jusque-là ne s'était risqué à le faire" ("laying bare of a feminine sexuality such as no one until then had risked doing it"; van Rossum-Guyon 83). Schor, investigating Sand's idealism, claims that "[i]dealism for Sand is finally the only alternative representational mode available to those who do not enjoy subjecthood [i.e., existence in themselves, as such] in the real" (Schor 54). What I think needs to be emphasized about *Lélia* is the way in which Sand underlines simultaneously this status of women as "deprived of subjecthood in the real" *and* their status as subjects of a different kind who might offer a different, better "real." Consider Lélia's depiction of the plight of "des cœurs purs" who might maintain "la flamme du céleste amour":

> ces âmes d'exception, éparses sur la face d'un monde où tout les froisse, les refoule et les force à se replier sur elles-mêmes, se chercheraient et s'appelleraient en vain. Leur union ne serait pas consacrée par les lois humaines, ou bien

Chapter One

> *leur existence* ne serait pas protégée par la sympathie des autres existences. C'est ainsi que tout essai de cette vie idéale a misérablement échoué entre des êtres qui eussent pu s'identifier l'un à l'autre, sous l'œil de Dieu, dans un monde meilleur. (1: 170 [61]; emphasis added)

This passage, which comes just a page before Lélia's evocation of an immortal flame concentrated in women, focuses, by contrast, on the difficulty women as "âmes d'exception" have in existing at all in a society whose laws are hostile to the possibility of women's existence as anything other than a utilitarian corollary to men's. Ultimately, and despite Sand's utopianism, *Lélia* cannot be an optimistic novel, cannot end on an uplifting note of "un monde meilleur," since Lélia, even as she seeks a different relation to the world and to God from within a community of women at the convent, still finds herself within a world, and within a religion yet to be "abattue et desséchée" ("hurled down and dried up"; 2: 156). What I called earlier a "feminine divine" may indeed be no more than a gesture toward a possibility found in passages like the ones we have considered here, but even as such, it is therefore more than, different from, a railing against what is *impossible*; it is a refusal to accept the nonexistent as the never-to-exist.

Perhaps this quasi(?)-optimism may have something to do with Sand's changing Lélia's (and *Lélia*'s) ending in the 1839 edition. On the subject of her revision of *Lélia,* Sand wrote, "Je veux achever un livre où j'ai mis toute l'âpreté de ma souffrance et où je veux mettre aujourd'hui le rayon d'espoir qui m'est apparu" (*Correspondance* 3: 595 [62]; also qtd. in *Lélia* 1: 11). Rather than being killed off by the mad priest, Magnus (the 1833 version), for example, Lélia now expires as she speaks to her friend Trenmor. She falls into his arms after a delirious monologue (the chapter is entitled "Délire") during which she continues her protest, calling herself "en désaccord avec tout" ("in disaccord with everything"; 2: 157) and fearing that this *désaccord* might be unchangeable. "Elle eût pardonné au ciel de l'avoir frustrée de tout bonheur si elle eût pu lire clairement dans les destins de l'humanité future quelque chose de mieux que ce qu'elle avait eu elle-même en partage" (2: 156 [63]), is a remark that we might want to read alongside Sand's comment that Lélia was born "cent ans trop tôt" ("a hundred years too early"), which, as Didier notes, belies an optimism on Sand's part (1: 42). As it is, Lélia's quest for a Truth that would not be the truth that snuffs out the immortal flame ends in failure: "Depuis dix mille ans je t'[la Vérité] ai sentie dan mon cœur sans pouvoir te traduire à mon intelligence" (2: 159 [64]). I would argue that this unhappy ending for the character Lélia points to a structure of continuing struggle with which Sand imbues this novel and her later works. For even as Lélia dies without having succeeded in her quest, the very phrase "sans pouvoir te traduire à mon intelligence" still assumes that there *is* another "intelligence," and another truth, to be understood and discovered. The intelligence that the male-female relation has "laissé sommeiller" in women is nevertheless there to be cultivated, and is even changed and nourished by the passionate "flamme immortelle" that men have only succeeded in fanning by their refusal of it.

It is impossible not to think of Irigaray's "La mystérique" in this context of burning, immortal flames and the impossibility of translating a divine Truth to Reason. Her writing of the place of the mystic—the only place in the history of the West where woman speaks and acts (*Speculum* 238/191)—could be describing Lélia's place at the end of the novel. Irigaray writes that the terms "mystical language" or "mystical speech" are the

> Noms qui s'imposent encore par la conscience pour signifier cette hors-scène, cette autre scène, pour elle *cryptique*. Indiquant par là le lieu où elle ne se maîtrise plus, cette "nuit obscure" mais encore ces feux et ces flammes où elle s'abîme pour son extrême confusion. Lieu où "elle" parle —ou lui mais par recours à "elle"—de l'éblouissement par la source de lumière, logiquement refoulée, de l'effusion du "sujet" et de l'Autre dans un embras(s)ement qui les confond comme termes, du mépris de la forme comme telle, de la méfiance de cet obstacle à persévérer dans la jouissance que constitue l'entendement, de la sécheresse désolée de la raison . . . (*Speculum* 238 [65])

Woman's immortal, divine flame, which, Lélia says, has secretly intensified even as the light of her reason has been damped, is located by Irigaray in a cryptic space that needs opening, but not onto or within reason. This space, which Lélia

Chapter One

calls her heart, is for Irigaray both dark as night and (almost) dumb. If Lélia cannot speak her divine truth to her intelligence, and if instead she has only an infinite and unsatisfiable desire, this is because, Irigaray writes, the very condition of the feminine mystic, of the mystic as feminine, is to be without the power to "spécifier ce qu'elle veut. Défaillante dans ses mots. Pressentant un *rester à dire* qui résiste à toutes paroles, qu'à peine on pourrait balbutier" (*Speculum* 241 [66]). If any audible sense can be made of her desire, her knowledge, it is perhaps only in song. "Mieux vaut donc," Irigaray continues, "se refuser à tout discours, se taire ou s'en tenir à quelque clameur si peu articulée qu'à peine elle forme *un chant*" (241 [67]). This notion of a kind of truth, *another* truth, or truth's other, being enunciated, however indistinctly, from the breaths and throats of women, leads us back toward the beginning of our discussion of *Lélia* and the moment of revelation she undergoes upon first entering the Camaldules convent and hearing song:

> Lélia, frappée d'admiration, s'agenouilla instinctivement comme aux jours de son enfance.
> Des voix de femmes pures et harmonieuses montaient vers Dieu comme une prière fervente et pleine d'espoir, et des voix d'enfants pénétrantes et argentines répondaient à celle-ci comme les promesses lointaines du ciel exprimées par l'organe des anges. (2: 18; see [50])

Lélia's divine humanity is to be found among women, and children. The women singing together articulate their prayer, their desire, in such a way as to be intelligible to the divine. And the children's voices, pregnant with the future, sound like divine responses.

In this context, Lélia's retreat to the convent can also be read as her enactment of the eroticism she cannot or will not find with Sténio, the man who loves her. It is in this feminine and divine space that she experiences and speaks her "délire," or what Irigaray calls "une jouissance si extrême, un amour si incompréhensible, une illumination si démesurée, que la nescience y devient désir" (*Speculum* 242 [68]). In her railings against God, Lélia is, she feels, taken over by a kind of ecstatic, painful delirium she can barely contain in speech. But when she does arrive at a word, it is precisely this: "Ceux-ci t'ont appelé Satan, ceux-là crime: moi je t'appelle désir" (2: 158 [69]). Lélia's delirium comes, of course, in the context of her desperate, despairing death. Her absolute inability to know, to know Truth, constitutes, and in a sense *is* her desire. Immediately following her passionate soliloquy, she dies, and believes she dies of desire.

> Et depuis dix mille ans, pour toute réponse à mes cris, pour tout soulagement à mon agonie, j'entends planer sur cette terre maudite le sanglot désespéré du désir impuissant! [. . .] Depuis dix mille ans j'ai crié dans l'infini: *Verité, verité!* Depuis dix mille ans, l'infini me répond: *Désir, désir!* (2: 159 [70])

Finally, what Lélia enjoys, *all* she can enjoy, is this painful, dark desire. She is "en proie à un délire sans nom, à un désespoir sans bornes." She "flotte dans les ténèbres et [ses] bras fatigués n'embrassent que des ombres trompeuses" (2: 158 [71]). Irigaray will ask where she can head "dans ce vagabondage nocturne? Sinon plus avant dans la nuit jusqu'à ce qu'elle devienne rayon transverbérant, ténèbre lumineuse. [. . .] Car vers où se diriger dans cette ignorance qui d'un embras(s)ement seulement peut recevoir sa science?" (*Speculum* 240–41 [72]) After depicting the "sweet pain" and unbearable torture her mystic must undergo for another knowledge, Irigaray will pose a question to which Lélia gives a final response. "Mais comment continuer de vivre dans une telle violence, si douce aussi soit-elle?" (244 [73]). For Sand's character, the response is that one cannot; one will ultimately be consumed by the burning violence of the desire to know and the desire to be.

Although the novel's initial question, "Qui es-tu?" never receives a complete answer, the complexity of Sand's analysis of male-female relations in society serves as a prolonged meditation on why it is that such a question is impossible to answer as of yet, and indicates the kind of radical changes and struggles necessary for the eventual possibility of an answer. Such an answer, *Lélia* suggests, would entail the creation of a space for another desire, a desire whose aim is not only *not* the acquisition of a given object, but may also not be even its own satisfaction in a jouissance that would extinguish desire. As I argued in the Introduction, Lacan in his twentieth seminar

Chapter One

spells out among other things the nature of the unethical nonrelation between the sexes. And to use a Lacanian turn of phrase, it seems to me that it is not for nothing that we see in George Sand's nineteenth-century heroine the representation of a woman who suffers that nonrelation in terms of the impossibility of giving up on her desire on the one hand, and on the other, the inevitability of being mortally wounded by a jouissance she quite literally does not want. If love cannot take place *ici-bas*—no more for Sand's Lélia than for Lacan—and if jouissance is both too little (phallic) and too much (*autre, en plus, féminine*), then we are left with a foreclosure of the possibility of any relation that would be a relation with another, capable of an acknowledgment of the absolute irreducibility of the other to the self.[22] But I think that neither in Lacan, nor in Sand, is this conclusion necessary, for there is the alternative—taken up by Sand—of underlining and problematizing the imposture of masculine subjectivity just as vividly as the masquerade of feminine subjectivity. I would hazard that when this happens, feminine jouissance may become not the only *other* jouissance in question; we would also have to deal with, if you will, *another "other" jouissance,* which is neither phallic nor the feminine "en plus" of phallic jouissance: a "masculine" jouissance?, which would not be limited to the phallic function inasmuch as it would not be wedded to the demand for finitude, completion, the covering over of the gap? In turning to Colette's multiple sexes and sexualities, we will be able to consider this perhaps far-fetched hypothesis of an altogether different jouissance.

Chapter Two

What Does a Woman Enjoy?

Colette's *Le pur et l'impur*

Toward the end of his career, Freud famously told his one-time analysand, then friend and benefactress, Marie Bonaparte,[1] that the most important question for psychoanalysis was the one he had not been able to answer throughout all his research and practice: "The great question, which has never been answered and which I have not been able to answer, despite my thirty years of research into the feminine soul, is 'What does a woman want?'"[2] This oft-quoted question defines the problem of sexual difference as synonymous with that posed by Woman's difference from Man. Her desire, as opposed to his, is a puzzle. And the reason for which her desire is a mystery is, as we have seen with Lacan and Irigaray, that her existence itself needs to be accounted for. If "femininity" is Freud's question in the essay of the same name, for example, it is indistinguishable from the question of how it is that out of a "bisexual" child a feminine woman can develop instead of a masculine man: how it is that there can be a she, instead of a he ("Femininity," *SE* 22: 119). The well-known maleness of this bisexual child is Freud's fundamental and, for him, invisible obstacle to accounting for the feminine difference he seeks to illuminate. As soon as the little girl is understood to be a little man, it is impossible to come up with a plausible reason why she would not continue in her manliness (attachment to the mother, "phallic" aggressivity, etc.). To explain the girl's turn to girl-ness, and then womanhood (neurotic, masculine, or normal), from little man-ness, Freud finds that he is obliged to ground himself on the very anatomy he began by saying could offer no solution to the question of the difference between men and women. "After all," Freud writes, betraying, perhaps, a sense of defeat in the face of the apparently overwhelming force that

87

Chapter Two

the having and not having of a penis carries, "After all, the anatomical distinction [between the sexes] *must* express itself in psychical consequences" ("Femininity," *SE* 22: 124; Strachey's brackets, emphasis added). Nowhere else in Freud do we find this particular *must*, this quality of necessity in the relation of the body to the psyche. Most often things are quite the opposite, and Freud is warning us (in the same essay in fact) not to assume a one-to-one correspondence between them; and reminding us, again in "Femininity," that it is fantasy that is sure to leave permanent traces in the mind, while the material of bodily experience is subject to an infinite range of interpretations and outcomes for the psyche. Here, though, the actual superiority of the condition of being male unmistakably informs his judgment. The little girl is immediately upset that she has been given inferior equipment. For Freud there is little, or at any rate insufficient, doubt that her physical difference will from the first be perceived as less than, worse than, and to confirm this, if he needed to, he might simply ask anyone to look around at others who are similarly (un)equipped ("Femininity," *SE* 22: 125), and also curbed, ruled over, trained to suppress their own impulses.

The fact that Freud is ineluctably influenced by the states of women and men in the world in which he lived, and by all of the assumptions about the natures of each that went along with these states is the ground both of penis envy's dubiousness (a dubiousness that he himself acknowledges in another essay[3]) and its radical potential as a concept. For if the phenomenon of penis envy in female infantile psychical development is either nonexistent or not necessarily existent (and thus not the thing that will explain the turn from the mother, the identification with the father, and later, a preponderance of jealousy, envy, depression in the female psyche), it is nonetheless indisputable that women are "complaining," falling ill, and that their illnesses are indeed intimately bound up with the relation between two opposite, opposed sexes. While little girls may not be getting upset as a result of a protuberance of flesh they see on some beings, but only on some, and not on themselves, they are nevertheless *getting* upset, and by precisely those "social customs," that "suppression of women's aggressiveness [. . .] imposed on them socially" to which Freud alerts his readers ("Femininity," *SE* 22: 116).

Colette

This is why Brennan is right to argue for an acceptance of "femininity" as a real problem that affects women (and, differently, some men) in Freud's day, and in our own, for that matter.[4] To overlook it, or rather—as is the tendency if we adopt a rigorously "equality feminist" stance—to reject it out of hand as misogynist and essentializing, is ultimately to ignore or to wish away the fact of domination that structures, and is acted out in, relations between the sexes. To focus solely on femininity as a pathology, of course, is to run other risks. Namely, such a focus risks ignoring the manifest and myriad pathologies of masculinity (or subsuming them under the quantifier "human," thereby de-sexing them), and risks overlooking the potential of femininity, despite and because of the pathology involved in it, the suffering it entails, to inform the way in which we can reimagine sexed relations, in order for *another* sexual difference to obtain, one based on neither dominance nor equality.

This attempt to reappropriate femininity in its literary and psychoanalytic guises is essentially Shoshana Felman's project in her *What Does a Woman Want?*, wherein she asks how our understanding of the title question might change when it is asked by a female speaker within a discourse focused on the feminine. The question of a woman's desire, Freud's question of sexual difference, "can be truly opened up and radically displaced," Felman argues, "by being repossessed, reclaimed by women" (3). Such a displacement should have far-reaching consequences for both literature and psychoanalysis. Felman continues:

> Can literature [. . .] reclaim the question [of femininity] as its own specific question, and consequently *be reclaimed by it*? [emphasis added] Can psychoanalysis? Is it in the power of this question to engender, through the literary or the psychoanalytic work, a woman's voice as its speaking subject? What consequences might such attempts at *en-gendering* a self-analytical female discourse have for the possibilities of reading, writing, thinking, analyzing, living, of women *and* of men? (3)

When a woman asks this question, that is, when it is asked self-reflexively, with one eye toward the world and its discourses and another toward the psyche and its idiosyncrasies, then the

Chapter Two

"outside," the context in which the question is posed, the discourse of psychoanalysis, for example, or of literature, will be as open to question as the questioner herself. And instead of this meaning an attack on literary or psychoanalytic thought, it performs a revolution in them, and allows them, as Felman puts it, to be reclaimed, precisely by the question of sexual difference. In terms of psychoanalysis, this is what the inadequate term "psychoanalytic feminism" ought to designate, and in the realm of literature, this means reading with an attention not only to signs of patriarchy, oppression, victimization, or empowerment, but to what emerges from different, differently sexed, voices.

In this chapter I propose examining such differences in Colette's *Le pur et l'impur,* a work best known for its inclusion of various "female" and "male" sexualities, though, as we shall see, what makes a sexuality male or female is for Colette not immediately apparent. The question of femininity has certainly been literature's as much as psychoanalysis's. Indeed, "What does a woman want?" might be said to be the riddle from which the whole of the nineteenth- and twentieth-century novel (and, it has been argued, the novel itself as a genre[5]) spins itself, from Germaine de Staël's *Delphine* at the beginning of the nineteenth century through to Hèléne Cixous's contemporary works.

Colette's *Le pur et l'impur* (originally published as *Ces plaisirs . . .* in 1932) holds a special place in this trajectory because it is among the first works in which the narrative voice, a woman's voice, self-consciously blurs itself with the voice of the author, and in which this very blurring is instrumental in how the question of sexual difference gets posed and addressed— all of this within the context of a narrative whose self-described *raison d'être* is to probe the mysteries of sexuality. *Le pur et l'impur* is usually described as a series of past episodes recounted in the present, episodes in which the chief concern is the nature and meaning of sensual pleasure. This is true, but what is most important about this work, I would suggest, is that it is a series of narrative episodes in which Colette the narrator, who is also always but not only Colette the writer, places *herself* in relation to characters, some historical, some not, whose sexual lives she is interested in exploring for the sake of "verser au trésor de la connaissance des sens une contribution personnelle" ("depositing into the treasury of our knowledge of the senses a personal contribution"; *PI* 584).[6] The knowledge that emerges is always also a knowledge of Colette herself, a knowledge of this voice of a woman who is not, she says, quite a woman (586). For all of its variety, for all of its explorations of different sexes, different pleasures, *Le pur et l'impur* is first and foremost a narrative preoccupied with the question of femininity, a question that Colette, by placing herself within it, takes beyond the register of desire to that of enjoyment.

Colette tells us in the opening pages of *Le pur et l'impur* (1941) that the work will speak sadly of pleasure. Its sadness is, of course, of a different order from what we encountered in Sand. There is no heroine here struggling to achieve an ideal, no anguished contemplation of the impossibility of love, no inevitable, passionate death. And yet an ideal is here, as a question to be explored by the narrator, who wonders about the "burden" of her exceptional, androgynous nature. The impossibility of love as a perfect complementarity is also here, for all of the episodes allude to love's dissatisfactions, its inevitable mismatchings or left-overs. And the presence of death haunts the entire book, written as it is in the form of a backward glance at a life already lived. But though these structural similarities obtain and will help us (at the conclusion of this work) to discern a particular kind of development in French women's writing about love, sex, self, and difference, the dissimilarities between these two writers' approaches is of course much more immediately apparent.

The fundamental difference between Sand and Colette when it comes to sex is that for the former the essential difference between masculinity and femininity inexorably determines the fates of women and men. Lélia is exceptional, but always an exceptional *woman;* there can never be a doubt as to that. Whereas for Colette, this basic distinction, while operative in her work, is not tied to identities called "men" on the one hand and "women" on the other. Instead, the difference expresses itself in the varying ways people live it, or are lived by it. It is not, for example, that one of her characters is more masculine or feminine, or is *more* or *less* hetero- or homosexual. Sexual difference and sexuality are in fact never matters of degree, as has sometimes been suggested with respect to Colette's

Chapter Two

"tolerant" views.[7] It is a question of how the difference inhabits one, and of its inhabiting each one differently. This difference in the difference, in turn, informs one's pleasures. Colette, the narrator gives us to understand, is one of the few inhabited, or burdened, by a "true mental hermaphrodism," which is to say that the difference between masculine and feminine within her refuses to resolve itself, remaining instead in a tension, despite the fact that she has at times wished for the clarity of feeling herself to be completely one sex. From this ambiguous and, as it were, authoritative position, she recounts the pleasures of those whose differences are more or less decided, in whom the balance has been tipped.

How does Colette's understanding of sexual difference as potentially, if not always, an ambiguous difference inform her insights into the nature of pleasure, which, like love, always falls short of what it might be? At the base of this question is the problem of jouissance as the beyond of the pleasure principle. Whereas pleasure disappoints by falling short, *jouissance* does not, and all of Colette's subjects find themselves in the thrall of something they do not necessarily desire or even consciously enjoy, but which they are nevertheless driven toward in their divers sensual, more or (oftener) less pleasurable, lives. Before going into these in some detail, I should first clarify as far as possible the notions of pleasure and jouissance with which I am working.

Pleasure and Jouissance

The distinction between pleasure and jouissance essentially corresponds to the difference in levels between Freud's ego and id. Jouissance, which is a function of the drive, always reaches its mark, unlike desire, which can be disappointed or displaced. Pleasure, in this schema, would be on the side of conscious desire and the self who says "I want, I like . . ." The subject knows what it wants and likes, its pleasure, but does not know (as we saw with Lacan in the Introduction) what it (id) enjoys. Jouissance, pleasure's underside, is highly unpleasureable (in terms of this particular, narrow definition of pleasure): the repetition compulsion at work. Addressing precisely this understanding of jouissance as drive, Renata Salecl writes:

> The subject of desire is the subject of identification: this is the subject who constantly searches for points of support in the symbolic universe [. . .]. Such a point of identification can be a teacher, lover, analyst, etc. But on the level of the drive, there is no identification anymore; there is only *jouissance*. Paradoxically, the subject is always happy at the level of the drive: although because of the drive the subject actually suffers terribly and tries to escape its enormous pressure, in this suffering *jouissance* is at work. (20)[8]

The subject who is "happy" at the level of drive is the Lacanian subject, that is, the subject of the unconscious, whereas the subject who suffers as a result of the "painful satisfaction" that is jouissance is the "subject of identification," the ego or I. Jouissance goes on in spite of this knowing self, independently of the I's intentions and desires, and at the same time inflects those desires, shaping or deforming them and the pleasures to which they are linked. Jouissance is pleasure's beyond in the sense of pertaining to a wholly different (but not wholly separate) register, that of unconscious drive and libido. Pleasure is what the ego enjoys, while jouissance is that enjoyment felt by the ego as what Salecl calls a "painful satisfaction." When analyzed, it appears as a senseless compulsion to repeat, a satisfaction that the ego finds itself seeking out without wanting to.

While I am making a (far too) neat distinction between jouissance and pleasure (unconscious and conscious), for my purposes here, the former realm constantly makes forays into the latter, rendering questions about desire (pleasure) and jouissance impossible to isolate one from the other. To mention only the most obvious complications, pleasure is not simply an outcome of satisfied, conscious desire (for either Freud or Lacan, or Irigaray), and desire in psychoanalytic thought is never merely about conscious wishes. Furthermore, the ego is not simply a conscious, intending, self-knowing instance, but a fundamentally disjointed one, distinct from the "I," the subject, in Lacanian thought. Without going into the specific reasons for that distinction,[9] it is clear enough that one only comes to say "I" in the process of a self-recognition that is also a misrecognition. (This is the basic message of Lacan's most-read essay, "The Mirror Stage.") The identification that happens in the development (not merely the chronological,

Chapter Two

"developmental" development, but in any development, at any time) of the ego is always, in Lacan's economical word, "asymptotic." "I" will never quite match that which is reflected back to me as me. The being who perceives some reflection of her- or himself and identifies that reflection as corresponding to "me," has necessarily also confronted the fact of the reflection's noncorrespondence, the fact that it fails to match "really" or totally what "me" is. Thus the ego, and its desires as well, are necessarily involved in an interplay of conscious and unconscious instances, in a tension between the two that fixes it on its imaginary plane.

And yet, even if desire is both conscious and unconscious, there is still a distinction to be made between desire and jouissance, for the former is always related to identification, whereas the latter is not (which is Salecl's point above). Conscious or unconscious desires, for Lacan, always come down to the desire to be recognized *as* this or that, to be confirmed in one's hopeful belief in the identity between, say, the fragmented mental and body parts I perceive and a totalized version of them that could be reflected back to me by what is therefore the object of my desire. As Lacan puts it, "desire comes from the Other, and jouissance is on the side of the Thing. [...] identifications are determined by desire without satisfying the drive" ("On Freud's 'Trieb'" 419; Fink's translation). While desire is satisfied by identifications, jouissance is most emphatically not. Why not? Because, Lacan explains, "the drive divides the subject and desire, the latter sustaining itself only in the relation it misrecognizes between that division and an object which causes it. Such is the structure of fantasy" ("On Freud's 'Trieb'" 419; Fink's translation). The subject and its desire are split by drive, but not (usually) overtaken by it, for desire persists by identifying (misrecognizing an identification between) the fact of that split, the fact that (again, to put this in terms of the mirror stage) I never completely match the image reflected back to me, and that therefore there seems to be a something missing, and an object supposed to be able to provide or embody that something (by recognizing, identifying me). In short, desire confuses a split with a lack, and designates an object or objects as what it takes to fill in the lack. And fantasy, as Lacan points out, is built precisely on this structure of inevitable misrecognition, allowing the subject to desire.

The subject is split (by drive), and even as conscious and unconscious desires go about seeking to fix the split through objects of identification, the drive carries on independent of such quests, having nothing whatever to do with identifications and the wish for, or lack of, wholeness. The drive persists, never minding, as it were, the fact of its misrecognition. As Jacques-Alain Miller puts it, commenting on Lacan's "Trieb," "the drive couldn't care less about the desire for recognition. No identification can satisfy the drive" (J.-A. Miller, "Commentary" 424; Fink's translation). Another way of putting this is to say, as Miller does, that "while the subject and desire are divided" or split, "the subject and the drive are not" ("Commentary" 426; Fink's translation). Jouissance, in this understanding, is not only limited, but also, unlike desire, undivided, whole.

Things become more complex when we speak of *feminine* jouissance, which, while certainly not divided or split, is nevertheless not to be thought of as "whole." While Lacan, as we saw in the Introduction, is categorical in his location of feminine jouissance beyond knowledge and hence beyond language, he keeps open the question of its being. Not *what is feminine jouissance?* When we ask that question, it is as if we are dealing with an entity about which we can say, at least, that "it" exists, and then go on to wonder about its nature, its attributes, and so on. Instead: given that we cannot say that feminine jouissance exists (not in the realm of articulated knowledge at any rate) but that it nevertheless may be believed in (Lacan says he believes in it), then what does this jouissance, this feminine, wordless drive-enjoyment tell us about that which we can know: desires, intentions, wants, needs, and so on? In other words, what does the belief, or lack thereof, in feminine jouissance have to do with the structure, and the experience, of desires, pleasures, enjoyments? If we were to try to take it into account (not to account for it, but to take it into account as an element in desiring, speaking subjects and their relations with each other), how might that change our understanding of selves, "masculine" and "feminine," and their desires and pleasures? A feminine jouissance beyond

Chapter Two

knowledge, since it cannot be pointed out or identified simply, must instead be gradually followed as we find its traces in painful, unconsciously sought satisfactions, such as those that inhabit Colette's characters and Colette the narrator/author.

At stake here, finally, is not an understanding of jouissance (what could it mean, finally, to "understand" drive?), but of the feminine and femininity, two different, but vexedly related terms. If the subject of jouissance is radically opposed to the subject of consciousness, if in fact this jouissance is driven to obliterate the self-contained sense-making of the subject of identification, and if, further, the jouissance with which we are concerned is inextricably bound up with the feminine, with, in fact, Woman (who for all her nonexistence nevertheless permeates the subjectivities of women and men), then what, Colette's narrative allows us to ask, becomes of the feminine in relation to pleasure and enjoyment? And what of femininity?

Colette: From Desire to Jouissance

In *Le pur et l'impur,* a series of characters suffer their various jouissances as they pursue pleasures. Madame Charlotte, with whom the book opens, cannot forgo the enjoyment she derives from feigning pleasure. In spite of her body, which "knows what it wants" (*PI* 564), she continues to perform her "deferent lie, [her] dupery, undertaken with ardor" (562) for her young lover who does not "satisfy" her. A bodily satisfaction, she knows, is technically attainable, but it would come at the price of jouissance, the complex satisfaction she gets precisely from denying herself a certain enjoyment and lying to the one she loves, thereby retaining a particular control over him and herself. Her jouissance thus thwarts her pleasure. "X," the seducer, relentlessly strives to push each of his conquests beyond all possibility of refusal even as he longs for at least one woman to "love him enough to refuse herself to him" (567). Damien, the Don Juan, secretly despises women, whom he cannot forgive for "going too far" in their pleasure and getting more of it than he. He begrudges them their pleasurable excess, which it is nevertheless his jouissance to cause. "La Chevalière" surrounds herself with sensual possibilities and simultaneously complains that no woman has ever allowed her to remain with her "very natural platonism [... with just] *the idea*" of love (594–95). The homosexual Pepe and the other "monsters" of his circle constitute a comforting refuge for Colette, and they themselves live out their desires "trembling with fright" and in a "nervous fragility" that, in Pepe's case, leads to suicide. The ladies of Llangollen inhabit what seems a sentimental and sensual idyll, but Colette does not fail to point out that this perfection seems to depend on the complete silence of one of the two, who, in the midst of what may be "perfect happiness," loses her tongue and even her own name.

It is doubtless a question of jouissance versus pleasure (drive versus desire) in *Le pur et l'impur*, but these are not the only two terms at play. As we have already pointed out, a third term is there from the outset, disturbing the more or less consistent struggle between drive and ego. What, *Le pur et l'impur* asks, might be a *feminine* enjoyment as opposed to a feminine desire? (Although Colette herself is of course not using the terms *pleasure* and *jouissance* in the particularly psychoanalytic way I am here, there is a clear distinction between the two registers in the novel. Accordingly, when Colette's word is *plaisir*, it will not always correspond to the pleasure I have just evoked in its relation to jouissance. Since, however, this relation is an ambiguous one, I will not insist on clarifying *which pleasure* is in question at every point. It may well be that the blurring between pleasure and jouissance will prove illuminating for the questions of the feminine and femininity in Colette.) In this reworking of the question "What do women want?" it is not only women who are at issue, but femininity itself, which for Colette is always an unsettled and unsettling notion. A feminist and psychoanalytic reading of this work needs to account for Colette's mingling of jouissance, pleasure, and femininity in a narrative that insists throughout on the sadness of its subject matter, pleasure, a sadness, Colette writes, that is best captured in a feminine face.[10]

If we keep this feminine face in mind, then *Le pur et l'impur*'s proximity to Colette's three "mother" books, *La maison de Claudine*[11] (1922), *La naissance du jour* (1928), and *Sido* (1930), becomes telling. Elaine Marks has argued that "*Le Pur et l'impur* belongs, in spirit and in point of view, with the Sido-dominated books" (216). And Lynne Huffer, in her

Chapter Two

Another Colette,[12] situates her reading of *Le pur et l'impur* as a continuation of her analysis of "Colette's search for the mother" in the Sido trilogy, which Huffer reads from a Lacanian and Kristevan perspective. (It should also be pointed out that, although the publication date for *Le pur et l'impur* is 1941, that edition is an only slightly revised version of the text that appeared first in 1932, under the title *Ces plaisirs*... Chronologically speaking too, then, the four works are close to each other.) Huffer argues that in *La naissance du jour* the mother-daughter relation reveals the tentative and liminal process of becoming a subject who speaks in a voice she can identify, at least in part, as her own. She makes the crucial point that this becoming in Colette is always that, and that far from proclaiming a straightforward feminine subject, Colette's text puts into relief the undermining of subjectivity that accompanies, indeed constitutes, her becoming in language. As Huffer puts it, "[In *La naissance du jour*] the daughter remains on the edge of subjectivity [...while] the mother becomes a figure, an object of representation, that stands for the subversion of subjectivity as the locus of speech" (43). For Huffer, this subversion is a Kristevan semiotic effect that troubles the Lacanian division between the imaginary and the symbolic orders, and Colette produces this effect through her representation of Sido as simultaneously beyond words and writing, beyond language, and as the engendering force behind Colette's literary creativity. When she proceeds from her consideration of the Sido books to *Le pur et l'impur,* though, Huffer wants to move away from a psychoanalytic reading in order to do justice to the heterogeneity of the latter text. She writes:

> As metaphors endowed with subjectivity, both the maternal and paternal figures are open to psychoanalytic readings that focus on the formation of mothers and daughters as subjects and the Lacanian rewriting of Freud's Œdipus complex. And yet, a rhetorical reading of Colette's texts that is founded only on psychoanalytic structures does not adequately account for the vast range of operations and transformations that constitute textuality, and obfuscates the historical, transindividual, and intertextual nature of literary discourse. (71)

Huffer's caution against a psychoanalytic approach that risks essentializing and ahistoricizing is important. Her own work, however, demonstrates that it is possible to bring psychoanalytic thinking to bear on Colette's writing without reducing its nuances to a psychoanalysis taken as a ready-made (already made) theoretical framework. And to say the least, Colette's works—especially the Sido books and *Le pur et l'impur*—written in the twenties and thirties, participate in the intellectual and cultural debates of the day, at least insofar as they are written in the same milieu, and clearly engage questions with which both feminist and psychoanalytic thought are also preoccupied at the time. In this sense, Colette, like Sand, is a perfect example of a writer whose work not only refuses to be subordinated to critical discourses, but actually challenges those discourses by putting forth "their" questions (e.g., feminine sexuality, maternity, perversity) in a novel form. In so doing, her writing encounters the fundamentals of psychoanalytic and feminist thought. My project is concerned precisely with the attempt to work with psychoanalysis's and feminism's most radical possibilities where sexual difference is concerned, possibilities that Colette's writing calls forth and that go against the kind of essentializing moves often attributed to psychoanalytic discourses. A reading of *Le pur et l'impur* that is both feminist and psychoanalytic, in my understanding, will not risk reducing the richness of Colette's literary discourse to a pat family romance devoid of historical specificity and mired in the story of an individual's development. Instead, such a reading will allow a sustained attention to Colette's negotiations of jouissance, pleasure, and femininity. More specifically, I am interested in how the question of the maternal—so overtly presented in the Sido books, and equally, though differently, important for this work from the same period—informs and throws light on these negotiations.

Felman, reflecting on a notion of reading autobiographically that includes reading psychoanalytically, provides a helpful understanding of why such an approach, far from failing to attend to "the vast range of operations and transformations that constitute textuality," or obfuscating "the historical, transindividual, and intertextual nature of literary discourse," can

Chapter Two

actually shed light on the dynamic elements of both literary and historical subjects. Reading psychoanalytically can do so because of what such a "method" (or countermethod) does not presuppose. Both psychoanalysis and feminism, at their most basic and most radical points, refuse to assume the truth of the subject. For both discourses, the subject is in process, in the making or unmaking of itself, as the case may be, but never simply, terminably defined. Felman suggests that "women's autobiography is what their memory cannot contain—or hold together as a whole—although their writing inadvertently inscribes it" (Felman, *What?* 15). Thus while performing psychoanalytic and feminist readings, Felman necessarily starts from a dynamic and incomplete picture, allowing a life, a text, to shape itself in her reading of it. In Colette's work, where characters and selves (including the narrative I) constantly reveal yet another veil as they unveil themselves (Charlotte's hidden face is but the most literal example), the project of reading autobiography otherwise is necessarily an open one, and demands, I would suggest, a literary critical version of Freud's free-floating attention.

When Marks argues that *Le pur et l'impur* belongs with the Sido books, she says this is because, like them, it is chiefly concerned with the themes of love and purity. Purity, in the earlier works, is always associated with Sido, the mother, and impurity with Colette, the daughter-writer.[13] Marks asks, "Why are Sido, the ladies of Llangollen, Pepe and the 'monsters' pure, and not Colette?" (218). She concludes that they are pure in that "they live in an independent world to which they give themselves completely. Never is Sido's attention distracted from the daily adventures of her house, her garden and her village; [. . .] never are the ladies of Llangollen and the 'monsters' distracted from the presence of the loved one" (219). Colette, on the other hand, is mobile, moving from one object of interest or passion to another in her writerly vocation, and is thus, apparently, exiled from what Marks calls her "kingdom of the pure."

> This feeling of not being pure may well have been one of Colette's personal concerns. Quite often the reader may sense it in her novels, short stories, anecdotes, meditations

and reminiscences. It is not merely by chance, however, that the works in which it stands out most clearly should also be Colette's masterpieces. Paradoxically, by their very existence, they attest to her long and patient effort to eliminate all impurities from her work, to discover, behind all the masks, her own voice and her own world. Despite all her self-doubt, Colette, by virtue of her fidelity to her work, was indeed one of the pure. (219)

Marks is doubtless right to see in a work like *Le pur et l'impur* a honing and perfecting of style and voice and a tenacious fidelity to whatever that voice might produce. But how is Colette faithful, or, more specifically, what characterizes the voice to which her fidelity attaches itself? I would suggest that, like the ladies of Llangollen, Colette is "fermement fidèle à une chimère" ("firmly faithful to a chimera"; 626), the difference being, of course, that Colette recognizes the chimera as such, and enjoys her fidelity despite, or because of, its fanciful, fleeting object. The chimera, of course, is more than an unreal product of the imagination (pure fancy); it is also a monster (lion, goat, and serpent), and so impure by its very nature. Thus, if Colette's textual fidelity guarantees her voice's inclusion in the realm of the pure, it is also that by which she refuses this purity, choosing instead a complex, monstrous tenor. While Marks's observation that Colette does somehow inhabit purity despite a general "feeling of not being pure" is not quite right, neither is it quite wrong, because throughout *Le pur et l'impur* Colette recounts her continuous seduction by the various sorts of erotic purity she describes and invents *as pure* in their monstrosity.

The question then becomes: what is the relation between the mother-daughter couple, with its meanderings around the theme of purity, and the discourse on sensual pleasure that makes up *Le pur et l'impur?* Where or how are the mother and the daughter, in their purity or impurity, in the work that "speaks sadly of pleasure"? How does the mother-daughter couple inform the sexual/sensual couple?

In order to answer this question, it is necessary to look through the lens Colette offers at the beginning of the book with the character of Charlotte, an engaging, no longer young

Chapter Two

"bourgeoise" who is having an affair with a man young enough to be her son. Colette's first encounter with Charlotte, who as we shall see is an echo of both Colette and Sido, is auditory. Shortly after entering an opium den and making herself comfortable in order to observe, she hears Charlotte skillfully simulating the ecstasy that her lover does not provoke in her. In Colette's subsequent conversations with her, Charlotte vacillates between revealing herself frankly and closing herself off from Colette's psychological inquiry.

Beautiful, refined, and amorous, Charlotte has been called a double for Colette. And indeed, the Colette of the book's action (that is, the narrator's representation of herself as she was eighteen years before the moment of writing) is about the same age as Charlotte, who is "probably forty-five" (557). Her physical aspect, as Sherry Dranch has pointed out in her "Reading through the Veiled Text: Colette's *Le pur et l'impur*," mimes that of the historical Colette. Dranch notes that "Physically, with her plump arms, her hands and feet at ease, Charlotte is very much a middle-aged Colette [. . .] she even wears a fox collar on her coat—and 'foxy,' as we know, was always an item in the lexicon that Colette employed to describe her own features" (177–78). The two women, then, are the same age, resemble each other personally, and are known by only one name. Not only does Charlotte's name mime Colette's visually and phonetically (the initial "C," the liquid "l" in the middle, and the closing plosive), it also echoes the double nature of Colette's name, which is at once proper (it comes from her father's name, Jules-Joseph Colette)[14] and assumed. Colette emphasizes a similar ambiguity in Charlotte's name, which floats somewhere between true or false (557), adding to the "idée de mystère que nous attachons aux êtres dont nous ne connaissons que la simplicité" ("idea of mystery that we attach to beings of whom we know only the simplicity"; 559–60). As we will see below, there is yet another way in which Colette is associated with Charlotte: along with the nominal, chronological, and bodily levels, we also find that the two are linked, subtly and deeply, on the erotic level.

But the identification we are dealing with is not between two, but among three. If Charlotte is linked to Colette as I have just indicated, and is her perfect contemporary, she simultaneously comes from another, older generation:

> Elle ressemblait, par le nez court et le visage charnu, aux modèles favoris de Renoir, à des beautés de 1875, si fort qu'en dépit du manteau vert olive à col de renard et du petit chapeau en vogue il y a dix-huit ans, on pouvait lui trouver je ne sais quoi de démodé. (557 [74])

Charlotte seems a woman out of 1875, a woman who would have been a woman already when Colette was born (1873). Charlotte thus evokes the world of Colette's mother with her *démodé* suggestion of Sido's generation. The imagery that dominates once Charlotte appears in the flesh recalls Sido with more specificity (who herself, like the other two, is also known by one name). Charmed by her appearance outside the door of the dark opium den that they exit together, Colette is then refreshed upon coming out with Charlotte into the "air libre, frais, encore obscur," and suddenly an "envie quotidienne de matins clairs, d'évasions vers les champs et les forêts, tout au moins ver le Bois voisin [the Bois de Boulogne]"; 557 [75]) causes her to hesitate at the edge of the sidewalk before starting on her way home. It is significant that references to the natural world immediately follow Charlotte's appearance. No sooner has Colette come close to this woman than she is stopped short by a desire for those natural scenes—bright mornings, fields, woods—with which Sido is always associated in her books.[15] Even Charlotte's speech has the magical power of a (phallic) mother's: what she says immediately becomes real:

> "Vous n'avez pas de voiture? dit ma compagne. Moi non plus. Mais à cette heure-ci on trouve toujours des voitures dans ce quartier..."
> Comme elle parlait, un taxi parut, venant du Bois, ralentit, s'arrêta, et ma compagne s'effaça.
> "Je vous en prie, madame..." (557 [76])

Each refuses in turn to take the taxi, deferring to the other, until Charlotte suggests that they share it, offering to drop Colette at

Chapter Two

home. Colette relishes the opportunity to be near her a while longer.

The two have spent the evening in the same house, but Charlotte has been with her young lover. We have already heard her voice twice: first, singing so beautifully that everyone hushed to listen; and second, singing out again during lovemaking "sur un rythme calme d'abord, si harmonieusement, si régulièrement précipité que je me surpris à suivre, d'un hochement de tête, sa cadence aussi parfaite que sa mélodie" (556 [77]). When Colette listens to her again now, at close quarters in the taxi, Charlotte's voice continues to seduce her as powerfully as her flesh.

> Le son charmant de sa voix, l'attaque râpeuse de certaines syllabes, une manière vaincue et suave de laisser tomber dans le registre grave la fin des phrases . . . Quelle séduction! . . . Le vent, par la vitre ouverte à la droite de "Charlotte," rabattait sur moi son parfum assez banal et une saine, une active odeur de chair, que gâtait celle du tabac refroidi. (558 [78])

Charlotte's voice, her smell, her flesh, overwhelm Colette in a pleasurable seduction. Understanding the import of Charlotte's maternalism in relation to the narrator who both is and is not a woman, requires that we look further into their erotic link.

The first two episodes of this book, of which Charlotte is the focus, constitute an introduction to the question of femininity as Colette will pose it. We will see that if Charlotte is, sensually, a feminine mixture of nonchalance and inhibition, it is because the Colette who encounters her is as well. And if Charlotte is simultaneously a figure of the omnipotent maternal and an image of the most compliant, even self-effacing, femininity, it is because this is the sort of contradiction that the narrated Colette labors under, and that the narrating Colette will probe.

At their first meeting, after the two women have entered the taxi, Charlotte speaks of her "pauvre petit" ("poor little one"), saying, "Il me donne beaucoup de souci" ("He gives me so much worry"). Colette, who has heard the sounds Charlotte produced while she and the "pauvre petit" were on the balcony above her, smiles and replies, "Pas seulement du souci? . . ."

("But not just worry? ..."), to which Charlotte rejoins, with a shrug of the shoulders, "Vous croirez ce que vous voudrez" ("Think what you like"; 558). During their next tête-à-tête, Charlotte will admit to her "mélodieux et miséricordieux mensonge" ("melodious and merciful lie"; 561), but in such a way that Colette guesses at the truth herself before it is spoken.

> "C'est si fatigant quelqu'un qu'on aime! ... soupira-t-elle. Je n'ai pas beaucoup de goût à mentir.
> —Comment, mentir? ... Pourquoi? Vous l'aimez?
> —Naturellement, je l'aime.
> —Mais alors ..."
> Elle m'infligea un magnifique regard de supérieur à l'inférieur, qu'elle adoucit après:
> "Mettons que je n'y connaisse rien," dit-elle poliment.
> (561 [79])

Colette proceeds to consider the "quasi public" pleasure of Charlotte, remembering the "romanesque récompense" that she had bestowed upon her lover, the

> plainte de rossignol, notes pleines, réitérées, identiques, l'une par l'autre prolongées, précipitées jusqu'à la rupture de leur tremblant équilibre au sommet d'un sanglot torrentiel ... (561 [80])

This "mélodieux et miséricordieux mensonge" constitutes Charlotte's "génie femelle," makes her a "rassurante amie des hommes," and is a "duperie entretenue avec flamme, prouesse ignorée qui n'espère pas de récompense" (562 [81]).

Charlotte's lie, which constitutes her femininity (her valiant, reassuring femininity), seems less a matter of deceit for Colette than of the capacity to wait. Immediately after the revelation of Charlotte's secret—a revelation, incidentally, that occurs in the silence of a pause in their conversation, while Colette awaits her response—Charlotte's patient, waiting posture is evoked: "Assise et les jambes étendues, *elle attendait* oisive, à mon côté, de reprendre la tâche dévolue à celui qui aime le mieux: la fourberie quotidienne" (562 [82]; emphasis added). Meanwhile, Colette herself is waiting to hear the truth, which is to say the lie, from Charlotte's own lips: "'Encore quelques

Chapter Two

instants, pensai-je, quelques instants de trouble entretien, et j'apprends de Charlotte ce qu'elle cache au farouche petit amant...'" (562 [83]) But in fact Charlotte chooses to talk instead about the housekeeping details of the opium den in which the two are sitting, informing Colette, the newcomer, of the little rules that prevail, and thereby extending her wait. In so doing Charlotte allows her to come to further conclusions.

"[T]out me plaisait en Charlotte," and so Colette sets about distinguishing her character from those feminine qualities she disapproves. First, whereas other women past their prime (*sur le retour*) designate their younger lovers with sundry "unacceptable" appellations ("petit époux," "méchant gosse," "gentil péché," "petite fille"), Charlotte calls hers, simply, "'mon garçon,' ajoutant à sa maternité ambiguë un accent d'autorité rond et sans langueur" (563 [84]). Second, Colette wants to distinguish her from a species of women that disgusts her:

> Déjà je voulais qu'elle ne ressemblât en rien à ces nonnes encombrantes que l'on heurte à tout carrefour. J'appelle nonnes ces prédestinées qui soupirent entre les draps, mais de résignation, aiment en secret l'abnégation, la couture, les travaux de ménage et les couvre-lits en satin ciel, faute d'un autre autel à napper de la couleur virginale... (563 [85])

These women, the picture of a stereotyped femininity, are simultaneously characterized by a fascination with things masculine that gets expressed in their obsessive relation to particular sorts of domestic duties (they "prennent un soin fanatique des vêtements de l'homme, du pantalon surtout, bifide et mystérieux" ["take fanatical care of a man's clothing, especially the biped and mysterious pants"]), and in what Colette calls "le pire perversité" ("the worst perversity"): they wish for their mates' illnesses, for the moment they can busy their hands with "tout vase souillé, tout linge moite" ("every filthy basin, every piece of wet linen") produced by the male's malady (563).

Charlotte, though, is like neither of these types, or at least the narrated Colette would have it so ("Déjà *je voulais* qu'elle ne ressemblât en rien à ces nonnes"). In Colette's fantasy of her, Charlotte is not an overbearing mother figure belittling the one she loves with foolish appellations; nor does she embody a femininity based on the desire to subjugate the masculine through its own sacrificial abnegation. The two women Charlotte *is not* represent two possible interpretations of the maternal as feminine. The first, an older woman infantilizing her younger lover, maintains in her erotic life a control and authority called maternal. This is the first type from which Colette needs to set Charlotte apart, for she is indeed bent on not losing control of herself in the relation with her boy, and she does in fact dote on his delicate health with maternal concern, managing his exposure to risks, and making sure that he takes his pills, eats his red meat, sleeps with the window open, and gets a reward for his good behavior now and then (559). How, then, does Colette distinguish Charlotte from the infantilizing mother-figures? Simply by noting that Charlotte's maternal relation, while simple and forthright (she calls her lover nothing more complicated or dressed up than "my boy"), is nevertheless "ambiguous." Charlotte *is* a mother, *is* maternal in her love relation, but what her maternity is is not altogether clear. Colette can only say that it is ambiguous. Thus the first description we find of a maternity that is not to be scorned is, literally, a wandering one (ambiguous coming from the Latin verb *ambigere*, "to wander"). The mother in Charlotte is both forthright and elusive. Straightforward and errant.

The second interpretation of the rejected maternal is embodied by Colette's ostensibly meek, submissive women who suppress their own desire for authority (their desire, as it were, to wear those mysterious, biped pants), converting it instead into pathological (to Colette at least) symptoms: obsessions with the details of domesticity that figure their lost purity (the virginal blue of the bedspread); the inability to relate to men except as patients, as surrogate children; their desire, even, for their mates to become ill in order to be spared the pain of the nonrelation that prevails, masking it with a care called "maternal" only to differentiate it from "erotic," since it does not extend beyond domestic and physical details into the emotional or intellectual lives of their lovers. Colette's "nuns" present a picture strikingly similar, in fact, to the "housewife psychosis" Freud mentions about twenty-five years earlier in the 1905 Dora case study. There, Freud attempts to piece together a

Chapter Two

picture of Dora's mother based on accounts he has been given, and this leads him to a more general observation about a condition he has apparently noticed in many women.

> I never made her [Dora's] mother's acquaintance. From the accounts given me by the girl and her father I was led to imagine her as an uncultivated woman and above all as a foolish one, who had concentrated all her interests upon domestic affairs, especially since her husband's illness and the estrangement to which it led. She presented the picture, in fact, of what we might call "housewife psychosis." She had no understanding of her children's more active interests, and was occupied all day long in cleaning the house with its furniture and utensils and in keeping them clean—to such an extent as to make it almost impossible to use or enjoy them. This condition, traces of which are to be found often enough in normal housewives, inevitably reminds one of forms of obsessional washing and other kinds of obsessional cleanliness. But such women (and this applied to the patient's mother) are entirely without insight into their illness, so that one essential characteristic of an "obsessional neurosis" is lacking. (*SE* 7: 20)[16]

Charlotte, it would seem, who so pleases Colette, suggests another alternative, precisely because she, unlike either Freud's housewife or Colette's nuns, is aware of her situation, and is even careful not to fool herself into complacency, as we shall see. At any rate, and from the beginning, Colette envisions in Charlotte an exception to the general rules that obtain for femininity.

> Charlotte appartenait, je m'en donnais tout bas l'assurance, à une autre règle. Son oisiveté aisée la rehaussait à mes yeux; peu de femmes savent, les mains vides, se tenir immobiles et sereines. J'observais ses pieds, ses doigts pendants et dépliés, tous les signes révélateurs de la sagesse, de l'empire sur soi . . . (563 [86])

Colette, again, is *reassuring* herself that Charlotte is different, that this woman is otherwise than most women. Her difference consists in her maternal ambiguity (the errant maternity we just noted) coupled with a certain idleness or ease that speaks of

Colette

self-control and serenity. For Colette then, the possibility of the existence of "another rule" for women, for women's being, is bound up with a peculiar notion: a wandering idleness, a serene errancy.

Colette sits with Charlotte in the dark, drinking the maté she has brewed and poured for her, and interrogates Charlotte's particular sadness, a sadness bound up with her pleasure. Colette herself has first come into the opium den in a state of some uncertainty, even agitation. At any rate, it is self-consciousness, as opposed to self-control, that characterizes her entrance into the narrative. When she first appears in the opium den, Colette is approached by a colleague who asks whether she has come out of curiosity. When Colette answers that it is her profession that has brought her, he smiles:

> "Je le pensais bien . . . Un roman?"
> Et je le détestais davantage, pour ce qu'il me croyait incapable—moi qui l'étais en effet—de goûter ce luxe: un plaisir tranquille, un peu bas, un plaisir inspiré seulement par une certaine forme du snobisme, l'esprit de bravade, une curiosité plus affectée que réelle . . . Je n'avais apporté qu'un chagrin bien caché, qui ne me laissait point de repos, et une affreuse paix des sens. (554 [87])

This commentary on the sort of atmosphere that prevails in the opium den is framed by Colette's observations of herself. She is incapable of enjoyment and she has within her only two things: a grief that she hides and that gives her no rest, and a sensual paralysis. It would appear, then, that the pleasing picture of maternal femininity drawn around Charlotte corresponds precisely, and inversely, to Colette's own state of being. Her own restless, hidden grief is countered in the ambiguity (errancy) of Charlotte's frank maternity. Both characteristics imply movement, but Colette's is an enforced mobility (she is not allowed to rest), whereas Charlotte's ambiguity is her own. Likewise, the terrible stillness of Colette's senses is doubled, and countered, by the serene stillness of Charlotte's hands. Whereas Colette's body is paralyzed, deadened, Charlotte's physical stillness is the result of a wisdom and control Colette lacks. The theme of deadened senses is itself as pervasive in

Chapter Two

this section of the book as is the opium that wafts through it, further tranquilizing Colette, who is glad of the calm and begins to hope "que nulle danseuse, nul danseur nus ne troubleraient la veillée, qu'aucun danger d'Américains, frétés d'alcool, ne nous menaçait et que le *Columbia* [phonograph] lui-même se tairait . . ." (555 [88]).

It is at the moment when Colette has sunken with her grief and her terrible sensual peace into the soothing absence of sensation bestowed by the opium smoke that "embaumait ce lieu banal" ("embalmed that banal place"; 554), and while she is wishing not only for no noisy interruptions but for less noise than there is, for a total lack of stimuli—it is at this moment that "une voix féminine, cotonneuse, rêche et douce comme sont les pêches dures à gros velours, se mit à chanter, et nous fut à tous si agréable que nous nous gardâmes d'applaudir, même par un murmure" (554–55 [89]). Charlotte's singing, which is soon cut off by her lover, later becomes her rhythmic, nightingale call during lovemaking.

That rhythm, which Colette is surprised to find herself following with a regular nodding of her head, is that of a woman *struggling against* her invading pleasure ("Une femme [. . .] luttait contre son plaisir envahissant"), and for all its beauty (it matches the perfection of her earlier melody), it introduces a chill into the tranquilized darkness of the narrative:

> Tout soupir mourut là-haut. Et les sages d'en bas sentirent, tous ensemble, le froid de l'aube d'hiver. Je recroisai et serrai sur moi mon manteau fourré, un voisin étendu ramena sur son épaule un pan d'étoffe brodée et ferma les yeux. Au fond, près d'une lanterne de soie, les deux femmes endormies se rapprochèrent encore sans s'éveiller, et les petites flammes des lampes à huiles battirent sous la pesée d'air froid qui descendait de la verrière. (556 [90])

The cold air descends from where Charlotte is, from the frigidity of her "melodious and merciful lie" (561), prefiguring the subject of the later conversation between her and Colette. Charlotte will awaken in Colette, who is suffering from the stillness of her own senses, from a grief that is never specified, a twofold desire: both that Charlotte *not* represent the maternal-feminine alternatives Colette herself wants to reject, as we have seen; and also that Charlotte find what she lacks.

Another element that informs Charlotte's difference from other versions of maternal femininity is the fact that she, unlike the others, knows how to wait. "'Comme vous devez bien savoir attendre, madame Charlotte!' [...] 'Assez bien, c'est vrai. Mais maintenant, comme disent les médecins retraités, je n'exerce plus'" (563 [91]). As much a mother to Colette as to anyone, Charlotte once again occupies the place of a "superior" explaining things to an "inferior." Colette persists:

> —On attend toujours ... Vous venez de dire: 'Je l'attends dans une huitaine'..."
> —Ah! oui ... [...] C'est vrai, je l'attends ... Mais je n'attends rien de lui. Il y a une nuance ..." (564 [92])

The waiting, the expecting, is something that Charlotte does well precisely because her expectation has no object. She waits: but she waits for nothing to come as a result of, or in recompense for, her waiting. Indeed, instead of underlining her dissatisfaction with her lover, she puts it quite another way. "Ce serait *trop beau*, l'amour d'un si jeune homme, si je n'étais pas forcée à mentir" (564 [93]; emphasis added). The excessive beauty of a love without her "deferent lie" (562) is, finally, curiously, what Charlotte rejects. If she would not dream of seeking out the pleasure she lacks, even though she knows it is attainable, it is because to attain it represents, paradoxically, a terrifying loss.

> —Madame Charlotte, ce qui vous manque ... 'véritablement'... est-ce que vous le cherchez?"
> Elle sourit, la tête renversée, montrant dans la lumière confuse le dessous de son joli nez court, son menton un peu gras, un arc de dents sans brèche:
> "Je ne suis pas si naïve, madame, ni si dévergondée. Ce qui me manque, je m'en passe, et voilà tout, ne m'en faites pas un mérite, non ... Mais une chose qu'on connaît bien pour l'avoir bien possédée, on n'en est jamais tout à fait privé. C'est sans doute la raison de sa grande jalousie, à mon garçon. J'ai beau faire—et vous avez entendu que je ne suis pas maladroite –, mon pauvre petit, qui a de l'instinct, prend

Chapter Two

> des colères sans motif, et me secoue comme s'il voulait à toute force m'ouvrir ... C'est risible," dit-elle. Et elle rit en effet.
> "Et ... ce qui vous manque ... est-ce réellement hors d'atteinte?
> —Il est possible que non, dit-elle avec hauteur. Mais j'aurais honte de la vérité à côté du mensonge. Voyons, madame, figurez-vous ... M'abandonner comme une imbécile, ne plus seulement savoir ce qui vous échappe en gestes ou en paroles ... Rien que cette idée-là ... Oh! je ne peux pas supporter cette idée-là."
> Elle dut même rougir, car son visage me parut plus foncé. Elle tournait de côté et d'autre sa tête sur le coussin blanc, agitée, la bouche entrouverte, comme une femme que le plaisir menace. (565 [94])

The prospect of pleasure is menacing, upsetting for Charlotte. The lack, filled, would be, she fears, an utter loss of self. Indeed, even this approach to pleasure in conversation with Colette serves to close her up in self-defense. She has come close, in Colette's description of her response to the question about her pleasure, to allowing that pleasure some sway over her. Her head is thrown back, her mouth open, her face flushed, and Colette, seduced or wanting to be, cannot resist expressing aloud her thought that "à cesser de mentir, Charlotte ne risquait que de devenir plus belle" ("in ceasing to lie, Charlotte only risked becoming more beautiful"). As with the boy who wants to open her, so with Colette, "elle se referma" ("she closed herself back up"; 565).

Charlotte's fear of filling up the lack or empty space with some content, with some particular pleasure, for example, calls to mind psychoanalyst Enid Balint's discussion of the notion of "being empty of oneself," which is worth exploring inasmuch as, for Colette, this lack in her alter ego, Charlotte, is crucial: it is the very thing that keeps her from both her own beauty and from any connection to others. She insists on keeping the lack unfilled, and she does so by closing herself off. I would like now to compare this state of affairs with one described by Balint, to suggest how Balint's work might be read alongside what we have already seen of Irigaray's notion of taking the negative upon oneself, and then to return to Colette, Charlotte, and the emptiness that links them.

"Emptiness," Death, Femininity

In her 1963 essay "On Being Empty of Oneself," Enid Balint presents the case of a female patient, whom she calls Sarah, who had broken down at age twenty-four and who said she felt empty of herself and as if she inhabited a void. Without going into too many of the details provided by Balint, let me summarize the main points in her presentation that will concern us here. Sarah's mother introduces her to the analyst by insisting that Sarah was a "perfect baby," and that "there had been no trouble at all until perhaps a year before the breakdown" (Balint 42). The mother herself "seemed a depressed woman with precarious self-esteem [. . . and] could not understand how her daughter could have changed so much" (41–42). It soon becomes clear, however, that Sarah has always had problems, and that these problems were intimately bound up with her parents' failure to recognize her, especially with the failure to recognize when she was in some sort of trouble. "It gradually transpired that she felt in a void or empty of herself, or both, in the presence of people who were, so to speak, in another world but did not recognise this fact, or failed to recognise that she was in another world" (46). To begin with, Sarah can only offer her own death as a solution or outcome to this state of affairs; she gradually comes to incorporate body feelings into herself, particularly the feeling of her uterus; she feels "herself to be inside her body—and parallel with that the external void began to fill up" (54). Over time, Sarah ceases to feel empty, and even develops an anxiety about the possibility of losing herself.

Balint prefaces her presentation of this case by suggesting that it might have a more general contribution to make:

> These observations might also contribute something to our knowledge of the special psychology of women. In my clinical experience the feeling of being empty or of "being empty of herself" is more frequently found in women than in men [. . .]. Further, this disturbance is linked with another, which in my experience is also encountered more frequently by women than by men; namely that they are full of rubbish, which is valueless and lifeless [. . .]. (40)

In a recent discussion of this case, Mitchell speculates on its meaning, suggesting the notion of a "dead mother," which she argues plays an important role in the construction of femininity (Mitchell, "Looking"). Rather than being empty, Mitchell wonders whether such women are instead "full of a dead mother." This dead mother is the presence of the maternal body without the spirit, and she is internalized by the daughter in preference to a nothing-at-all. The actual mother, whose psychic maternity has been damaged in some way ("a depressed woman with precarious self-esteem") has been unable to recognize and foster such a maternity in her daughter, who then lives with an incorporated dead maternal mark, a sterilized fecundity, a negative maternity rather than the nothingness or void that is its only alternative.

This dead maternal mark (as opposed to a nurtured and fecund psychic maternity) speaks to Irigaray's negative in a manner not usually forwarded: namely, it suggests that the encounter with this negative, let alone its acceptance or taking on, would entail also the exposure of and to an internalized, feminine death, a dead maternity that, if it is to be revitalized, resuscitated, needs first to be recognized in its dangerous force: from birth, for a mother wounded in her fecundity, emerges an intimate death that is not a simple mortality, but a death-in-life, or rather a death *as* life, the only life there is, for both mother and daughter. The location of the death drive in the vicissitudes of sexual difference is thus inextricably bound up with the foreclosure of the maternal—this buried negative that is relentlessly kept at bay lest it emerge as that dreaded nothingness at the core of being, a nothingness that is even less than a wounded or defunct creativity. The taking upon oneself of the negative is then also an engendering, a giving birth to eros, to the life drives. It may be then, that this self-disappropriation that is tantamount to the actualization of the negative within, amounts also to a revitalization of the dead mother, a revitalization that allows a buried fecundity to re-emerge, or emerge for the first time, as a fecundity that does not demand or pretend to know completely its creation, nor the other with whom it may create. A psychical femininity then, for men as well as for women, would emerge from its burial (we can recall here Irigaray's reading of *Antigone*[17]) when the insufficiency, the limit, or the incompleteness can be both acknowledged and survived—a condition that is constantly running up against the resistance of a more or less universal phallo-imaginary that, as Irigaray argues, demands the whole of it, the complete being, being complete.

Maternity and Enjoyment

Charlotte will not seek out what she lacks—and in terms of her conversation with Colette, what she lacks is sexual enjoyment—because of her dread of an absolute loss of self. Her lover's violent shakings, Colette's prying questions and spy-glances serve only to close her off from them more securely. But we are nonetheless permitted a brief look, a fragmentary image of what would be Charlotte's enjoyment were she to open herself: "Elle sourit, la tête renversée, montrant dans la lumière confuse le dessous de son joli nez court, son menton un peu gras, un arc de dents sans brèche." Her face takes on a deeper shade, and "[d]eux points de lumière rouge s'attachaient au va-et-vient de ses grandes prunelles humides et grises" ("two red points of light were fixed on the back and forth of her large, moist gray eyeballs"; 565). Charlotte close to, or "threatened" by, pleasure is a confused, partial, and almost diabolical sight. She herself recoils from this sight when Colette attempts to show it to her, telling her that, beautiful as she has just become, she imagines Charlotte would only risk becoming more beautiful were she to cease to lie to her lover (and allow herself the "shameless" and "naive" enjoyment of that which she lacks). But

> Je [. . .] ne réussis qu'à la rendre assez froide et circonspecte, telle que je l'avais vue dans le taxi. Peu à peu elle se reprit, se referma. Le temps de quelques paroles et elle me barra le domaine mental qu'elle semblait mépriser de si haut, et qui porte un rouge nom viscéral: le cœur; —elle me défendit aussi la caverne d'odeurs, de couleurs, le sourd asile où s'ébattait sûrement une puissante arabesque de chair, un chiffre de membres mêlés, monogramme symbolique de l'Inexorable . . . (565 [95])

The key point here is that Charlotte, in fleeing pleasure, refuses the possibility of intimacy with her interlocutor in favor of a sort of loyalty to her lover, or more precisely, to the self she

Chapter Two

does not confront, find, or fear losing in her controlled relation to him. Charlotte's withdrawal from feminine proximity, where an erotic relation to a man informs the context, is important because Colette will end her work by evoking another female tête-à-tête, a scene in which two women, this time, succeed in coming together "in spite of a man" (653).

But Colette's and Charlotte's mutual attraction is as clear as their mutual inhibition. We could read the episode as Colette's attempt to seduce or draw out a woman who captivates her, an attempt that, despite its failure, nevertheless betrays in certain moments a particular link between the two women, who communicate with silences and half-gestures. Charlotte closes herself off when pleasure approaches, and the Colette who narrates this closure also puts into play, less overtly, her own shutting down.

The episode begins, as we saw above, with Colette's picture of herself as she is when she meets Charlotte: incapable of enjoying and subject to a deadening of her senses (554). The section ends with Charlotte's hiding herself (literally, with a veil) away from pleasure (566). The question at hand, then, would seem to be that of the inability to enjoy, their need, in fact, to avoid enjoyment. The temptation is to read Charlotte as a representative of frigidity in women, a figure of antipleasure that inaugurates a book about pleasure. But it is of course more complicated, for Charlotte, who in fact *does* evoke a feminine coldness, is also woman-as-maternal. Furthermore, whereas Colette strongly criticizes the frigid "nuns" capable of enjoying only a maternal relation to men, a relation described in pathological terms, Charlotte—also cold, also maternal—is not counted among them. Quite the contrary, if Charlotte is a figure for a stereotypical femininity, what is striking is the fact that the narrator embraces her—indeed, is seduced by her— and does not reject her. Her presence both soothes and stimulates Colette, who, sitting silently beside her in the dark, feels as if she has just confided in her, as indeed she will (562).

The narrative embrace of Charlotte will be best thought through by considering further the relation between the maternal in Charlotte and Colette's representation of herself with respect to it. Colette has not, in fact, set up an opposition between maternal femininity on the one hand and pathological femininity on the other. Instead, she has put them in the same character, a character who in turn reflects them in Colette, so that the relation between the women is both familiar and strange. Charlotte's "ambiguous maternity" is as much in relation to Colette, as we have seen, as to her young lover; and yet at the same time the two are utterly unknown to each other. Charlotte remarks, "Que c'est agréable de se connaître aussi peu! Nous parlons là de ces choses qu'on ne se confie pas entre amies. Des amies—s'il y en a—n'osent jamais se confier ce qui leur manque véritablement . . ." (564 [96]). Friends may not, but these two, related strangers do. And Charlotte is not the only one who confides a secret here. Colette, too, briefly and obliquely, makes her own confession. Or rather, it becomes a confession, a shared secret, once Charlotte responds to it, literally bringing it into existence after the fact of its utterance. After Charlotte has underlined the nuance between waiting and expecting, and reflected that love would really be too beautiful without her lie, she elaborates on the structural cause of that lie: the difference between the heart and the body and what each knows:

> De cœur, je suis toute dévouée à cet enfant. Mais qu'est-ce que c'est que le cœur, madame? Il vaut moins que sa réputation. Il est bien commode, il accepte tout. On le meuble avec ce qu'on a, il est si peu difficile . . . Le corps, lui . . . À la bonne heure! il a comme on dit la gueule fine, il sait ce qu'il veut. Un cœur, ça ne choisit pas. On finit toujours par aimer. J'en suis bien une preuve. (564 [97])

The heart's ignorance of what it wants puts the body, as it were, in a position where lying becomes inevitable. But the body, nevertheless, is the place where the deceit stops: it cannot be fooled. Colette does not respond immediately, and Charlotte asks whether or not she understands.

> —Très bien, assurai-je promptement. Madame Charlotte, ajoutai-je avec une *chaleur involontaire,* il est probable que je vous comprends le mieux du monde."
> Elle me paya par un sourire, contenu tout entier dans son regard:
> "Ce n'est pas rien qu'un mot pareil." (564 [98]; emphasis added)

117

Chapter Two

Colette's secret—that she too understands what it is to feel that the heart and the flesh are at odds—is also her identification with Charlotte, the ultra-feminine woman who nevertheless belongs to a separate rule. Colette is *the* other person in the world who best understands Charlotte. Both women describe themselves in terms of a reining in, an inhibition of the senses, which is itself opposed to the frightful, or impossible letting go of enjoyment (Charlotte's "just the idea of it!" and Colette's inability to enjoy; 565, 554). Like Colette's nuns, Freud's manically cleaning housewife, and Balint's empty inhabitant of a void, their enjoyment is walled away from them. Charlotte figures Colette's own inhibition and at the same time, the Charlotte section of *Le pur et l'impur* is a metaphor for how it is that Colette understands the process of coming out of this inhibition and loosening the reins. The first step she takes, in effect, is to embrace, in the form of Charlotte, the blocked sensuality with which she is burdened. This embrace becomes the creation or re-creation of a literary maternal. Literary because it is written, because it is *in the writing itself* that the engendering takes place. And maternal in that Charlotte, as we have seen, functions as an object of identification who evokes the narrator's mother and the motherly more generally. But, as we shall see, Colette's maternal engendering, which succeeds in producing the rest of this book that she predicted would one day be recognized as her best, rests on more than this tentative identification with Charlotte.

To sum up: Charlotte's metaphorical role has at least two moments to it. First, she is described in terms of her maternal characteristics, and is compared to Colette's mother through the various metaphors mentioned above. It is important here to remember that by "Colette's mother" here I am referring not to the mother of the biographical Colette, nor simply to the mother of Colette the narrator, but to a psychical mother of the Colette who is herself, like Charlotte, a character in the work. Which brings us to the second moment of Charlotte's metaphorical role: Colette's identification with her. Like Charlotte (only less overtly) Colette fails to enjoy, and also like Charlotte, Colette's femininity, despite its pathology, is exceptional, belonging to another rule.

At this point we should recall this book's status as a fragmented group of narratives that take place in the narrator's past, and finally ask why it is that Colette identifies the date of her encounter with Charlotte so precisely, albeit casually. As we saw above (pages 102–03), when Colette describes the somehow old-fashioned air of the ambiguously maternal woman, she refers both to the period Charlotte's figure evokes ("those favorite models of Renoir, those beauties of 1875") and to the time in which she meets Charlotte: "eighteen years ago" (557). As *Le pur et l'impur* was written in 1930 and 1931,[18] this situates that cold dawn of their meeting during the particularly difficult winter of 1912: Sido had died that September.

The "well hidden grief" (554) with which Colette enters both Charlotte's domain and the narrative itself is a daughter's grief for the death her mother. It is, of course, a narcissistic loss for her, inasmuch as we have seen that she now seeks out, or seeks to (re)create, a mother with whom to identify herself. At the moment of the narrative's beginning, though, Colette is in an inbetween space: no longer able to identify with the dead mother, she is nevertheless incapable of withdrawing that identification from her, incapable of losing her. The encounter and attempt at intimacy with Charlotte, indeed the very invention of Charlotte, constitutes, or *will have constituted* (for we must remember the temporal structure of this text and its at least two Colettes) the creation of another mother in order for the daughter to be able to perform two essential, life-preserving acts. First, to regain an identificatory relation to a maternal ideal, and concomitantly, to render herself the acknowledged author, mother of that ideal.

And for Colette, this creation and identification hinge on a reconstituting of the erotic, as well as a resistance to the erotic, which Charlotte represents, even as she sings out her quasi-pleasure in public. Colette's creation of an erotic and maternal ideal resonates with Irigaray's call for the regeneration of the mother, as well as of the mother-daughter relation. In "Le corps à corps avec la mère," Irigaray seems almost to be writing out a credo of Colette's narrative encounter with Charlotte:

> Nous avons aussi à trouver, retrouver, inventer les mots, les phrases, qui disent le rapport le plus archaïque et le plus

Chapter Two

> actuel du corps de la mère, à notre corps, les phrases qui traduisent le lien entre son corps, le nôtre, celui de nos filles. Nous avons à découvrir un langage qui ne se substitue pas au corps-à-corps, ainsi que tente de le faire la langue paternelle mais qui l'accompagne, des paroles qui ne barrent pas le corporel mais qui parlent corporel. (Irigaray, *Sexes et parentés* 31 [99])

The narrative attempt to speak the corporeal between Colette and Charlotte ultimately fails, as Charlotte bars the former from the "red and visceral" sensual realm. Charlotte takes on a certain sensual death (corollary to Colette's deadening of the senses) in order to maintain her authority over self and other, self and lover, in her erotic enjoyment. This is because that enjoyment is driven to the other's expiration, not the self's. So that when Colette speculates on whether her Don Juan friend, Damien, might ever have encountered Charlotte, the answer comes to her suddenly and clearly:

> Et qu'eût-il dit de rencontrer celle qui abuse l'homme en simulant, par grandeur d'âme, le plaisir? Mais je suis bien tranquille là-dessus: il a *fatalement* rencontré Charlotte, et peut-être plus d'une fois. (586 [100]; emphasis added)

The two—he who is certain of the pleasure he gives while resenting the (comparatively) little he receives, and she who makes sure always to seem to receive more than she will ever allow herself—are fated to have met, according to Colette. Their meeting is inevitable because they are necessary to each other. There can be no Don Juan obsessed with his potency (585) without a Charlotte determined to prove it for him, with her authority and her self-control intact, her half-closed eye "lucide et attentif à la joie de son maître" ("lucid and attentive to her master's joy"; 586). They have *fatally* met, and Charlotte is, in this sense, a *femme fatale,* because there is and must be absolutely no mystery to be uncovered behind her feminine veil. Her pleasure *will have been,* unquestionably and without fail, from the beginning. Her drive is, finally, to rid herself of drive as jouissance, to banish enjoyment's death, enjoyment's drive, from within her, giving it instead to the other, and to him only. This is the self-control bespoken by her hanging hands, the reason behind the shame she would feel at "the truth next to the lie" (565).

Charlotte's particular sensual death produces her ambiguous, ultimately unproductive, maternity, as well as her authority, such that nothing escapes from her body (a thought she "can't bear"; 565), much as Mitchell's "dead mother" allows Sarah to hold something (as opposed to the nothing she fears) within herself. But whereas Mitchell speaks of a maternity that engenders a death, a terrible mortality, Colette embodies what we could call the inverse of this logic. She is suddenly inhabited by a new and unfamiliar, dead mother, a mother much more difficult to identify with than the narcissistically gratifying, nurturing, living mother. In her unspoken grief, she seeks to resuscitate that dead mother, to give it flesh and sensation, through her encounter with an ambiguous maternal figure somewhere between life and death, between an all-powerful feminine, fantasized as lacking nothing, not even that which she lacks ("one is never completely deprived of a thing that one knows well for having possessed it"; 565), and a pathological feminine enjoyment (the nuns, the infantilizing older women). Confronted by an unspeakable mourning, Colette finds, for the first and only time in her life, that she secretly wants to be a woman, all woman, and to renounce the burden of her "hermaphrodisme mental" ("mental hermaphrodism"; 586). The autobiographical intertext to this quasi-autobiographical fiction is doubled: the narrated Colette, according to the chronology the author scrupulously provides, is not only grieving the death of her mother at this moment. She has also just conceived a child. The month after her mother's death, Colette became pregnant with her only daughter, to be named Colette, and called Bel-Gazou.

In effect, and as we have seen, Colette has outlined various versions of feminine enjoyment: the hyper-neurotic nuns, the falsely puerile *dames* with their young lovers, Charlotte's more complex withdrawal, and the enjoyment of the two women speaking together. Charlotte both emphasizes and puts a stop to this last pleasure. After the two have confided in each other something of their erotism, Charlotte muses on the pleasure of such an intimacy between two who are otherwise strangers (see p. 117, above). But she will soon stop the intimacy, and Colette

Chapter Two

herself will eventually take a greater distance from the figure of a woman who so fascinated her. Recalling her later, and hypothesizing that she surely encountered her friend Damien, she goes on to describe the imagined meeting, and Charlotte ceases to embody one woman, reverting instead to a type.

> Elle lui a versé sa vocalise brisée, cependant qu'elle tournait sa tête de côté, et que ses cheveux couvraient son front, sa joue, son œil mi-fermé, lucide et attentif à la joie de son maître ... Les Charlotte ont presque toujours de longs cheveux ... (586 [101])

Attracted by Charlotte's mixture of an old-fashioned femininity and a maternal authority, Colette ultimately resists the invulnerability of that self-control, the unfailing consistency with which the veil is drawn over the face, hiding both enjoyment and its lack, enjoyment *as* its own lack. Colette's apparent critique of both the Charlottes and the Damiens of this world quickly turns into self-reflection:

> Dans un temps où j'étais—où je me croyais—insensible à Damien, je lui suggérai que nous ferions, pour un voyage, une paire de compagnons courtoisement égoïstes, commodes, amis des longs silences ...
> "Je n'aime voyager qu'avec des femmes," répondit-il.
> Le ton doux pouvait faire passer le mot brutal ... Il craignit de m'avoir fâchée et "arrangea tout" par un mot pire:
> "Vous, une femme? Vous voudriez bien ..." (586 [102])

Damien's first comment wounds Colette and shows her that she is perhaps not so "insensible" to him after all. But what makes it "worse" is his underlining the substance of his remark: you are not a woman, though you might want to be.

It should now be clear that the story of *Le pur et l'impur* is that of the invention of (a) woman in the context of two obstacles that threaten to derail such an invention. On the one hand, there is the apparent need to reject the existing forms and pleasures of woman, up to and including Charlotte, and on the other, the sudden absence of the mother. The first obstacle parallels Freud's observation that the little girl lacks incentive to resolve her Œdipus complex and enter a world that defines her as castrated and generally inferior.[19] And the second would

Colette

seem to rob the woman of a major source of consolation for, or even an alternative to, such a world: the identification with a vital, powerful mother. What womanly response might there be? In short, how can one be a woman?

What this reading of Colette's self-writing suggests is that her enjoyment, once assumed, would obliterate, in its drive, a certain femininity (that of the nuns, of Freud's psychotically housewifely housewife), a femininity that is itself threatened by jouissance. Charlotte herself, to the extent that she is on this side of femininity, reveals the threat it constitutes: the possibility of complete loss of (self-)control and hence acknowledgment of the emptiness of the self, that brings us again to Mitchell's dead mother. This femininity, these selves, are not so much empty as they are full of a dead mother. It is this dead mother that is the *sine qua non* of femininity understood as that which jouissance threatens. One keeps her, holds her, and refuses to let her go, which is at the same time holding onto an absolute deadness.

The prospect of life, as well as of enjoyment, is dangerous because it means the unbearable pain of giving up this mother, who, even if she is dead, is still internalized and apparently essential to one's being. Pathological femininity, it would seem, consists in having a mother that is a deadening, paralyzing internal weight. It is obviously not satisfactory to assume this femininity as the essence of woman and therefore to call for a turn from the mother in such a way that rejects the feminine, and hence sexual difference, completely (opting instead for what Irigaray calls the economy of the same, or what Freud, in his terms, identified as a masculinity complex). And yet clearly some sort of turning, some fundamental change, is needed if emptiness is not to engulf the subject.

Colette's feminine enjoyment points to a possible rethinking of jouissance in its close relation to the death drive. Or, rather, it points to the beyond of jouissance's tie to the death drive. If jouissance, as opposed to pleasure, constitutes in its insistent pressure a threat to the subject, to the *one* who says I, then feminine jouissance does this and more. It threatens to obliterate the feminine *one*, and thereby suggests the possibility of something other than this one, something, at least, in excess of it. In *Le pur et l'impur,* that excess becomes the

Chapter Two

writer's self-invention, the invention of a Colette who will have been the author, the daughter, the mother of her text and whose enjoyment it will have been to create it and be created within it.

But once feminine jouissance is seen in this light, the question arises: how is it that it has not always been driving the female subject toward a new creation in excess of herself? The question, first, would seem to imply that feminine jouissance itself is or would be, when assumed, this new creation, when in fact it is only its hint, the *soupçon* of a beyond that, as a hint, as a too-brief glimpse behind an obscure veil, threatens. But given this, we can answer the question by saying that yes, in fact it does always, potentially, drive the subject beyond herself, when and if she decides to assume her own unbearable reflection within it. For Charlotte, to look at the spectacle of herself "not knowing what escapes [me] in gestures and words" is impossible, and her veil, finally, shields her own eyes from what they might see. But Colette will have decided to take on her particular burden, the mental hermaphrodism that keeps her from being "all woman." It is only by risking the loss of that possibility that she accedes to its beyond. But not without resistance, not without initially wanting to throw off her burden as does Charlotte, and lay it down like a sacrifice.

> Si la parole décrétale de Damien me fâcha, c'est que j'espérais alors dépouiller cette ambiguïté, ses tares et ses prérogatives, et les jeter chaudes aux pieds d'un homme, à qui j'offrais un brave corps bien femelle et sa vocation, peut-être fallacieuse, de servante. (586 [103])

Her body, "bien femelle" and mutely pregnant, is not yet the body she will have taken on by the time Colette becomes the narrator of herself. Like Charlotte, she first makes herself a master's servant, averting her gaze from an ambiguity nonetheless insistent for the attempt to sacrifice it. Looking back on a moment that preceded an assumption and creation of herself, the narrative displays, in addition, the way that Colette's enjoyment, including the enjoyment of the writing self, allows her to incorporate a re-created maternal without ending up, or stopping, in a static identification with an idealized mother (whether dead or living). By acknowledging the jouissance that inhabits her—that mental hermaphrodism with which her "strongly organized being" is burdened (586)—rather than relegating it to an impossibility (Charlotte) or an abomination (the nuns), she converts the threatening, deathly drive into a creative one.

Le pur et l'impur, in its erotic wanderings, is significant for women's writing, for *l'écriture féminine,* because it makes this fundamental, libidinal shift, a shift that sheds light on why it is that Cixous claims that among twentieth-century French writers, Colette is one of three whose writing produced an inscription of femininity.[20] The narrative turns, but not away, not in aversion: instead, the narrator has turned *into,* has engendered her mother, herself, her daughter. How this can happen out of the deadness of femininity's "mother" is the question that feminine jouissance might be a response to: femininity (as pathological) is not the whole of the story; there is an elsewhere *within* it, a jouissance that would destroy it, and, if survived, come to function as a drive on the side of life, eros.

Chapter Three

Nathalie Sarraute
After the Feminine Subject

> Alors vous voyez, j'ai renoncé, je suis l'univers
> entier, toutes les virtualités, tous les possibles . . .
> l'œil ne le perçoit pas, ça s'étend à l'infini . . .
> Nathalie Sarraute
Tu ne t'aimes pas [104]

In this chapter, I argue that Nathalie Sarraute's writing can offer an important direction to contemporary thinking about ethics and sexual difference. To elect Sarraute as a writer who speaks to the question of "ethics and sexual difference" or even "women's writing" may seem perverse, and calls for some sort of initial explanation. Sarraute's work, from *Tropismes* (1939) to the 1989 text to be discussed here, often blurs, disregards, or specifically rejects the difference between the sexes in favor of other idiosyncrasies of a writing or written subject. It is precisely for this reason, I will argue, that her work is important to current discussions of writing and sexual difference. For it is the premise of this book that in order for sexual difference to be addressed and re-created in writing or elsewhere, there must be a risky turn to a position feminism emphatically rejects: what we could call, what Sarraute does call, the neutral.

What feminists know and have known—before Irigaray's "any theory of the 'subject' has always been appropriated by the 'masculine,'"[1] before Simone de Beauvoir's "a man is in the right in being a man" (Beauvoir 1: 14/1: xxi; Parshley's translation), or Virginia Woolf's "it is the masculine values that prevail" (77)—is that protestations of neutrality come down to a male-sexed universalizing. As Jean-François Lyotard observed regarding the catch-22, the injustice, of the feminine position, "women can only be part of modern society if their differences are neutralized" (13). And yet, Woolf also wrote, "it is fatal for anyone who writes to think of their sex" (108), and de Beauvoir similarly claimed, "What woman essentially lacks today for doing great things is forgetfulness of herself" (2: 545/2: 702; Parshley's translation). Even Irigaray suggests that the "wonder" of sexual difference lies beyond its conventional avatars, women and men: to move us, she writes, it is necessary and sufficient that it (sexual difference as wonder) *surprise,* "qu'il soit nouveau, *non encore assimilé-désassimilé comme connu*" ("that it be new, *not yet assimilated/disassimilated as known*"; *EDS* 77, *ESD* 74–75). This general tendency within feminism, within patriarchy, toward a desire for *another* version of femaleness, if not of both sexes, most often reveals itself in a fantasy of androgyny that entails a rejection of reigning conventions and regulations of sexual difference. Woolf attempts to imagine an androgynous writing, one in which both sexes, and the difference between them, are present (107–08). De Beauvoir laments that "what we need is an angel—neither man nor woman—but where shall we find one?" (1: 29/ 1: xxxiii; Parshley's translation). And Irigaray too imagines angelic go-betweens:

> Les anges, messagers très rapides, et qui transgressent grâce à cette vitesse toutes clôtures [. . .]. Ils annoncent que ce trajet est accessible au corps de l'homme. Et surtout de la femme. Ils figurent et disent une autre incarnation, une autre parousie du corps" (*EDS* 22 [105])

As Irigaray will go on to emphasize, this new, other body, and other being, is entirely unforeseeable, unpredictable. It is impossible to say what we might encounter as we create it.

Such an acknowledgment and imagination of the unforeseeable is what I will contend Sarraute approaches, to the point of arguing for it, in *Tu ne t'aimes pas.* This is not to attempt to place Sarraute among a possible group of those who produce feminine writing, such as that famously indicated by Hélène Cixous in her essay "The Laugh of the Medusa."[2] Sarraute's writing rather moves away from (perhaps beyond) this feminine in its extended reflection upon the question of the identity

Chapter Three

of one who is reflecting upon herself. Who, Sarraute asks, are the subject and the object of a phrase such as "you don't love yourself"? Unlike other women writers before her, Sarraute does not begin with the assumption, or hypothesis, "I am a woman," and its possible meanings. Instead, Sarraute sees her writing as concerned with "interior dramas," the Sarrautean tropisms in which "j'ai la conviction qu'il n'y a aucune différence entre les hommes et les femmes, comme il n'y en a pas dans leur système respiratoire ou sanguin" ("there is, I am firmly convinced, no difference between men and women, just as there is none in their respiratory or circulatory systems"). Any assertions of a text's masculinity or femininity are, for Sarraute, "fondées sur des préjugés, de pures conventions" ("based on prejudices, on pure conventions"; Sarraute, Response 29).[3]

The interior drama would have a merely conventional relation, if any, to sexual difference. Masculinity and femininity would be as relevant to this domain as they might be to the physiology of the circulatory or respiratory system. Setting aside the actual pertinence of sexual difference to those systems,[4] and taking up what Schor calls "Sarraute's refusal to be read as a woman writer" (*Bad Objects* 128) as it is expressed in her work, we will be able to hear in this refusal something distinct from a wish for neutrality understood as identity or sameness. Sarraute's conviction that in writing there is no sexual difference, I will suggest, provides her work with an open space in which "another incarnation," another subject, takes form.

A fundamental fact about this subject, apparent from the beginning of *Tu ne t'aimes pas,* is that it is not singular but plural. In an essay concerned with portraits of men in women's writing, Schor argues that this plural subject is a challenge to traditional forms of representation that Sarraute's prose shares with other women's writing. In Schor's words,

> one of the major differences between men's and women's writing, at least in France, is that *there are, so to speak, no "images of men" in women's writing* because that writing is marked from the outset by a profound suspicion of the image and its grounding phallicism. Rarefaction, multiplication, pastiche, and disfiguration are some of the operations to which the image, the male image that is, is subjected

Nathalie Sarraute

in French women's fiction from La Fayette to Sarraute. (*Bad Objects* 131)

Tu ne t'aimes pas would seem to back Schor up on this point, because in it Sarraute explicitly addresses this impossibility of a coherent image coextensive with identity. The narrative "we," a manifold and polyvocal subject, has never managed to develop for itself such an imago:

> —[. . .] c'est là justement une de nos déficiences . . . ces images de nous-mêmes que les autres nous renvoient, nous n'arrivons pas à nous voir en elles . . . [. . .]
> —[. .] elles glissent sur nous, elles n'adhèrent pas, tout ce qui remue en nous les fait bouger, elles ne peuvent pas se fixer. (15 [106])

According to Schor (in her reading of female portraits of men in works by La Fayette, de Staël, and Sarraute), this profound suspicion of the coherent, representable image on the part of women writers results in "a morcelizing of the masculine imago [that works] to dethrone the visual from its hegemony over representation in favor of the tactile. And the promotion of the tactile inevitably leads to an end to mastery" (*Bad Objects* 130). Whether or not an emphasis on touch suggests or can accomplish an end to mastery is debatable.[5] However that may be, Schor suggests that if this female morcelizing of a hegemonic representation is possible, and even inevitable, it is because women themselves historically lack a strong, well-defined self-image, a prerequisite for a practice of representation that possesses the power "to fix the Other in a static image, a stereotype" (131). Only those who have an inflated self-image reflected back to them, the hypothesis goes, are capable of such objectifications of others. Bereft of that empowering self-image, women have never relied, at least not to the extent men have, on stable and stabilizing concepts of representation and representability: they have had no one reflecting back to them a coherent, "larger-than-life" image of themselves that would reinforce such a concept. Thus, Schor concludes, we can "understand why it is that for women writers, for whom the mirror has for centuries remained empty, the representation of men is bound up with the death of the image of man" (131),

Chapter Three

and with the emergence of different concepts and literary practices of representation.

Schor's analysis of representation in French women's prose implicates another term that will be important in our approach to Sarraute's writing: experience. In Schor's reasoning, it is possible to discover a more or less direct relation between the experience of women and their writing: women have a certain (fragmented, not totalized) experience of subjectivity, and therefore their writing manifests an uncertainty or suspicion with respect to the possibility of solid, full identities. This logic, which emphasizes the plasticity of identity (a plasticity recognized and experienced by women and disavowed by men), is, it must be acknowledged, circular. It rests upon an understanding of experience as prediscursive, which in turn re-enforces a generalized account of that identity called woman, an account that leans on the transparency and immediacy of her experience. Experience comes first and forms the woman; the woman then writes, and her writing necessarily reflects the kind of subject into which her experience has made her. In other words, rather than presupposing an essential female identity, the argument assumes a female experience that comes before, and causes, the discourse produced by women. Arguing in another context, historian Joan Scott explains the effects of such appeals to experience:

> The effect of these kinds of statements,[6] which attribute an indisputable authenticity to women's experience, is to establish incontrovertibly women's identity as people with agency. It is also to universalize the identity of women and so to ground claims for the legitimacy of women's history in the shared experience of historians of women and those women whose stories they tell. In addition, it literally equates the personal with the political, for the lived experience of women is seen as leading directly to resistance to oppression, to feminism. (31)

When it comes to her reliance on a fairly straightforward understanding of experience, Schor's claim about female representations of men in French women's writing probably fits Scott's description. Although her primary aim is certainly not to argue that "women are people with agency," and although in most of her writings Schor is very far from positing essentials that are then inevitably expressed in particular instances,[7] her description of feminine representations grounded in women's lived experience does in fact "universalize the identity of women," understood in this case as subjects who experience the other side, or the contrary, of men's experience in patriarchy (wholeness, complete images), and it does assume that this shared history is directly infused into women's "stories," which in turn become, inevitably, stories or representations that resist or counter the dominant forms. Thus the very possibility of such resistant representations is seen *to rest on, to follow from, a pre-existing women's experience.*[8]

We might ask, taking up this question of experience: and so what? Is it not the case, at least since Woolf's novels, indeed, since Sand's Lélia's generically unconventional "history of an unhappy heart," or de Staël's *Corinne,* that many women, and many of their artistic creations, do testify to this different experience of subjectivity, of reality and its representability? Surely this is not disputed? Perhaps not, and yet it must be interrogated, because, as Scott explains, resting upon a transparent, prediscursive (which is to say an always already legitimated and legitimating) ground called experience "closes down inquiry into the ways in which female subjectivity is produced, the ways in which agency is made possible [. . .], the ways in which politics [or any representations] organize and interpret experience—the ways in which identity is a contested terrain, the site of multiple and conflicting claims" (31). To pass directly from woman's experience to woman's writing, though at times intuitively appealing, is to exclude questions about how and who we understand "woman" to be, and thus ultimately is to essentialize not only experience, but also female identity. It is to assume *a priori* the identity of the person to whom an experience is attributed, rather than to ask, for example, how that experience constitutes, in part, an identity. Is experience, even as self-consciously narrated and interpreted, the whole of what makes us who we are? Is there not something beyond what "happens" to me or what I say I have experienced that is at work in the constitution of a self? Scott suggests, "It is not individuals who have experience, but subjects who are constituted through experience" (26). She goes

Chapter Three

on to argue that to rest claims about representation on the authority of experience is to presume that a given discourse flows from experience, and to exclude the reverse, *that our experiences are always informed by how we talk about them, and never immediately available to us in themselves.*[9] Finally, Scott's argument can be taken beyond the fact that experience is never an immediately available datum, beyond the observation that experience is always *narrated,* and hence, interpreted. Experience is also necessarily inscribed by the ways in which we *do not* talk about it, by, specifically, its unconscious articulations, so that to say one is the sum-total of one's experiences is to say that one is the sum-total of much that is inaccessible to conscious knowledge.

The next question we have to ask is whether the reliance on a supposed female experience is not in fact very much in line with the logic of Sarraute's work. For does not Sarraute's style suppose a prediscursive reality that the author experiences and then attempts to craft into a written expression that would match that experience as closely as possible? Sarraute has spoken of her writerly vocation in just such terms. In a 1996 interview with Monique Wittig, for example, Sarraute's description of how she came to writing, the obstacles she encountered to representing what she wanted to represent, and the example of the relative insubstantiality of her literary characters sounds perfectly in keeping with an understanding of experience as the prime motor of discourse.

> *Monique Wittig:* Vous avez commencé à écrire *Tropisme[s]* en 1932?
>
> *Nathalie Sarraute:* Oui. Jusque-là je n'avais pas trouvé aucune forme qui puisse m'intéresser pour rendre ce que je ressentais. Quand j'ai commencé à écrire, les formes romanesques qui existaient ne me permettaient pas de mettre au jour ces mouvements intérieurs insaisissables. Ces mouvements ne pouvaient pas s'accommoder des formes préexistantes. Quand j'ai écrit mon premier Tropisme, j'ai essayé de rendre une sensation, un mouvement intérieur dont le personnage, si l'on peut dire, n'était que le simple support, à peine visible. (Wittig, "Le déambulatoire" 4 [107])

Sarraute here describes her writing as a process of experiencing some prediscursive feeling, and then attempting to find or create a form that might accommodate it, an effort that results in, among other things, a particular way of representing characters. The interior and immediate experience she has leads directly to forms that, in Schor's words, "resonate with feminist critiques of representation" (*Bad Objects* 130). For Arthur Babcock, Sarrautean representation proceeds as it does precisely because the writer recognizes language as that which kills pre-linguistic experiences. In her prose, according to Babcock, there is an imperative to tear oneself away from language, "Because the danger of language is that it will suppress the living substance that exists before language and that is the purpose of writing" (Babcock 69). For Sarraute, Babcock argues, it is always a matter of language coming after "a tropistic substance that exists first" (70). In the above-cited interview with Wittig, however, Sarraute proceeds to throw this neat picture, where unmediated experiences precede and cause the written form and content of representations, into some doubt. Even as she alludes to the "reality" to which she would try to get through her writing—that original, *insaisissable* feeling— she also moves away from it.

> Dans mon dernier livre, *Ici,* il m'a semblé m'approcher davantage de ce qui est la "réalité." [. . .] "Ici," on ne sait pas qu'on est dans le *for intérieur.*[10] Ce qui apparaît occupe tout. Et quand cela apparaît, on établit des cloisons pour que cela occupe justement tout l'espace qu'on lui réserve.
>
> Et par-derrière comme dans un déambulatoire des paroles circulent, se tiennent toujours prêtes à surgir, *soit qu'on les fasse venir ou qu'on les repousse. Il y a là toute une interaction* qui m'a intéressée. *J'ai eu l'illusion* encore cette fois de me rapprocher, *si cela a un sens,* de la "réalité."
> (Wittig, "Le déambulatoire" 7–8 [108]; emphasis added)

As if they were in a special enclosure made just for them to move about in, words circulate and come forth. The enclosure, or ambulatory, where words walk about in a state of readiness (whether or not the subject wants them there) is behind "here," behind immediate consciousness, and behind even the thought, which seems to take up all space, to occupy everything. Language does not come later, as a simple after-effect of experience, it enters, whether or not one seeks it, shaping experience *as* an interaction. In this spatial inversion of the notion of a

Chapter Three

prediscursive "reality," a reality met with before any words, it is language that lies behind or before experience, and the *interaction between them* that constitutes reality. The traditional reading of Sarraute as discounting the primacy of language in favor of a pure experience fails to acknowledge this complexity in her writing. Babcock, again, insists on "Sarraute's conviction that the naming of psychological qualities and relationships is a falsification, a handy convention that we use instead of looking for the real truth" (Babcock 57), thereby eliding Sarraute's persistent doubts about, and complications of, "the real truth." While Sarraute certainly cannot be said to argue for the view that language simply precedes reality, neither does her writing espouse a naive apprehension of the Truth or the Reality that exists in some ideality *beyond* language.

We might suggest then that on the question of representation and experience Sarraute finds herself in fundamental agreement with the psychoanalytic insight that human beings are *beings who speak,* who are inhabited by language in such a way as to be split by it. Because of this split, the experience of reality is never immediate, nor absolutely opposed to the medium of language. Instead, "experience" would be understood as part of an interaction that comprises the linguistic and the sensual and that does not neatly distinguish between the two, does not place the one beyond the other. The sensual is always also linguistic, and vice versa, language happens always in the context of bodies. As we will see, Sarraute's work often dwells on the ways in which the "tactile" or perceptual is from the beginning bound up with words. The key point here is not what Babcock calls "the extreme view" that "there is no reality outside language" (68) or even the notion, specifically rejected by Sarraute, that "everything begins with words."[11] Rather, the point is that nothing is untouched by language, even, or especially, that which feels beyond it. At the very least, such feelings are in a relation with language that is inescapable, even if inadequate.

All of this is to place Sarraute, as Schor does, within a twentieth-century literary tradition that questions and rethinks the nature of the subject and that has also seen the attempt to rethink feminine subjectivity. Certainly Sarraute has been foremost among French writers in creating and articulating new literary forms that announce and dissect a particularly modern version of the self, a project that has been explicit at least since her 1956 *L'ère du soupçon,* essays in which she gave her account of the novel as a genre that was necessarily transforming itself. (Paul de Man called it "the diagnosis of the current state of a literary genre which has become problematic"; qtd. in Jefferson 61n1). But Sarraute's work presents a challenge not only to the genre of the novel and to largely nineteenth- and early twentieth-century notions of representation; more important for our purposes here, her work also confronts feminist theory's representations to itself of a sexed subject, representations that have often been strongly indebted to appeals to the "lived experience of real women" as a ground upon which to rest, rather than as a terrain to investigate. Whether or not "Sarraute's search for the neuter is another stunning denial of gender," as Leah Hewitt has put it (63), is, to say the least, open to question.[12]

Feminist attempts to articulate a sexed subject face constantly the risk of that subject's reification, its being destined, for example, either to a repetition of the (positive) essentialism of the masculine subject, or to a (negative) vision of the subversion and destruction of the prevailing order, a vision that forgets or fails to imagine another kind of creation, and another kind of creating subject.[13] Arguably the most important response to this risk has been Irigaray's articulation of a sex, and a subject, which is not one, but at least two. In *Tu ne t'aimes pas,* Sarraute echoes this feminist and psychoanalytic concept of an I who is, from the first, a we.

>—Mais ils te l'ont dit: Tu ne t'aimes pas. Toi . . . Toi qui t'es montré à eux, toi qui t'es proposé, tu as voulu être de service . . . tu t'es avancé vers eux . . . comme si tu n'étais pas seulement une de nos incarnations possibles, une de nos virtualités . . . tu t'es séparé de nous, tu t'es mis en avant comme notre unique représentant . . . tu as dit "je" . . . (9 [109])

The emphasis is immediately placed on the *as if:* the fiction of identity, or more precisely, its necessarily fictive composition, is this narrative's starting place, not its conclusion. Even before this passage, the first typographical sign on the first page alerts

Chapter Three

us to the difference of the Sarrautean subject: the dialogic dash introducing the conversation it—they—are having with themselves. Outside, this subject may form an apparently single unit; inside, it is taken for granted that "I" is a plural pronoun. Thus the narrator, or one of its incarnations, responds to the above observation:

> —Chacun de nous le fait à chaque instant. Comment faire autrement? Chaque fois que l'un de nous se montre au-dehors, il se désigne par "je," par "moi" . . . comme s'il était seul, comme si vous n'existiez pas . . . (9–10 [110])

The Sarrautean subject is not only plural, but in a state of continual flux. The I or the we who has heard the phrase "you don't love yourself" is already different from the we who contemplates the remark later. Even at the instant the remark was heard, "we" can only designate the subject partially, for there is never a full complement, so to speak, of all the voices who make up "us," in attendance.

> —[. . .] Ce n'est pas à nous tous que ce "nous" s'applique . . . Nous ne sommes jamais au grand complet . . . il y en a toujours parmi nous qui sommeillent, paressent, se distraient, s'écartent . . . ce "nous" ne peut désigner que ceux qui étaient là quand tu as fait cette sortie, ceux que ce genre de performances met mal à l'aise, ils se sentent atteints . . . (10 [111])

To say the least, this is not a self-identical subject. At any given moment it differs from itself, even while it is keenly, often painfully, aware of the apparently single picture it presents to the world in which it lives and speaks. Its experiences, both "internal" and "external," are crowded with second guesses and prolonged analyses of what constitutes them (the experiences), both for "us" and for those outside us who see some of our faces. Sarraute's prose here and elsewhere is both disarming and seductive, and these qualities are bound up with what is often felt to be the immediacy of her writing. The reader is simply given the Sarrautean conversation to listen in on. Without pretext or explanation, the prose *is there,* announcing in its presence both its strangeness to and its intimacy with the reader who may find it. I would emphasize here that this sense of immediacy is precisely *of the writing,* and not of anything, any experience, the writing describes. More precisely, the immediacy of Sarraute's prose in *Tu ne t'aimes pas* lies in her attempt to investigate the terrain of experience *not* as something that merely happens to someone (an ineffable *frisson* that language inevitably kills), but as a process of multiple events, events that include the registering and the narration of vague or precise associations, histories, sensations, recognitions. This attempt does not limit itself to a subjective internality. Germaine Brée calls the style of this work "un audacieux bouleversement technique" ("an audacious technical overturning") that hinges on "l'élimination d'une 'conscience centrale' nouant les fils du roman, remplacée ici par une foule de voix" ("the elimination of a 'central consciousness' knotting the threads of the novel, replaced here by a crowd of voices"; 41). And these voices also come from outside the interior crowd, constantly implicating it in an external "reality" that is always yet to be fully apprehended, comprehended, constituted. Brée continues,

> Le "for intérieur" d'où émanent ces voix évolue dans une sorte d'anarchie mais maintient des rapports avec une société extérieure qui l'investit, vers laquelle on délègue des "émissaires," des "représentants" aussi différents et interchangeables que les "visages" que tout individu montre à la société qui l'entoure [. . .]. Au cours des années, Nathalie Sarraute a souvent fait allusion au "gant retourné." La métaphore s'applique parfaitement à ce "roman." Toutes les voix du monde de ses écrits y trouvent leur place; mais situées à l'intérieur du *terrain* de ce moi fragmenté. (42 [112])

The voices, though they emanate from a *for intérieur,* do not and cannot form one consciousness or self because they do not, cannot apprehend themselves as one. What Irigaray refers to as the (possible, yet to be) wonder of sexual difference, not yet assimilated and not yet known, would seem to find a place here, where the subject itself is never, in Irigaray's words, the whole of the subject.[14] And the so-called immediacy of Sarraute's prose, as I indicated above, contains in fact an exploration of what is usually apprehended as experience's immediacy. Thus it can be read as an attempt to formulate mediation where none seemed possible, necessary, or desirable.

Chapter Three

Sarraute's writing would locate any space of sexual difference or another subject not in a utopian future or not-yet moment, but in the now, a now to which there is, however, no immediate access, and in a subjectivity or subjectivities that are also impossible to conceive as immediate.[15] Writing thus becomes a process of revealing, representing mediations that are already there but are usually invisible, and of creating new mediations that might allow for the assimilation and knowledge of a newly perceived or created present and presence. This is why we find in Sarraute no feminist arguments for the "rights" of "women" or for their inclusion in an already existing universal. Nor do we find narratives preoccupied with struggles for the identification and satisfaction of authentic desires. Instead, Sarraute's writing in *Tu ne t'aimes pas* is far more in line with an Irigarayan notion of becoming. In *J'aime à toi*, for example, Irigaray describes the difference between what, traditionally, feminisms have concerned themselves with, and what it is that she argues for:

> Pour ce devenir, il ne suffit pas d'accéder aux besoins ou aux désirs immédiats d'une femme, et pas plus de lui accorder simplement une aide pour obtenir l'objet qu'elle souhaite, fût-il intellectuel. [...] *C'est de médiations et de moyens de distanciation dont les femmes ont surtout besoin.* L'immédiat est leur tâche traditionnelle—associée à un devoir purement abstrait—, mais il les resoumet à l'autorité spirituelle des hommes. Ainsi accorder à une femme ce qu'elle veut sans lui enseigner le détour de la médiation revient à se comporter en patriarche, fautif à son égard. (*J'aime* 17 [113]; emphasis added)

In yet another revisiting of the question of what a woman wants, Irigaray suggests that this question can take us only so far, and that to go further it is necessary to leave it behind, in the domain where its answer hinges, ultimately, on what men might or might not (be able to) grant women. According to Irigaray, it is not enough first to discover, then struggle for, then obtain what one wants, because this trajectory on its own only results in a repetition and a continuation of a logic that is faulty, and at fault, with respect to sexual difference and women. Instead of the profound question of desire, Irigaray proposes that of mediation and distanciation. She further proposes that any future in which sexual difference might emerge depends upon the resolution, by women, of the "opposition entre subjectif et objectif en ce qui concerne l'identité, notamment historique, du genre féminin" ("opposition between subjective and objective as regards feminine identity, especially in its historical dimension"; *J'aime* 19, *I Love* 5).

These two concerns (mediation versus immediacy and the subjective/objective opposition with respect to identity) are Sarraute's in *Tu ne t'aimes pas*. As I noted above, the plasticity and plurality of identity are the starting point in this work, not a utopian notion. And rather than setting themselves the task of imagining this plurality, the narrative voices instead try to imagine how the conception of a unitary subject is possible; a subject, in the phrase of the book, that loves itself. Such a notion calls for explanation.

> –Ils s'aiment véritablement? [. . .] Mais comment font-ils donc?
> –C'est très simple. Ils sentent que tous les éléments dont ils sont composés sont indissolublement soudés, tous sans distinction . . . les charmants et les laids, les méchants et les bons, et cet ensemble compact qu'ils appellent "je" ou "moi" possède cette faculté de se dédoubler, de se regarder du dehors et ce qu'il voit, ce "je," il l'aime.
> Exactement comme cela nous arrive quand nous regardons les autres, ceux qui ne sont pas nous—et que nous les aimons . . . Eux, ils s'aiment aussi eux-mêmes . . . (Sarraute, *Tu ne* 14 [114])

The unitary, self-contained, and self-same subject, a compact fantasy made up of (only) two instances, one objective and one subjective, is able to love itself precisely because of its singleness: it is the subject par excellence of the One/Love both Jacques Lacan and Irigaray discuss. Illusory though this unity may be, it produces certainty and resoluteness. Sarraute wonders if it is not "le plus enviable des dons" ("the most enviable of gifts"; 14), and proceeds to entertain the possibility that this "they" who love themselves constitute a privileged group, endowed perhaps with a fuller subjectivity than "we." The voices imagine that these others have been given something "by good fairies," either at birth or over the course of their development, that has allowed them to become so gifted. We, who were

Chapter Three

not "made for happiness," have somehow missed out on the necessary ingredients for this self-loving subjectivity. Perhaps they have had special help, then. They were given, from childhood on, "des regards d'amour, d'admiration . . . ils se voyaient reflétés dans les yeux des autres . . . et cette image . . ." (15 [115]).[16] But here another voice interrupts, remarking that this is precisely what "we" have never been able to do: see ourselves in the images of ourselves that others send back to us. Whether because of our conscious effort, or, as is more often the case, whether the images simply don't stick, this subject has never internalized those reflections long enough to contemplate them as forms that correspond to it.

In order to press this question, the voices begin to ask whether or not they are really an exception, whether this subject too might not in fact love itself, or, on the other hand, whether there are many others who do not love themselves. This questioning begins with the recollection of a person, a recollection that itself begins not with the person, but with a piece of him, his hand. First there is a hand, with no other part visible; then there is the person's look: whoever it is is looking at his hand, "[e]t dans son regard, tant d'amour . . ." ("and in his look, so much love . . ."; 20). At this point, the voices begin a kind of interrogation that proceeds as a series of propositions and denials. One voice notes that those who love themselves (as this man does) start by loving everything they can perceive of themselves, from their hands to other body parts, to their reflection in the mirror. Another voice interjects, "—Et nous? N'y a-t-il pas eu des moments quand nous aussi . . ." It is immediately cut off: "—De brefs moments, plutôt d'étonnement . . . Est-ce moi, vraiment? . . . Mais venait très vite un autre et encore un autre reflet . . . Et puis nos regards occupés ailleurs ne s'arrêtaient guère pour contempler . . ." (20–21 [116]). There follows a repetition of suspicion and denial:

> —Oui, mais notre main, à nous aussi, quand on y pense . . .
> —Mais justement nous n'y pensons pas. [. . .]
> —[. . .] Pourtant en nous aussi deux cigarettes . . . et même une seule parfois . . . C'est sans doute un effet plus fréquent qu'on ne croit . . . [It's a question of the handman's comments about cigarettes and his digestive system.]
> —Mais rien de tel ne s'est glissé en nous à ce moment. Aucune comparaison entre lui et qui que ce soit . . .

>   —Pourtant ne semble-t-il pas que même à ce moment, un bref souvenir...
>   —Vite repoussé... ne méritant pas l'attention [...]
>   —Ça rappelle que nous n'étions pas seuls en train de le regarder, de l'écouter. Quelques personnes étaient assises comme nous à cette table... elles le contemplaient aussi en silence...
>   —Mais alors... ces gens si attentifs et silencieux, est-ce qu'ils ne seraient pas comme nous? Est-ce qu'eux aussi, comme nous?...
>   —Cesseraient d'exister en sa présence?
>   —Ne s'aimeraient pas eux-mêmes? Nous ne serions pas une exception? (21–24 [117])

This last question is answered in the negative, and it is explained that the others' self-love was actually being nourished in the presence of one in whom self-love was great and perfect. And again, "they" are contrasted with a we who are multiple. Imagining "ourselves" seen, through the eyes of others, as single, as some*one*, the reaction is a combination of incredulity, naïveté, and perhaps a touch of haughtiness: "'Oui, nous... réduits à cela...' 'Nous si nombreux... incernables... incommensurables...'" ("'Yes, us... reduced to that...' 'We so numerous... unencompassable... incommensurable...'"; 29).

"Happiness"

As opposed to this incommensurable we, others, who are "made for happiness," look within themselves and find a self. They are trained from babyhood to see themselves as everyone else sees them, so that they feel themselves to be "real" babies, boys, girls, women, and men, and nothing else. Real women and real men are an agreement that rests on the convention of identity internalized, taken in from without. This other subject, however, insofar as it distinguishes itself from those who say "I" (and even from itself when it says, of necessity, "I") consists of "de bien étranges répartitions de populations" ("strange distributions of populations"), including frisky youths, adolescents gathering with tottering old folks, old folks with young ones, and many, many children (32). Others construct a tiny, but hard and solid, statue of themselves, and then work to become it. But this subject's statue—when it has one that

Chapter Three

allows it to show to the outside "un beau 'je' présentable, bien solide" ("a presentable, quite solid 'I'")—quickly disintegrates. "Qui se souvient clairement de ce que ce 'je' était?" ("Who remembers clearly what that 'I' was?"). As soon as the statue is left "seul parmi nous" ("alone among us"), it shows itself to be a mere snowman, and promptly melts (37, 39).

The book's early tone of ironic self-pity (we are not made for happiness, we're ungifted, unfavored) soon changes to one of comic experimentation with identity, self-love, and happiness, and then to contempt for these existential gold-standards. As Anthony Newman notes, "Everything in *Tu ne t'aimes pas* finds itself under the knife of a massive, global irony that concerns the desire of the one who doesn't love himself to be like the one who loves himself. In sum, if it is this, more or less, that the text *says,* what it *means* is pretty much the opposite" (101). Those who love themselves and therefore live in happiness are in fact "victims" whom nothing can help. Attempts to disabuse them only lead to accusations ("you don't love yourself," for example) and anguish. And attempts to be like them ("Un instant . . . attendez . . . je crois que je vais y arriver . . . Voilà . . . j'y suis . . . je sens que je m'aime . . ." ["Just a second . . . hold on . . . I think I'm going to get there . . . There . . . I'm there . . . I feel that I love myself . . ."; Sarraute, *Tu ne* 58]) end in distraction and comedy, as when the voice who momentarily finds "Happiness" complains to the others about their insistent questions and snide remarks, and thereby loses it:

> —[. . .] Je voulais retrouver cette sensation qu'on a quand on vit dans le Bonheur . . . j'y étais déjà . . . mais vos continuelles interruptions . . .
> —Nous voulions seulement t'aider . . .
> —Maintenant, il faut que je recommence . . . Où en étais-je? (63 [118])

But the victims of unity of self and Happiness are not only externalized, and smugly pitied or scorned by this subject. On the contrary, it knows the ruse well because it too has been duped, at least at times. "'Mais souvenez-vous . . . ,'" one of the voices demands, "'il y en a même parmi nous . . . [. . .] Vous reconnaissez que vous vous êtes tendus vers le Bonheur . . . et avec quelle nostalgie ... vous y êtes allés ...'" (52 [119]). There is a quick defense, another qualification of another suspicion:

> —Nous avons été entraînés ... vous savez combien nous sommes influençables, crédules ... Alors toutes ces réclames, cette continuelle propagande, ces illustres modèles exposés, ces conseils, ces encouragements, ces récits de ceux qui s'y trouvent ... on n'a pas pu résister ... D'ailleurs vous qui êtes si forts, vous qui ne vous en laissez pas conter, vous nous avez suivis ...
> —Dites plutôt que vous nous avez tirés avec vous, aidés par ceux du dehors, nos proches, nos parents, nos amis ... ils nous ont enrobés dans ce qui coulait de leurs regards, de leurs paroles ... (52 [120])

But however they got there, to Happiness, once there they felt restless, claustrophobic, clumsy, as if they might break something, and mischievous, looking for hidden faults and finding, chiefly, boredom (55). Nevertheless, the subject is implicated in what it criticizes and disdains, and the reader soon suspects that the subject disdains "Happiness," self-love, and the unity of identity precisely *because* it is implicated in them. One thinks of an episode in Sarraute's *Enfance,* in which the young Nathalie is looking at blossoms and trees in bloom and a green lawn with pink and white daisies:

> le ciel, bien sûr, était bleu, et l'air semblait vibrer légèrement ... et à ce moment-là, c'est venu ... quelque chose d'unique ... qui ne reviendra plus jamais de cette façon [...] mais quoi? quel mot peut s'en saisir? pas le mot à tout dire: "bonheur," qui se présente le premier, non, pas lui ... (Sarraute, *Enfance* 66–67 [121])

Similarly, in *Tu ne t'aimes pas* the voices console themselves in their inability to "know Happiness" by pointing to Happiness's inadequacy. After a voice reminds the others that, after all, not knowing happiness has its advantages too, another seconds the idea: "C'en est un [avantage] déjà de ne pas être obligés de plaquer ce nom de Bonheur sur toute sensation encore intacte, vivante ... de l'écraser ..." (64 [122]).

Sarraute's insistence that language kills the experience has often been noted. But in this case, the observation is not limited

Chapter Three

to the fact that the name can never measure up to or capture the ineffable experience, which it therefore tarnishes or ruins. Sarraute is concerned here to underline the reality that the word itself creates, a reality that has its own killing force. "Happiness," like loving oneself or being confident one is a unified whole, is dubious not just because it misses some unique, elusive mark, but because it constitutes a strict ideal that stifles and regulates any possibility of freedom. In failing to name one thing (a sensation), the word also names and constitutes something else, and comes to have a regulatory force. Not to know it is thus to refuse to be under its rule.

>—Et de ne pas voir partout répandu cet enduit lisse, luisant, clinquant... sans une tache, sans une fêlure...
>—Et cette vigilance épuisante, cette continuelle surveillance. Un régime policier. Le moindre écart, le moindre soupçon de liberté qui pourrait mettre le Bonheur en danger et on est rappelé à l'ordre, ramené dans le Bonheur pieds et poings liés... (65 [123])

The rebellion against Happiness produces, in others, the shock of a broken taboo. They refuse to believe when they are told it is a trap, an enslavement, a matter of dupery (69). Or else they defend themselves and their kingdom by shooting out looks of pity and astonishment. The voices reflect that it is better to keep quiet, since there is really nothing that can be done for Happiness's victims (67).

And yet there was one instance in which it was really too much, when one of those "evil-doers" was holding up a particular Happiness, and went too far in his imposition of the rule. The Happiness in question was that "of maternity, of paternity," and it was being dangled before another of happiness's victims who was deprived of it.

>—[N]ous nous sommes élancés, nous sommes montés à l'assaut... "Quel Bonheur? Ce n'est pas le Bonheur! —Pas le Bonheur? Nous avons été pris, interrogés... Ce n'est pas un bonheur d'avoir des enfants? Est-ce que par hasard les vôtres ne vous en auraient pas donné?" (67 [124])

And the victim turns "pitying" or "incredulous" eyes on us. Again, the objection here is not that "Happiness" fails to describe something (the indescribable joy of maternity, for example) but rather that it *does* describe something absolutely alien, thereby erecting a false front, a fortress in which there is no room for a maternity that, in the subject's faltering phrases, "comporte aussi . . ." ("includes also . . .") or "n'est pas toujours . . ." ("is not always . . ."; 67). Language kills, yes, but this is not its only function. The narrator(s) imply that it might also make room for something that is not an easy fit. That it might gesture toward, evoke, suggest, even tell in silence, especially the silence of Sarraute's ubiquitous ellipses. In other words, language might function as a medium *for* the unknown, rather than as a denial of it, a diversion from it.

Love, Language, Selves

Later in the book, as its subject is attempting to speak of what was apparently "un amour partagé" ("a mutual love"), Sarraute directly addresses the relation between language and the inexpressible. Rather than oppose the two, she evokes their simultaneity and their location *at a distance.*

> —Quand quelque chose . . . comment l'évoquer? . . .
> —Etait-ce une couleur, une ligne, une à peine perceptible nuance, une intonation, un silence . . . mais ça ne se laisse . . .
> —Ça ne se laissait jamais capter par aucun mot . . . [. . .]
> —N'est-ce pas Cézanne qui a dit à propos d'autre chose . . .
> —Mais était-ce vraiment quelque chose d'autre dont il a dit que "ça s'enchevêtre aux racines mêmes de l'être . . . A la source impalpable du sentiment"?
> —Le sentiment, lui, est là-bas où les mots circulent, se posent, désignent . . .
>
> — C'était amusant d'y faire de temps à autre une excursion . . . (123 [125])

Feeling is what never gets contained in a word just as it is also precisely the realm where words throng, looking to land somewhere and designate, as in the ambulatory Sarraute evokes in the above-cited interview. There would be no feeling, which is itself "impalpable," in isolation from the impossible attempt to

Chapter Three

name it, nor from the declaration that "[c]e que nous ressentons n'est inscrit nulle part" ("what we feel is not inscribed anywhere"; 130). Thus the we of *Tu ne t'aimes pas* is not simply distinct from those who, for example, *do* love themselves, *are* self-identical, or *do* believe that they find and use words adequate to their feelings. Quite the contrary, this subject is both the we who, as it were, know better, *and* the he, the you, the they, the I, and the me who, quite literally, run to their mother-tongue, their mother and their tongue, to be reassured, confirmed in their need to know that the interior disorder can be contained, made manageable, or simply *made,* by words.

The voices talk about those among them who are capable of extracting and naming what cannot be named, that which simply happens, "ni vu ni connu . . ." ("neither seen nor known . . ."). They remember one who was capable of producing a "Je suffrais" ("I suffered"), and a "Je pleurais" ("I cried"). And even a "Ce que je m'amuse" ("I'm having fun"; 130–31). He simply absented himself for a second unbeknownst to "us" in order to go outside and report, "I'm having fun," in order to close in what was scattering and escaping. Then he could return among us, secure that everything was in order.

> —N'est-il pas comme l'enfant qui brusquement, en plein jeu, quitte ses camarades, court vers sa mère, en reçoit un baiser et revient rassuré, fortifié . . . (131 [126])

The game, the place where "we" are and where the unknown happens, is a realm of risk and the impossibility of certainty, security, or definition. Language, the kiss of the mother-tongue through which, for example, "feelings" can be delimited, picked out, and identified, brings not simply form to what happens but mediation, indirection, simultaneously rendering events foreign and articulate, estranged and speakable.

The subject, overflowing and breaking up, runs to language, and language embraces the subject at a given moment, forming for it a link, a tie between the overflow, the risk, which is hot to the point of boiling, and the frozen inertness of the known, embalmed and exhibited in a glass coffin (132–33). The mother-tongue is herself not the killer—her kiss not quite the kiss of death—but is a link to death, and may tend toward that end when used as a blind, a false front. She is already there

Nathalie Sarraute

(again, like the words in the ambulatory), and may be called upon, or else will emerge on her own, but the way in which she emerges is not already set in stone. The fashion and the effect of language will depend upon an interaction, among the child, the mother, and the game; among the subject, language, and the "fragile, perishable" (133), but not simply pre- or extra-discursive, experience.

Thus far, I have noted the plurality of Sarraute's subject, her complicated understanding of representation and experience, and the way language acts as a necessary liaison between, and interaction of, the two. I have also suggested that Sarraute's at least partial definition of experience and of the subject as unknown and unknowable links it with Irigaray's emphasis on the sexed subject's fundamental incompletion in the recognition of both the other's and her own status as not entirely knowable or appropriated. Probably the most serious doubt such a parallel has to confront, though, stems from Irigaray's emphatic distinction between multiplicity, which she rejects, and twoness, which she tries to elaborate. Pheng Cheah and Elizabeth Grosz summarize the development of Irigaray's thought around this key distinction.

> It is widely accepted that Irigaray's critique of phallogocentrism involves an exposure of the violent logic of the one, a Platonic monologic that reduces the other to a pale copy or deficient version of the same [. . . and that] Irigaray regards [. . .] as the theoretical underpinning of a variety of historical patriarchal social and cultural structures as well as phallocentric discourses on femininity and feminine sexuality [. . .]. However, [. . .] it will [. . .] be somewhat of a surprise to many of her readers that Irigaray regards multiplicity as complicit with the logic of the one. In her view the multiple is the one in its self-willed dispersal into unrelated atomistic singularities, many others of the same. The alternative model she offers is the paradigm of the two, a mode of original relationality or being-with-the-other in which the otherness of the other is respected. (Cheah and Grosz 6)

Is Sarraute's "moving mass" (16) of a subject, with its multiple, clamoring voices, a subject she likens at one point to a flock of birds or a school of fish (87), in any way comparable

Chapter Three

to Irigaray's being-two? I propose looking at the ways in which it manifestly differs from Irigaray's dual subject, before considering further their possible links.

First, as I've mentioned, there is the fact that Sarraute's subject is made up of a throng of voices, as numerous as the stars in the sky (17). And it is not a question of many "I"s or many "me"s, but always of an "us" that refuses those terms. "'[E]ntre nous, ces "moi," ces "je," nous ne les employons pas . . .'" When someone said, "You don't love yourself," it meant the defeat of any lingering illusions of singularity.

>   —[. . .] [N]ous nous sommes vus avec plus de netteté que jamais désintégrés en une multitude de "je" disparates . . . qui pouvait-on aimer dans tous ça?
>   —Et puis ces "je," ces "tu" se sont effacés . . .
>   —[. . .] comme d'eux-mêmes dilués dans des masses informes . . . des "nous," des "vous" . . . faits de nombreux éléments semblables . . . (86–87 [127])

Sarraute's subject sees itself as having passed through a moment when singular "I"s and "you"s had some significance, to a moment in which it sees such clear, atomizing distinctions merely make it impossible for it to speak. In her interview with Wittig, Sarraute cites Beaumarchais, from *The Marriage of Figaro*,[17] to describe the subject in *Tu ne t'aimes pas* as "a formless assemblage of unknown parts" (Wittig, "Le déambulatoire" 7). Indeed, we might read Sarraute as specifically rejecting two as too small a number when it comes to the self, for it does come up in *Tu ne t'aimes pas*, in a recollected conversation with someone to whom the narrator felt she could speak openly.

The question is put tentatively, whether the other feels himself to be a very compact and unified whole that is clearly delimited and that you can look at from without. The man responds in the affirmative, and then adds the complicating nuance that in fact "il y a deux hommes en moi, je suis tantôt l'un tantôt l'autre, pas les deux à la fois," to which the narrator replies, "deux êtres contradictoires . . . [. . .] C'est bien peu . . ." (17 [128]). Of course, as we shall discuss shortly, Irigaray's being-two is not about being inhabited by two contradictory beings, but for the moment, it is enough to note that Sarraute's we is many more than two, a multitude upon which she repeatedly insists.

The second major difference between these two visions of the subject concerns, of course, sexual difference. Despite the fact that Sarraute's narrative voices are usually masculine (because, she says, the feminine pronoun just doesn't work as a universal), there have been attempts to read her prose as putting forward a particular identification with, or vision of, the feminine. We have already seen Schor's argument that Sarraute's writing is in at least implicit accord with feminist critiques of the subject. But there have been more emphatic attempts at linking her prose to an argument about the feminine.

Raylene Ramsay, for example, reads *Enfance* as introducing what she calls a "'complementary' or telescoping movement [. . .] between the masculine and the feminine," a back and forth that dramatizes the child Natacha's torn affections and loyalties between her divorced mother and father as representatives of the two opposing poles of sexual difference (Ramsay, *The French New Autobiographies* 57). A propos of Sarraute's consistent taking on of a masculine voice, Ramsay suggests,

> At the level of the *énoncé* [. . .], it may be the case that Sarraute identifies more closely with the critical, investigative "masculine" voice of her own writing enterprise. Yet, at the level of the *énonciation,* aware that words are flattening and inadequate and that single, reasoned judgments are simplifying, it is the uncertain, "feminine" voice of seeking and emotion that seems to exemplify what is most characteristic of Sarraute's work. (57)

However, we must admit, it is precisely about this level that Sarraute is speaking when she declares, "On the level on which the interior dramas I strive to bring to light are produced, there is, I am firmly convinced, no difference between men and women"[18] (Sarraute, Response 29; also qtd. on p. 128). The voice characterized by uncertainty, seeking, and emotion, then, does not, for Sarraute, have a content called feminine.

What insists in Sarraute's prose, in *Tu ne t'aimes pas* just as much as elsewhere, is a dogged refusal of any final, or finally meaningful, sexual identification. When we try to follow genders, grammatical or personal, over the course of a work,

Chapter Three

we are likely to come up empty-handed, or else to find ourselves constructing overelaborate formulae that equate certain words or phrases (the "elle" that stands for "une personalité forte") with certain traits (self-deluded femininity?).[19] Reading attempts at such interpretations leaves us less convinced than struck by their inevitable failure to respond to the shiftings of the Sarrautean subject, its first person plural that will not settle into a singular. Ramsay articulates one such attempt to locate sexual difference in *Tu ne t'aimes pas:* "Gender is grammatically determined ('une forte personalité' is a woman). Or it becomes a shifting, potentially multiple complex beyond the 'real man' and the 'real woman.' Gender emerges from the feeling experienced by some of the more introspective interlocutors of being androgynous or a mixture of both man and woman" (Ramsay, *The French New Autobiographies* 142). The problem here is that androgyny comes up in this book only once, and then to be dismissed immediately as one more impossibly "simple" form of identity, one that "they" often ascribe to themselves, but to which "we" cannot or will not limit ourselves:

>—Comment font-ils pour se sentir si nets, si simples?
>—Ils doivent s'y entraîner très tôt . . . [. . .]
>—Une fois qu'ils ont pris ce pli de se sentir tels qu'on les voit, ils le gardent toujours . . . à chaque étape de leur vie, ils se sentent être des femmes, des hommes . . .
>—Et rien que cela. De "vraies" femmes, de "vrais" hommes . . . [. . .]
>—S'ils cessaient de se sentir si "vrais," comment seraient-ils? On serait peut-être très surpris . . .
>—Il y en a bien qui se sentent comme un mélange d'homme et de femme . . . mais toujours le plus simple des mélanges . . . (30–31 [129])

Androgyny is presented merely as one among the many whole, compact modes of being that "we" see around us but do not share. Thus to claim, as Ramsay does, that the we in *Tu ne t'aimes pas* is "intimate," "individuated," and ultimately gendered insofar as it is to be identified with "the character, experience, and situation [of] an aging woman," Nathalie Sarraute (142), a "woman writer" who is confessing (158), is to do nothing more than bring us back to the beginning. For,

Nathalie Sarraute

while the logic of *Tu ne t'aimes pas* might allow for the possibility of agreeing with such a proposition,[20] it also suggests, primarily, its meaninglessness. Who is this "Nathalie Sarraute," or this or that I or you?, is, of course, the book's first and last question, so that to say that the book's subject is its female author is to have said nothing at all. The book itself will continue to ask, for example, what or who "a" "woman" writer might be. On the question of sexual difference, then, suffice it to say that Sarraute has little to offer directly, because she considers it a question that does not come up in the universe of tropisms, which Schor calls "those multiple, minute stirrings that lie midway between the inchoate formlessness of the semiotic and the rigid armature of the symbolic" (130). In that almost pre-linguistic[21] realm where words and sensations are melting into an inevitable, mutually constituting interaction, it is as if there is not yet any clear distinction made between male and female, men and women. (There are certainly no "real men" or "real women"—those chimerical embodiments of convention—as we have seen.)

Instead, there are possibilities, virtualities, which do not include the following sexed terms: "'real' women, 'real' men, 'real' fathers, mothers, sons, daughters, grandparents," but do include the (unsexed or not yet sexed terms?): "young people, adolescents," "old people," and "children" (32). One of the most important challenges of reading Sarraute in the light of feminism is to take seriously her writing's insistence that it has no place for sexual difference. In doing so, we may be able to grasp something more fundamental to her work, something that it shares, I will argue, with Irigaray's thought, and that is essential to the possibility of thinking about a sexed subject in an ethical context.

After the Feminine Subject

For both Irigaray and Sarraute, the important point about the plurality of the subject is its nontotality. In short, it is impossible to know the self, because the self is always more than its I, or, as Irigaray puts it, "Tu n'es ni je ne suis le tout, ni le même, principe de totalisation" ("You are not, nor am I the whole, nor the same, the principle of totalization"; *J'aime* 164,

Chapter Three

I Love 105). If there is, as yet, for Irigaray, no sexual difference in Western cultures' institutions and identities—no culture of sexual difference—this absence is intimately bound up with the principal of totalization, especially epistemological totalization, that she critiques. And if "there is no sexual difference" in Sarraute's writing, this is because for Sarraute sexual difference has to do with the "real" women and men of whose identities she is so suspicious, and not, as it does for Irigaray, with a new horizon of being in the world.

This distinction between what each writer is talking about when she addresses sexual difference allows us to understand how Sarraute, who refuses to be read as a woman writer, who insists there is no sexual difference in her work, can nevertheless be read parallel to a radical attempt at rethinking sexual difference. When she repeats that sexual difference is not what she is concerned with, she is speaking precisely about conventional representations of men and women in the world and the differences between them. For Sarraute, such differences are particular and should not be transferred from the domain of the idiosyncratic and the personal onto the literary or generic. As she puts it, "I think these distinctions [calling male or female the qualities or defects of a text] are based on prejudices, on pure convention. They are unverifiable assertions which rest on a very small number of examples, examples where the male or female author claims to possess certain qualities he believes proper to his sex" (Response 29).[22] When Sarraute discusses sexual difference in relation to writing, then, she is speaking about, in short, so-called "real women" and "real men" as they exist in either literary or lived conventions, and it is in that light that her refusals have to be understood: "The female condition is the last thing I think about when writing" (Boncenne 92).[23]

What Sarraute manages to avoid by *not* infusing something she would call female into her texts is what Gayatri Spivak has called the "misfiring" of the name of woman. According to Spivak, as long as feminism holds on to "woman" as its sole essence and cause, it will be doomed to essentialize that name (and all who bear it) in the name of history (especially the history of women), and thus to repeating a history it wishes to overturn. (Her point is logically similar to Scott's vis-à-vis experience, discussed above.) Insisting on the power, not to

Nathalie Sarraute

mention the adequacy, of the word "woman" to name an identity that would be shared by millions, Spivak suggests, is to forget what "woman" must always fail to name, and here she is referring directly to the Derridean deployment of "woman" and the "feminine" to name (and misname) "the non-truth of truth."[24] Counter to what she calls "Derrida's anxiety about not compromising the living feminine in the interest of a gynegogy which would sell itself to the death-story of the patronymic," *and* counter to egalitarian feminism's dogmatic reaction against both deconstruction's and psychoanalysis's critiques of the subject, Spivak suggests

> that we should not share this anxiety for the name, we should not identify the guarding of the question with *this* particular name. [. . .] We must remember that *this particular name,* the name of "woman," misfires for feminism. Yet, a feminism that takes the traditionalist line *against* deconstruction falls into a historical determinism where "history" becomes a gender-fetish. (217)

This is exactly what cannot happen in Sarraute's prose: the history, the story, cannot become a "gender-fetish," and cannot be fetishized convincingly along the lines of gender, because its subject is not named, not written in terms consonant with stable, stabilizing, genders. It is as if she were saying, with her "there is no sexual difference in my writing": If you want to see "real men and women," look elsewhere (and they are paraded around in no small numbers); in here, it's something else that's being written.

In *Tu ne t'aimes pas,* Sarraute indicates explicitly that it is a philosophical tradition into which her we does not fit, at least not completely, a tradition that finds its roots in the Socratic "Know thyself" and in ensuing interpretations that take the imperative to be totally fulfillable, and set about defining the self (as member of a family, as citizen, as subject, as individual, as separate from others, as alienated, as split, and so on). It is an imperative over which the subject puzzles, and toward which it moves, over the course of the narrative, pairing it with other duties, especially self-love, self-identity, and unity of self. Toward the end of the book, the voices remember an instance when one of them uttered, out loud and in some sort of public,

Chapter Three

the phrase "Chez moi c'est pathologique" ("With me, it's pathological"; 207).[25] The immediate question debated among them is whether or not this was said for others, on the outside, and thus in order to display and show off an I, or whether it was part of a Sarrautean (internal and critical) *sous-conversation*. The voices argue: some accuse those who said it of performing, of grandstanding: "Vous vous êtes dressés devant eux, le torse bombé, une main sur la poitrine . . . 'Chez moi c'est pathologique . . . '" Others protest their innocence: "Rien de pareil, vous l'inventez, nous étions tournés vers nous, nous l'avons dit comme si nous parlions à nous-mêmes . . . " (207–08 [130]). The proof that an exhibition has taken place turns on the demonstration that "we" too do affect the subjective stance par excellence, that of looking at oneself from without, objectively, the self-reflective first task of philosophy:

> —Mais avant même qu'ils puissent faire un mouvement, vous vous êtes échappés [from one of their "cells" within which you were about to shut yourselves], courant vers eux, [. . .] Attendez un instant, ne m'enfermez pas . . . pas entièrement . . . je me suis scindé en deux . . . une opération que vous recommandez, [. . .] je sais me regarder du dehors, je peux me voir, me connaître . . . Connais-toi toi-même, n'est-ce pas? vous le prescrivez . . . j'en suis capable, vous voyez, je viens me placer auprès de vous, à la même distance où vous êtes, et de là je me regarde avec la même impartialité, la même impitoyable clairvoyance . . . J'ai su assimiler vos enseignements, j'ai retenu vos classements, j'applique vos règlements, [. . .] regardons ensemble ce qui est là en moi . . . hé oui, c'est triste à dire, mais on ne peut pas le désigner autrement: c'est, "pathologique." (208–09 [131])

This we, who has gradually, in fits and starts, approached and admitted its own ability, or sporadic tendency, to love itself, now recalls its having taken on, dressed up in, the regalia of self-love as self-knowledge. Like an obedient (philosophy) student, the subject followed the formulae that are meant to lead to a complete vision, an objective clairvoyance. It goes without saying that this moment—much as in the Socratic dialogues and in contemporary philosophical engagements with identity and difference—this moment comes in order to come up short, to be shown to be impossible. Equally important, though, is that it comes also to be shown to have taken place nevertheless.

In this sense, *Tu ne t'aimes pas* is less an examination of why its subject does not love itself or form a "compact whole," than it is, throughout its first half especially, an exploration of how and why anyone does (seem to); how and why even "we," despite our protestations, have occupied this position of wholeness, this self-loving posture. Recalling getting up before others, assuming such a stance, the subject at last attempts to think what the relation might be between this apparently unifying act and the plural being it knows itself to be, and is mystified to begin with.

>—Nous n'y comprenions rien, nous ne cherchions pas à comprendre...
>—C'était un de ces phénomènes étranges dont on dit qu'on n'en croyait pas ses yeux, rien de ce qu'on sait ne permet de l'expliquer... (212 [132])

This subject, it would still like to claim, can know nothing of pretensions to one-ness or completeness. And yet the entire book is directed to this moment at which its subject admits to itself that it, too, shares in the self-love it disdains and holds to be impossible. Which is also to admit that the main opposition it has set up and rested upon throughout, that between them (who love themselves) and us, is in doubt. Only at the book's end do the narrating voices finally imagine those outside of them as vulnerable to them. Only at this point do they attempt to imagine their effect on others.

>—Mais maintenant, après tout ce que nous avons vu, ne pouvons-nous pas nous demander si ce que nous leur avons fait éprouver quand nous nous sommes dressés devant eux...
>—Un seul bloc serré, refermé sur soi. [...]
>—Ça a déferlé sur eux, indifférent à leur présence.
>—C'est venu on ne sait comment et puis on ne sait comment c'est passé...
>—Une force aveugle...
>—Un ouragan qui les a faits se courber...
>—N'ont-il pas eu un peu peur?
>—Peur?
>—Oui, pourquoi pas? ce n'est pas impossible, c'était si brusque, si violent... ils ont pu sentir d'abord une légère, passagère frayeur... (212–13 [133])

Chapter Three

At no other point in the book do the voices consider the feelings of others to be as mysterious and subject to question as its own. To the contrary, "they" (every one of them a simple, compact whole) usually stand for everything with which "we" do not and cannot identify because of our excessive nature: the fantasy of the One/Love, the self-loving one, the subject who knows itself. What happens at this point is a reversal. It is suddenly the we who take the place of the compact whole, the solid block, and the significance of loving oneself is revealed in the reactions of those affected by the event. It has nothing much, in fact, to do with the self, and everything to do with those who—as a result of the self's unifying, its forming a solid, single point—are able to identify themselves, to see themselves in light of it, in contrast to it, in relation with it. This, the subject seems to be grasping, is nothing other than what it itself does when it looks without it, identifying itself (in all its non-self-identity) in opposition to those who love themselves.

Sarraute's subject would have expected some sort of devastation as a result of its violent, furious sortie. The strong, overpowering, and it should have thought destructive force of its "hurricane" did not destroy, did not elicit defensive reactions:

> —Notre "sortie" involontaire n'avait pas provoqué chez eux ce qu'il aurait fallu attendre, pas la plus faible rétorsion, l'ébauche d'une rebuffade. Et même . . . (212 [134])

The we's sudden and violent taking on of an emphatic I has somehow had a salutary effect on the others. After a possible, passing fear, "'tant de fermeté, de force, d'assurance, de désinvolture princière, de parfaite liberté . . . ' 'les a raffermis . . . ' 'les a rassurés . . . ' 'les a rehaussés . . . ' 'Ils se sont sentis traversés par une vague bienfaisante . . . '" (213 [135]). There is a realization that this is what they have wanted, a release from the subject's refusal to be identical to itself, from what Lacan called the "asymptotic" relation of the I to the image of the self reflected back to it. Seeing the complex, plural subject as one provokes "admiration, tendresse, reconnaissance . . . ("admiration, tenderness, gratitude . . . ") for the release it effects (213), for the illusion it confirms. What "we have given them for a few seconds" is "what the one who loves himself gives them constantly." We have succeeded in becoming "the one, among all, the most gifted at loving himself," and in so doing, encounter the gratitude and relief of others, and realize that it is this with which we were reproached when told, "You don't love yourself": with not giving out, and participating in, the fantasy of wholeness that strengthens, reassures, and raises up. Not to gather one's self up and present it to others, definite and willful, is to inflict a wrong of some kind:

> —Si nous l'écoutons maintenant, ce "Vous ne vous aimez pas" qui nous avait tant surpris, il y a déjà assez longtemps, nous y entendons surtout un reproche, un blâme pas seulement pour le tort que nous nous faisons à nous, mais pour ce que nous leur faisons subir, à eux. (215 [136])

Finally, this gathering cannot be disowned. It is, in fact, an interaction that the entire book enacts. Sarraute indicates as much by drawing a parallel between the we who makes itself into an I before others and the act of running to language in order to contain a reality that seems otherwise to overflow its bounds. The one among "us" who ran to the mother-tongue to receive its kiss (*I'm having fun*), to be "reassured, fortified" (131), foreshadows the we's final sortie, which has the same effect upon those who witness it as language's kiss had on the subject, reassuring and strengthening them, providing a kind of fixed point around which it is then possible to form. Both moments create a "bienfaisant" feeling—"c'est si bon, bienfaisante" (131); "Ils se sont sentis traversés par une vague bienfaisante" (213)—formed out of the containment and definition provided by a sudden access to language, which the subjects call a gift of love, a gift that can only be bestowed by "[c]elui entre tous le mieux doué pour s'aimer" (214 [137]). Any attempt at language entails the chance of such beneficence, just as it also inevitably risks delineating borders of both the other and the self that are immediately inadequate and straightening. While the bulk of Sarraute's work is arguably preoccupied with this straightening effect upon the multiple, excessive self (effected by others, by "them," or by the subject's own recourse to language), what *Tu ne t'aimes pas* brings into relief is that without such recourse, inadequate and confining though it be, others cannot emerge as anything but statues, straw men

157

Chapter Three

who are to be either scorned or feared in their simplicity. In other words, when otherness is confined within the multiplicity of the self, it is nothing but sameness multiplied, or, again, as Cheah and Grosz put it above, describing Irigaray's argument, "the multiple is the one in its self-willed dispersal into [. . .] many others of the same" (6).

If agreeing to and confirming a certain version of identity has a strengthening, reassuring, and uplifting effect, and failing to reflect that version is necessarily to do a kind of wrong, to weaken, trouble, and lower the self that would know itself whole, then such a weakening, troubling, and lowering is precisely what thinkers of sexual difference, most notably Irigaray and Cixous, argue is necessary for a transformation of the subject from male/neuter to sexed, male and female. But the subject's transformation cannot stop at that. The effort to think toward another sexual difference does not culminate in this troubling move, as Irigaray's later work especially emphasizes. There has to be, further, a continuation of thought without the groundings provided by what she calls the logic of the same, of identity, a continuation of thought that will somehow positively value its troubling work, its non-sameness.

For Irigaray, leaving the ground of identity, of the Universal as One, is concomitant with a rethinking of what can constitute a ground, of what can constitute *and* ground a being. What she proposes is a new formulation of the universal, a universal based on the plurality of sexual difference. Her *being two,* taking its number from the two sexes, is the model she takes because of the specific sort of transcendence it implies, on both the inter- and intra-subjective levels. To be two, and to be of two, means for Irigaray to acknowledge that the other is irreducible to the self, and that even the self is never wholly identical to itself, belonging as it does to a universal gender, to a kind, which transcends its individuality and which the subject must remake, constituting her or his expression of the universal. In this sense, the universal of sexual difference can only be conceived as a process, and as not yet having arrived—both in terms of a contemporary cultural poverty that does not allow for it, and in terms of its own fluid nature. She writes, "La culture de cet universel n'existe pas encore. L'individu a été considéré comme particulier sans interprétation suffisante de cet universel qui est en lui: femme ou homme" (*J'aime* 85 [138]).

What Sarraute's subject confronts in *Tu ne t'aimes pas* is not so much the impossibility of being one in favor of its intimate sensation of being many, nor the impossibility of others ever knowing the self. Rather, it confronts the inescapable fact that, feel what it may, it reaches the other and appears to the other in a form it cannot comprehend—even as radically dispersed—on its own, in a form that only takes shape thanks to its mutual constitution by those without and those within. To say "I" is meaningless then, not simply because we are too complex, but because we literally do not exist unless there is already (or has already been) a we through which to be constituted.

This is where Sarraute's subject jibes with Irigaray's "new incarnation." In both visions, there is the primary acknowledgment that the subject is only itself because of and in mediation. "We" are given to ourselves only through others' (inadequate, or excessive, or mistaken) reflections and our acceptances and rejections of them. Language, then, is explored for the sake of discovering to what extent it might function not simply as a naming tool, or as Irigaray puts it, as a discourse of basic needs rather than of the creation of culture. "Le langage lui-même en reste généralement au niveau des besoins, y compris celui de maîtriser la nature, les objets, les autres, notamment en les nommant" (*J'aime* 77–78), a situation that ends up denying the need for an engendering communication, "non seulement sous la forme de transfert d'informations mais d'échanges intersubjectifs" (79 [139]). Such a language as Sarraute's in *Tu ne t'aimes pas,* I would argue, performs precisely this switch from denotation to communication, and in such a way as to be engaged in the creation of a reality that is just finding its words as they are written into utterances.

This highly volatile, shaky, yet forthright language does not operate on the basis of already given assurances, identities, or objects, but instead heads toward the possibility of new ones. In Irigaray's terms,

> Il serait question [. . .] de trouver une nouvelle économie de l'exister et de l'être qui ne soit ni celle de la maîtrise ni celle

Chapter Three

> de l'esclavage mais plutôt *de l'échange sans objet constitué, échange vital, échange culturel: de paroles, de gestes,* etc. (*J'aime* 80 [140])

Sarraute's prose does enact such a new economy, while also acknowledging the force of that language and culture that reign. In order to enact it, she writes the subject, writes as the subject who is no longer one and not yet the other (in Irigaray's sense of the other of sexual difference). Whence the impossibility of reading Sarraute's prose as a writing of sexual difference; but whence also its primary openness to a new thought of sexual difference geared toward the future. A fundamental shift then, has already taken place when the Sarrautean narrative begins, and continues to unfold as it proceeds. The openness of her dialogic prose echoes Irigaray's call for a movement out of the fixed and the past toward the unfinished and the future:

> Ainsi, entre la transmission hiérarchique d'un langage et d'une langue, d'un ordre et d'une loi, qui seraient déjà là, et l'échange actuel d'un sens entre nous, il y a une différence d'économie subjective. Le premier modèle de transmission ou d'enseignement est plus parental, plus généalogique, plus hiérarchique; le deuxième est plus horizontal et intersubjectif. Le premier modèle risque d'être asservi au passé, le second ménage un présent pour la construction d'un futur. (*J'aime* 81 [141])

To Irigaray's question, "how to make a *we?*" as opposed to a series of more or less disconnected Is and yous (85/48), Sarraute's prose responds with the impossibility of any gathering that would be complete. Incompletion itself, and its acknowledgment, are what lead, in Sarraute's writing, to the possibility of a we, of a dialogue where the unexpected gets said, where responses do not always come, where even at book's end, there is no finishing, but instead, notably, a question mark. Having vacillated between scorning and acknowledging self-love throughout the course of the book, and having finally assumed the personage (among others) of the one who is even the most gifted at self-love, Sarraute's narrators end their conversation with an incomplete fragment that serves to punctuate the work. Returning to the position of the we who do not manage to dwell in self-love, and recognizing that this causes others to undergo a kind of suffering, they speculate tentatively that, could they but remain there, "ce serait bon pour tout le monde . . ." "'Si on pouvait . . . ' 'On ne demanderait pas mieux . . . ' 'On ne demanderait pas mieux?' 'Pas mieux? Vraiment?'" (215 [142]). More than expressing suspicion of the security and complacency of self-love, these last questions punctuate the book with the only mark that refuses to be final inasmuch as it calls for a response: the question. The epigram with which this chapter begins, in which one of Sarraute's narrative voices recalls its I having given up trying to be one, having accepted itself as "l'univers entier, toutes les virtualités, tous les possibles . . . [. . .] ça s'étend à l'infini" ("the whole universe, all virtualities, all possibles . . . [. . .] it extends to infinity") frightens the listener, who moves away, closing himself up and suggesting she talk with "quelqu'un de plus compétent" ("someone more competent"; 17–18). The words would seem to indicate a psychotic character that, as Sarraute puts it at another point, knows no boundaries when it comes to the self. But the point of Sarraute's unbounded subjectivity is not to set it free of all limitations; rather, it is to reveal the subject as perpetually unfinished, never having drawn the last, defining, delimiting line of its self-portrait. Which brings us back to Naomi Schor's remarks on portraits in French women's writing. Where Schor sees no proper images of men in French women's fiction, we can add that in Sarraute's *Tu ne t'aimes pas,* the many (incomplete and open) images of selves that appear and reappear reveal themselves in order to discover what it is that they are not (yet), and what they might be in the light of a subjectivity imagined not on the model of the individual, but on the model of many "we"s who cannot say "I," not even when there is an attempt to break them down into smaller units. The plural is simply the most basic requirement for the subject to speak, to assume a voice: "un 'je' . . . non, [. . .] il fallait un 'nous,' un 'vous'" ("an 'I' . . . no, [. . .] a 'we,' a 'you all' was needed"; 87).

The experience this subject constitutes in and through the work is not that of an individual claiming for itself the parameters appropriate to its identity, even to its emergent identity. In

Chapter Three

this sense, Sarraute's subject leaves behind what we have discussed of Irigaray's universal-as-being-two, where transcendence is figured on the model of the fundamentally unknowable other gender, a transcendence that in turn informs the perpetual incompletion of self-knowledge. Sarraute, in effect, skips over the ground of sexual difference as she proceeds toward another subject. But for both Sarraute and Irigaray, an essential point is that the subject *is* its (always intersubjective, always manifold) lived experience; that the subject *will have* constituted itself and that experience as the very interaction, the ever-changing mediation, between the two.

Paradoxically, by insisting on this radical openness even to the point of refusing to posit as basic a distinction as sexual difference, and by concentrating instead on the intricate, intimate turnings of the self within the "medium" of language, Sarraute's writing allows a space for entirely new, unpredictable expressions of sexual difference. It does not, of course, prescribe such expressions, and can hardly even be said to formulate them explicitly, but such is the roominess of her subject's definition that one does find subtle, but specific, transformations enacted: a radically pluralized subject contests the complacency with which "the happiness of motherhood" is proclaimed and enforced. And language becomes, as we have seen, a maternal kiss that enables a subject to gather itself, at least enough to go on with its game, the experience of which can threaten to explode the very possibility of a self.

Conclusion
The Psyche of Feminism

In recent discussions of the current state of feminism,[1] contemporary feminist thought is largely divided between an "old guard" primarily concerned with equality, and a "new guard" associated with various "posts" (-modern, -colonial, -feminist). The post- group challenges the stable identity of "women," while the old guard widens its eyes in alarm at the inverted commas, attentive as it is to the struggles of real women.

This polarization may be no more than the residue of a split soon to be left behind by a third stream in feminist thought, a stream that has internalized both the political urgency of the "olds" and the attention to difference of the "posts," personified by feminists who have assumed their rights, but at the same time eschew egalitarian feminism as hopelessly mired in naïveté or a chimerical ideal of equality.

This, I would hazard, is one reason why we hear much less being said about "women's rights" today. It is also why this is not something to deplore. As long as feminists remain within the discourse of the "fight for equality," we will inevitably be placing ourselves in the irresponsible position of those who are demanding more pieces of an unacceptable pie. But on the other hand, as long as we continue to react scornfully *against* egalitarian feminism, we are wasting time trying to throw off and repudiate a tradition that has undeniably been an influence on our thinking. If it has accepted its "rights" and if it assumes difference to be of paramount importance, then what is the direction of feminism?

The short and inadequate answer to this question is: psychoanalysis. I put it so bluntly in order to emphasize one simple point that has run through this book. Namely, that feminism—whether in the form of a plea for equality, a rebellion, a

Conclusion

movement, or an interpretation—*is psychoanalytic*. It is concerned to articulate a relation, some relation, between the sexes, and in so doing must and does confront the primary questions of desire, enjoyment, and the tendency toward the shattering of the self that Freud called the death drive. But to say that feminism is inherently psychoanalytic is, as I argued in the introduction, also to assert that psychoanalysis is necessarily feminist, concerned as it is with the human psyche as sexual and sexed.

What reading Sand, Colette, and Sarraute helps to bring home is just this inextricable tie between the two discourses. Their writing, as I have tried to show, also offers an enrichment of our feminist and psychoanalytic claims. Sand's Marcie, the female character without a destiny, perceptible only through glimpses provided by her male interlocutor, suggests, as does the character Lélia, an extension, into the realm of affect, of Lacan's dictum concerning the existence of Woman. The ambiguously maternal jouissance of Colette's Charlotte, and of the narrator herself, further complicates the Freudian understanding of femininity, and adds to the possible interpretations of Irigaray's *feminine*. And Sarraute's chaotic self, a we that cannot unite and yet cannot but acknowledge its apparent solidity in the face of others, would seem to beg the question of sexual difference. In fact, her "subject" verges on another sort of ground, one that is equally important for both feminism and psychoanalysis: that of the self's continual dissolution and birth.

I began with an exploration of the relationship (actual, possible, and imagined) between feminism and psychoanalysis. The Introduction reviews the history of their entanglement and then argues, through a reading of Lacan and Irigaray's respective articulations of sexual difference, for the centrality of a radical psychoanalysis to feminist thought, especially to feminist attempts to reconfigure or reimagine, in ethical terms, relations between men and women, masculine and feminine.

It may be asked whether or not I need Lacan's thought for this work, and it might even be suggested that Lacan gets in my way when it comes to thinking about a feminist ethics. The importance of Lacan for this book comes down, I think, to his insistence on the nonexistence of Woman with a capital W. Now, it could be argued that this point hardly needs Lacan to

Conclusion

make it. Indeed, I get there with Aristotle, too, or with Wittig or Irigaray. Possibly even with Sand, who argues against capital W Woman's exclusion from Being. My answer is that Lacan does this in tandem with a radical reading of Freud, with, in short, psychoanalysis. And this is significant because I am proposing that feminism needs a psychoanalytic thought in order to go beyond arguments that ultimately get stymied in a too complete reliance on reason and the human subject as a producer of reason. With psychoanalysis, one cannot ignore the fact that reason does not begin or end with the ego, but goes beyond the ego into the unreason of unconscious thought. Fantasy, the life of the unconscious, has to be taken into account if there is to be any meaningful grappling with feminism's main concerns: inequality, difference, oppression. Lacan's focus on sexual difference is also what makes a feminist engagement with his work exciting: there is room to expand on Lacanian thought in a specifically feminist direction.

Chapter 1 takes up two attempts to reimagine the sexual relationship in the work of George Sand, where the emphasis is on the social and political injustices of women's lot and the impossibility of their desire. Chapter 2 deals with a relatively little-read work of Colette's, *The Pure and the Impure*, in which the narrator speculates on pleasure, especially sensual pleasure, as the key to any understanding of masculinity and femininity. Chapter 3 investigates Nathalie Sarraute's 1989 work *You Don't Love Yourself*, asking whether it is possible, or perhaps even necessary, for psychoanalytic feminist thought to entertain the question of neutrality put forth in Sarraute's prose. I conclude that, despite the risks, the turn to a Sarrautean neutrality, to the idea that there is someone *after* the feminine subject, is indeed needed because of the room it provides for entirely unpredictable expressions of sexual difference and ethical relations.

What I hope to have contributed to feminist literary scholarship in particular, then, is a demonstration of psychoanalysis's importance to feminist thought. But more than this, I have tried also to present the potential fruitfulness of the relation between literary and psychoanalytic discourses. Perhaps I have done this most overtly with Colette, whose narrative creation of what I have called a psychic maternity speaks directly to the problem of femininity as pathological. Her engendering of the mother conjures up feminine jouissance as the elsewhere *within*

Conclusion

femininity, an elsewhere that threatens it, and that comes to function on the side of eros. Of the three writers I have chosen, perhaps Sarraute is the most difficult to imagine speaking to a feminist psychoanalysis. Her writing would seem, for example, to focus on language at the expense of bodies, but one of the points I make is that, for Sarraute, there is no neat separation between the two. A woman's body, for example, is always a linguistic as well as a physical phenomenon, and this is what makes it fruitful to read Sarraute in the context of psychoanalytical thinking, which, quite simply, asserts that the body and language are so inextricably linked as to allow for something called "the talking cure," in which bodily ailments are cured with words. Sarraute's insistence on a conception of the self that is infinitely numerous and never unitary runs counter to Irigaray's focus on identity as two and not merely multiple. Still, it gives us a chance to come to a deeper, perhaps more nuanced understanding of the Irigarayan sexed subject, because Sarraute also creates a self that acknowledges the necessity of its constitution by another, in relation to another. Indeed, the drama of Sarraute's narrative voices lies in their gradual realization that they have no existence without the intervention—however inadequate, grating, or even violent it may be—of the other.

Much of this work is either implicitly or overtly concerned to argue against equality as an ideal for feminist thinking. It is very possible that this constitutes a weakness of the book. I have asked myself, for example, whether the need to critique egalitarian feminism has held me back in my attempts to think beyond it. I cannot help but suspect that it has. But that said, I am not convinced I would or should want to change this tendency in my work. I am not convinced because aside from writing this book over the past few years, I have also been teaching, and not infrequently teaching courses in women's studies programs. In these programs, it is too often the case that much valuable feminist scholarship is dismissed before it is heard, and that the ideal of the equality of the sexes is alive and well as the very limit of most women's studies curricula. Something like Irigaray's suggestion that "gender neutrality" might be a ruse that forecloses any possibility of engendering *two* sexes is too frequently ignored in the very place within the university set aside for feminist thinking. Naturally, I find this distressing

Conclusion

and have attempted to address it in both my teaching and my writing. It is distressing, moreover, in a way that relates directly to this book. I could illustrate this with countless examples. But to take just one: Sand's character Lélia runs through that 1839 novel at a feverish pitch, desiring nothing more nor less than to be. She finds ultimately that there is nowhere for her desire to go, nothing for *her* to be in herself and for herself. And Sand presents this impossibility specifically in terms of the world of men leaving no place for a female identity. I think that as long as feminists avoid sexual difference, avoid the task of trying to conceive of and engender a subject who is not defined *as* her relation to man (even if this is a relation of equality), there will be precisely nothing for women to be in and for themselves, and hence no possibility of an ethical relation between two subjects. The exhilarating achievement that was the formation of Women's Studies departments and programs twenty or so years ago has led, I fear, to a fate identical to that of Sand's heroine. This is, perhaps oddly, the point to which writing this book has brought me: a concern with the possibility of saving feminism from itself—saving it, more precisely, from knowing too well, or understanding too quickly, the identity of its object and its subject: women.

By refusing to know in advance who "you" or "I" are, who men and women are, feminism is able to take what I think is its necessary risk. It is by now a familiar one. In his 1984 seminar "Women in the Beehive," Jacques Derrida spoke of this danger in precisely this context of the institutionalization of feminism that necessarily carries with it assertions of power:

> [...] but there is a more dangerous and adventurous question. It is that whoever asks questions by definition not coded on these principles of progress risks to appear—in the eyes of women who are activists for women's studies—reactionary, dangerous, only limiting the progress of their positive research. [...] So a problem arises: if you keep the philosophical axiomatics, implying that *women* are subjects, considering women as subjects, then you keep the whole framework on which the traditional university is built. If someone tries to deconstruct the notion of subjectivity within women's studies, saying "well, woman is not a subject, we no longer consider woman as a subject"—this would have two consequences: one radically revolutionary or deconstructive, and the other dangerously reactive. (191)

Conclusion

Both psychoanalysis and feminism, at their most basic and most radical points, refuse to assume the truth of the subject. For both discourses, the subject is in process, in the making or unmaking of itself, as the case may be, but never simply, terminably defined. To the extent these discourses fail to recognize this incompleteness into which the human is constantly being reborn, they fall into a "dogmatic slumber." As I noted in the Introduction, according to Irigaray, the first move toward engendering an ethical relation between sexed subjects lies in an address to another that states, "je reconnais que tu es, que tu existes, que tu deviens. Dans cette reconnaissance, je te marque, je me marque de l'incomplétude [. . .] Tu n'es ni je suis le tout, ni le même, principe de totalisation" (*J'aime* 164 [143]).

I have suggested above that psychoanalytic thought represents an answer to the ills of feminism. No one would claim that Irigaray advocates an uncritical embrace of psychoanalysis for feminism's projects. Nor do I want to suggest that deeply ingrained doctrines of equality can be rethought *only* by recourse to the body of work Sigmund Freud inaugurated. The point is at once more complicated and less audacious than such a claim would allow; namely, that the history of feminism's entanglement with psychoanalysis demonstrates the potential of these fields mutually to transform each other, making new modes of thinking possible.

For feminism, a new mode of thinking becomes necessary as soon as we are confronted by the poverty of responses possible to the question of women's rights. What does a woman have a right to? What do women deserve and want, and how can they get it? When the answer is "equal rights," further discussion and discoveries are shut down as soon as irreducible and asymmetrical differences between women and men appear and seem to negate the moral force of equality's claims. But when feminist work includes the analysis of its own ends, it becomes possible to see both the logical and real (the philosophical and political) obstacles to those ends, obstacles interior to feminism itself.

As I noted in chapter 3, Irigaray proposes first, that feminist thought is in need of mediations if it is to be truly transformative, and second, that it is such mediation that might make it possible for women to resolve the opposition between subjective and objective with respect to feminine identity.[2]

Conclusion

The problem of a resolution between subjective and objective for feminine identity has perhaps the more readily apparent relation to what it is psychoanalytic thought implies for feminism, for it allows us to begin any attempt at a resolution from the insight that the process through which we become subjects presupposes the constitution of a reality made up of objects whose separation from the emerging subject is accepted as a fact. In other words, we can begin by understanding the opposition between subject and object not as a rift to be transcended, but as the fundamental means by which any identity emerges and becomes subject to the Other. At the same time, psychoanalysis does not understand this opposition as therefore fixed or unproblematic: precisely the contrary. The recognition of the psychical processes of object relation and subjectification demands that they be taken on as possible working sites, so to speak, as, in other words, processes continually in flux and open to change on both psychological and political fronts.

The matter of mediation is more complex in terms of its relation to what I am calling the psyche of feminism, and it is here that I think we are able to see more clearly why it is that claiming psychoanalysis for feminism need not be reduced to the mere application of one mode of knowledge to another. First, we can point out how Irigaray describes the significance of mediation as opposed to immediacy for women and, in our terms, for feminism. After insisting that giving women what they want (granting them the objects of their desires) amounts to acting faultily with respect to them, she continues:

> En rester à l'affect dans les relations entre femmes risque également de capter leur liberté dans un attrait qui les exile d'un retour à elles et les éloigne de la construction d'un vouloir et d'une histoire spécifiques. Doter les femmes d'une conscience propre dans la vie privée et publique, et de médiations qui leur permettent de l'exercer, manifeste souvent plus d'estime à leur égard qu'un amour sensible immédiat à plus d'un titre leurrant, aliénant, utopique, par manque de culture de la différence sexuelle. Nul besoin de faire miroiter au cœur des femmes quelque nouveau soir promis aux relations limité à l'intérieur de leur genre! [...] L'homo-sexualité n'est-elle pas ce qui les [the laws that govern patriarchal culture] structure, consciemment ou non, depuis des siècles? Une organisation parallèle et du même

Conclusion

>type les questionne peu à côté d'un remaniement des principes de leur économie. (Irigaray, *J'aime 17–18* [144])

The key point here is that for both psychical and cultural change to occur, there must be a passage beyond the immediate, including the satisfaction of immediate desires, which can, after all, be the source of powerful and positive affects—the vitalizing thrill of winning turf, say, or the glow of happiness that narcissistic relations to others like ourselves can bestow. This passage beyond the immediate involves an effort to step back from immediate satisfactions in order to confront their grounds, which are the same grounds that prevent what Irigaray calls an alteration of the principles according to which, for example, females, among themselves or not, live the distinction between subjective and objective in terms from which sexual difference as Irigaray imagines it is absent. What would be the point, this argument for mediation asks, of proposing that all women join Antigone in her rock, to bury themselves and their difference along with her, and in accordance with Creon's law, which they merely reproduce, albeit as a mirror opposite?

What Antigone (a paradigmatic figure for both feminism and psychoanalysis) suggests, on the contrary, is that there is a transcendence (beyond Creon's law) that obligates sexuate human beings, and that this transcendence (which may or may not have to do with gods) is constituted in and as a relation between two who cannot know each other finally, definitively. What is explosive about Antigone's act is not its defiance of the law or its implicit claim for her own humanity; it is the fact that her act implies that neither she nor Creon can know the rules of their world; it implies, in other words, that Antigone might have her own relation to the gods, to nature; and implies even that it is possible that Creon might be able to listen to what she would say. It is this listening, of course, which fails to take place in Sophocles's tragedy; but this failure does leave open what Irigaray calls an abyss, a chasm in the social world of the play: evidence that within the patriarchal order, constituting it, is a violent refusal to account for differences that point to that order's limitations and blind spots, to the holes in its own stories of the universe and spirit.[3] Creon fails to listen to Antigone because he already knows too much: the truth stands revealed

Conclusion

to him, and hence so does the law. The kind of listening Irigaray calls for "presupposes that the already existing world, including its philosophical or religious forms, not be considered finished, already made manifest or revealed" (*J'aime* 182, *I Love* 117).

Irigaray's analysis of *Antigone* and her transformation of Hegel's negative into the yet-to-be-created limit of sexual difference speak directly to and from the properly psychoanalytic practice of listening, and in such a way that, I argue, is meant to emphasize that activity's ethical, creative status. In effect, her work extends Freud's observation that sessions with each new patient constitute absolutely new knowledge of the field he seeks to establish. If nothing else, psychoanalysis proposes that the acts of speaking and listening (listening in a silence "sans présupposés, sans impératifs secrètement à l'œuvre" ("without presuppositions, without demands secretly at work"; *J'aime* 182, *I Love* 117) can and do transform subjects.

It is no accident then that Irigaray's thinking begins and becomes transformed in the study of the psychoanalytic project, with its persistent interrogations into the mysteries of, to use Freud's terms, of the psychical consequences of the anatomical distinction between the sexes. And her particular way of addressing herself to psychoanalysis—as well as the particular way in which she allows psychoanalysis to address her thinking—exemplifies why it is that we can claim that the relation between feminism and psychoanalysis might lead us outside of the feminist divide between the political and the philosophical, between questions of justice and identity. For psychoanalysis has come to function for feminism as one sort of mediation through which it can bring itself to radically new formulations of its project.

Because it works as a mediation—a mediator between feminism and its possible selves—and not as an answer, it is not necessary to identify the new stream in feminist thought as psychoanalytic feminism *tout court*, though this is certainly one of its manifestations. What is far more important is that feminist thought has been increasingly able to turn psychoanalytic inquiry not only upon psychoanalysis, but upon its own struggles with phallocentric culture and law. This can lead, and has led, to new knowledges. Again, I think Irigaray's work is

Conclusion

one of the clearest examples of how this can happen. Her current work barely mentions psychoanalysis as a theory or a practice, but her formulation of the possibility of an ethics in which there exist two sexed subjects continues to draw on *and to develop* psychoanalytic thought. This fact—the fact that Irigaray's so-called departure from psychoanalysis constitutes an extension of it—deserves the attention of scholars working at the limits of psychoanalytic thought at the beginning of its second century.[4]

And we can also imagine other directions into which this psychoanalytic mediation might lead. How, for example, might this still developing engagement affect problems with the institutionalization of feminism in the field and in departments of women's studies? It can be argued that it has been largely due to the institutional and intellectual growth of feminism that psychoanalytic thinkers have begun in the last decade or so to attempt, with renewed energy and seriousness, to address questions of race. Here is another instance in which psychoanalysis itself owes to other discourses the expanding and redefinition of its own limits. But will institutionalized feminism be capable of making space for its own transformation? Can it ask itself again, and with renewed seriousness, whether it prefers burial on familiar ground with familiar sisters to an opening of itself to the risks that mediation and distanciation bring? Can solidarity permit its own, perhaps temporary, perhaps permanent, undermining in order to rework the ground that has been the foundation for women's studies (one of whose perpetual slogans is "Take back the night!")? Antigone takes to the night in a descent into the abyss within patriarchy itself. Psychoanalysis takes to the night to interpret its dreams and to discover, for one thing, that within the most terrifying nightmares lurks an equally terrifying (because unconscious) fulfilled wish. If feminism's dreams are not subjected *by feminism* to a medium, to a mediation that can encounter its darkest wishes (the wish to continue to be dominated by a reliable Father's Law, for example), then surely the night into which we will descend will be a long, repetitive dream from which we will not permit ourselves to wake.

Appendix
English Translations

To aid those readers who prefer to see excerpts in English, I have provided English translations of French quotations. The longer translations are gathered here in the appendix, keyed in the text by the number in brackets that follows the French reference. For the reader's convenience, I have provided page references to published English translations where possible. However, in most cases the translations themselves are my own, as I have preferred to give as literal a rendering as possible of the French. When I have used someone else's translation, I make note of this in the reference.

Preface

1 What tie other than that of force could exist between he who has the right to demand and she who has not the right to refuse? [...] What exchange of feelings, what fusion of minds is possible between the master and the slave? (George Sand, *Lélia*)

2 I understood that death was a mysterious life; and that the horror of travel, the fear of the unknown, the disgust with the new, the mistrust of change, inflated the faint little noise that was but the brief snapping of the imagination at the limit of darkness. "Death" was the ogre of my grandmother. In my life there was no room for death; my life included the immensity of the unimaginable. Death died in its own name, like "nothing," like "God," like "certain," and everything that was unimaginable. (Cixous, *Dedans* 21–22)

Introduction
Psychoanalytic Feminism: Sexual Difference and Another Love

3 Now, Freud describes a state of affairs. He does not invent female sexuality, nor for that matter male sexuality. He accounts for them, as a "man of science." The problem is that [...] he interprets

English Translations to Pages 11–21

women's sufferings, symptoms, dissatisfactions, as a function of their individual histories, without questioning the relation of their "pathology" to a certain state of society, of culture. (Irigaray, *This Sex* 70)

4 In reality, the self-proclaimed universal is the equivalent of an idiolect of men, a masculine imaginary, a sexed world. Without neutrality. (Irigaray, *ESD* 121)

5 As paradoxical as this formulation may sound, we say that it is to be the phallus, that is the signifier of the desire of the Other, that the woman will reject an essential part of her femininity, namely, all of her attributes in the masquerade. It is for that which she is not—*that is, the phallus*—that she means to be desired at the same time as loved. But she finds the signifier of her desire in the body of him—*supposed to have it*—to whom her demand for love is addressed. (Irigaray, *This Sex* 62)

6 If the man in fact manages to satisfy his demand for love in the relation with the woman in as much as the signifier of the phallus constitutes her as giving in love that which she does not have—inversely, his own desire for the phallus will cause its signifier to emerge in its insistent divergence toward "another woman" who can signify this phallus under varying titles, as virgin or as prostitute. (Lacan, *Ecrits* 290)

7 The choice she is offered would be between a radical censoring of her drives—which would lead to death—or their hysterical treatment, their hysterical conversion. This alternative, in fact, is not really one. The two operations are consistent with each other. (Irigaray, *Speculum* 72)

8 But what does it mean to deny it? Is it in any way legitimate to substitute a negation for the perceived apprehension of inexistence? (Lacan, *XX* 132)

9 From the fact that one can write *not every χ is inscribed in $\Phi\chi$* we can deduce by way of implication that there is one χ which is inconsistent. This is true on one condition alone: that, in the all or in the not-all in question, it be a matter of the finite [. . .]. Only, we may be dealing on the contrary with the infinite [. . .]. When I say that Woman is not-all and that it is because of this that I cannot say Woman, it is precisely because I am putting in question a jouissance that, with regard to everything that serves in the function $\Phi\chi$, is of the order of the infinite. (Lacan, *XX* 94)

10 Is it in any way legitimate to substitute a negation for the perceived apprehension of inexistence? This too is a question that, for me, it is only a matter of initiating. (Lacan, *XX* 132)

English Translations to Pages 22–30

11 For a long time I have desired to talk to you by being a little bit more among you. I had also hoped, I can admit to you, that the so-called school vacation would have thinned out your audience. Since this satisfaction is refused me, I return from it to that from which I started the last time, which I called *another satisfaction*, the satisfaction of the word. (Lacan, *XX* 61)

12 a new being. Except that the thing doesn't work without a meiosis, without a completely manifest subtraction, at least for one of the two, just before the very moment when the union is produced, a subtraction of certain elements which are not for nothing in the final operation. (Lacan, *XX* 63)

13 You will be as one, the law decrees. It does not say how this is possible. It obligates without showing the path.
   What we would discover is how *two* can be made in order one day perhaps to become a *one* in that third which is love, for example.
   Currently there is a kind of *one* [...] which is merely an enslaving complementarity [...]. In order that the *one* of love might perhaps one day be achieved, it is necessary to discover the *two*. (Irigaray, *ESD* 66; Irigaray's emphasis)

14 It is as an imposter that the Legislator—he who claims to institute the Law [in this context, the Father as opposed to the Mother]—presents himself as making up for the deficiency. (Lacan, *Ecrits* 311)

15 she [woman] has, in relation to what I designate the phallic function of jouissance, a supplementary jouissance. You'll notice that I said *supplementary*. If I'd said *complementary*, where would we be! We would fall back into the whole. (Lacan, *XX* 68)

16 I recognize you signifies that I recognize that you are, that you exist, that you are becoming. In this recognition, I mark you, I mark myself with incompleteness, with the negative. Neither you nor I are the whole [*le tout*], nor the same, the principle of totalisation [...]. The *mine* of the subject is always already marked by a disappropriation: gender [*le genre*]. To be man or woman amounts already to not being the whole of the subject [...] but also to not being completely oneself [...]. *I* is never simply *mine* inasmuch as it belongs to a gender. Thus, I am not all: I am a man or a woman. (Irigaray, *I Love* 105–06)

17 So that one could say that the more man can confuse the woman with God, that is, that of which she joys, the less he hates, the less he is—both spellings—and, since after all there is no love without hate, the less he loves. (Lacan, *XX* 82)

English Translations to Pages 34-39

Chapter One
George Sand and the Impossible Woman

18 I accepted the honor of participating in the collaboration of the newspaper *le Monde* only as an act of devotion towards M Lamennais, who had created it and was in charge of it. As soon as he abandoned it, I withdrew, without even asking myself about the causes of this abandon; I did not have a liking, and I lacked the facility, for that type of interrupted and, so to speak, choppy work [demanded when writing for serial publication in a daily paper]. Having not had the opportunity in time and place to continue the *Lettres à Marcie,* I soon forgot the species of plan that I had conceived. I was reproached, in some *emancipation* newspapers, for having retreated in the face of the difficulties of the enterprise. Chance alone forced me to stop myself. (Sand, *Marcie* 166)

19 [Your] worries afflict me and retrace only too much those that often devour my own heart. I am no more heroic than you, Marcie [. . .]. Marcie, our spirit is sick [. . .] I am so sad and beaten down today, in my anguish I so confuse your misery and my own, that it is impossible for me to give you advice. (Sand, *Marcie* 179, 180-81)

20 You believe yourself fit for a man's role in society, and you find society quite unjust in refusing it to you.
    I fear, Marcie, that the impotent promises of a new philosophy may have harmed you. Whether you have ill-understood the true thought of Saint-Simonism, or whether Saint-Simonism, in its hesitations and searchings, has not found the meaning of your destinies, you have drawn from it the desire for the impossible. (Sand, *Marcie* 193)

21 But what confidence can women inspire in upright judges when, presenting themselves as reclaiming the part of their dignity refused them in the conjugal house, and especially the sacred part of the authority over their children which they are refused, they would ask as compensation not peace in their household, not the liberty of their maternal affections, but speech at the forum, the helmet and the sword, the right to condemn to death? (Sand, *Marcie* 202)

22 It is because of her vocation of artist-creator that Consuelo succeeds in assuming her sensuality and in becoming a complete woman. Lélia and Blanche [of Sand's *Rose et Blanche*] are transformed into statues—thus into passive objects—by sensuality. Consuelo refuses this static quality and refuses to be an object for the man she loves. She chooses to be an active subject by creating works of art. In *La Comtesse de Rudolstadt* Sand presents us with

English Translations to Pages 39–43

a positive vision of feminine sexuality and a truce in the war between the sexes. (MacCallum-Schwartz 177)

23 She [Consuelo] can accept her sensuality and satisfy herself without losing her will *because she has found the man that Lélia sought in vain—the superior man* who treats her as an equal. (MacCallum-Schwartz 177; emphasis added)

24 it seems to me very probable that you will be called by better circumstances, by the unexpected encounter with these fortunes [which life *en famille* brings] the secret of which the angel of our destiny whispers sometimes in our ear, and that you will realize your first wish. If fortune continues to mistreat you, you will be stronger than it; you will turn your aspirations towards sublime heights, you will find between mysticism and philosophy an exceptional role, a mission of virgin and angel; if your soul does not attain it, you will suffer long before resolving to risk your wisdom on uncertain promises, on deceitful hopes. You will die rather than accept fortune and pleasure from some impure source. (Sand, *Marcie* 202–03)

25 Search the social hierarchy, in all the ranks of power or industry, for some position wherein the thought of installing yourself does not seem risible to you. You can only be an artist, and nothing prevents you from this. (Sand, *Marcie* 196)

26 whenever we perform an act of strength, we raise ourselves above vulgar human nature. You know that great moral destinies are condemned to a sort of isolation, and that the spirit of wisdom [. . .] has amply recompensed those who withdraw themselves from the common way in order to enter voluntarily into an interior life. (Sand, *Marcie* 173–74)

27 A man must not obey a woman, it's monstrous. A man must not command a woman, it's cowardly. (Sand, *Correspondance*)

28 Some women have raised this question: In order for society to be transformed, must not woman intervene politically in public affairs starting today?—I dare to respond that she must not, because social conditions are such that women could not honorably and loyally fulfill a public mandate. (Sand, *Correspondance* 8: 401)

29 Wish to be their equals in order to renounce that cowardly pleasure of dominating them by ruses. Wish to be their equals in order to hold joyfully to the vow of fidelity which is the ideal of love and the need of conscience in a pact of equality [. . .]. Wish to be

177

English Translations to Pages 43–53

their equals in the name of that Christian feeling of humility itself, which means nothing else than the respect of the right of others to equality [. . .]. A man must not obey a woman, it's monstrous. A man must not command a woman, it's cowardly. Man and woman must obey their vows, honor, reason, their love for their children. These are the sacred ties, laws superior to the counsel of our pride and to the transports of human passions. (Sand, *Correspondance* 8: 406)

30 [Political overtures to the world of women] function as concessions on the part of existing powers, and not as the establishment of new values. [They are] too rarely thought through and affirmed by women themselves, who often stop at *critical demands*. Which is permitting a worldwide ebbing away of those points obtained in their struggles, for the lack of assuring some foundations other than those upon which the world of men is erected? (Irigaray, *ESD* 6; emphasis added)

31 And as for these dangerous attempts that some women in Saint-Simonism have made to taste pleasure in liberty, think of them what you will, but do not risk it yourself; it is not made for you. You would never be able to love by halves, and, if you love one day, you will love forever. You would have accepted a free homage, and soon you would be horrified at this right to infidelity [. . .]. What would be this new society where the beautiful souls would not have the right to extend their wings and to develop in their full expanse, where the strong [i.e., the morally strong, who love strongly] would be *by law* the plaything and the dupe of the weak? And how would this not happen ceaselessly under a regime that authorized it, since it happens so often under a regime which prohibits it? Strange remedy for the corruption of a society, to open wide for it the doors of license! (Sand, *Marcie* 176–77)

32 [Woman] always wants *more*, write certain psychoanalysts (notably, Jacques Lacan), assimilating this *always more* to a pathology [*sic*]. In fact, this always more is but the status of sexuate feminine desire. Unsatisfiable, certainly, in everyday life. But not pathological for all that [. . .]. She enjoys *touch* in some sense indefinitely. (Irigaray, *ESD* 64)

33 What's it to you, young poet? Why do you want to know who I am and whence I come? . . . I was born like you in the valley of tears, and all the unfortunate who crawl upon the earth are my brothers [. . .]. Can there be anything so strange and mysterious in a human existence? [. . .]

You ask if I am a being of another nature than you! Do you think I don't suffer? [. . .]

English Translations to Pages 54–57

You ask if I adore the spirit of evil! The spirit of evil and the spirit of good, they are one spirit, they are God [...]. Good and evil are distinctions that we have created. God does not know them any more than happiness and misfortune. Do not ask then, neither of heaven nor of hell, the secret of my destiny. It is you that I could reproach for throwing me ceaselessly above or below myself. (Sand, *Lélia* 1: 65)

34 I expressed the keenness of my solicitudes for you too frankly, Lélia; I have wounded the sublime delicacy of your soul. (Sand, *Lélia* 1: 66)

35 Wiser and happier than I, you lived only to enjoy; more ambitious and less submissive to God, perhaps, I lived only to desire. (Sand, *Lélia* 1: 160)

36 Any creature, mediocre as it may be, can inspire or feel that delirium of an instant and take it for love. The intelligence and aspiration of most people go no further than this. The being who aspires to joys always noble, to pleasures always vividly and sacredly felt, to a continuous association of moral love with physical love, is an ambitious being destined for an immense happiness or an eternal pain. There is no middle ground for those who make a god out of love [...]. Whence does it come then, that one refuses to pure women the faculty to feel disgust and to manifest it to the impure men that deceive them? [...] a proud woman cannot know pleasure without love: this is why she will find neither the one nor the other in the arms of most men. As for these men, it is much less easy for them to respond to our noble instincts and to nourish our generous desires than to accuse us of frigidity. (Sand, *Lélia* 2: 13–14)

37 It is a question of a sort of inverted initiation, centrifugal instead of centripetal [...]. An adolescent boy leaves the female group to integrate into the male group. For him, initiation has the value of a laying claim to a status. What can a girl do? A prisoner in the gynaeceum, she can try to leave it. To go where? This is the whole problem of women's liberation. Between the gynaeceum and the society of men, there does not yet exist a unisex society to receive her [as we saw so plainly explained in *Lettres à Marcie*]. What remains for her then is revolt-initiation [...]. For the adolescent girl, initiation can only be permanent flight. (Michel Tournier 340, qtd. in Penrod 86)

38 The noises of the party have grown distant. I hear the orchestra taking up the interrupted air; they are forgetting you; they have given up searching for me: we can be free for a time. Speak. (Sand, *Lélia* 1: 162)

English Translations to Pages 58–63

39 Lélia's drama consists not exactly in not knowing how to enjoy, but in having desired intensely and in suffering from an imbalance between the immensity of desire and the limits of jouissance. (Béatrice Didier, in Sand, *Lélia* 2: 197)

40 could enjoy nothing, because I wanted to enjoy splendidly all things . . . tormented by an insatiable desire *to be* something. (Sand, *Lélia* 1: 165, 166; emphasis added)

41 because we are both of us women. It is not impossible that if words, full and well established, have always been used, aligned, amassed by men, the feminine could appear as that herb—a bit mad, a bit spindly in the beginning, that comes to grow between the interstices of the old rocks and—why not?—ends up loosening the cement slabs. (Duras and Gauthier 8)

42 I wrote *Lélia* without order, without a plan, by fits and starts, and with the intention, in the beginning, of writing it for myself alone. I had no system, I belonged to no school, I hardly considered an audience; I had not yet formed a clear idea of what having a public meant [. . .]. Was this modesty? I can affirm that it was, although it hardly seems modest to attribute to oneself so rare a virtue. But since, for me, it was not a virtue, I say the thing as it is. *It was not an effort of my reason,* a triumph over the natural vanity of our kind, *but rather an unawareness of the fact,* an innate want of foresight, a tendency to absorb myself in an occupation of the mind without remembering that beyond the world of my dreams there existed a world of realities upon which my thought, serene or somber, could have any effect whatever. (Sand, *Lélia* 1: 53; emphasis added)

43 What paternal eye opened then upon the human race the day it thought to rend itself by placing one sex under the domination of the other? Is it not a fierce appetite that has made woman the slave and the property of man? What instincts of pure love, what notions of holy fidelity could have resisted this mortal blow? What tie other than that of force could henceforth exist between he who has the right to demand and she who has not the right to refuse? [. . .] What exchange of feelings, what fusion of minds is possible between the master and the slave? (Sand, *Lélia* 1: 170)

44 touched each other with astonished hands. They could scarcely get over finding each other so beautiful still, admiring each other, loving each other, and, different as they were, recognizing each other. (Sand, *Lélia* 1: 156)

45 proud and cold in your sleeping face, there was a something male and strong that almost prevented me from recognizing you. I found

English Translations to Pages 63–69

that you resembled that beautiful black-haired boy I had just dreamed of, and, trembling, I kissed your arm. (Sand, *Lélia* 1: 161–62)

46 "I even remember a word that I could not explain to myself," answered Lélia. "You made me bend over the water, and you said to me, 'Look at yourself, my sister: don't you find yourself beautiful?' I answered you that I was less so than you. 'Oh, you are much more so,' you replied, 'You look like a man.'"
"And that made you shrug your shoulders with disdain," said Pulchérie.
"And I did not guess," answered Lélia, "that a destiny had just been realized for you, whereas for me no destiny whatsoever would ever be realized." (Sand, *Lélia* 1: 162)

47 It is time that I rest, and that I seek God in his mystical sanctuaries in order to ask him if he has made for women nothing more than men. (Sand, *Lélia* 2: 22)

48 Woe! Woe unto that savage half of the human race, who, in order to appropriate the other half for itself, has left to it only the choice between slavery and suicide! (Sand, *Lélia* 2: 25)

49 To lose a child that one has nourished with one's milk and carried for an entire year attached to one's breast is no crueler to the heart of a mother than was for me the sudden and terrible detachment that took place at that moment between Sténio and me [. . .]. Do you find that I have shown an instant of spite to Pulchérie or to Sténio? Have I not tried to console the latter for his shame, and to ennoble the former in the eyes of the poet? Have I not offered the child my eternal friendship, my solicitude and my maternal guidance? (Sand, *Lélia* 2: 12)

50 Lélia, struck with admiration, knelt down instinctively as in the days of her childhood.
Women's voices, harmonious and pure, climbed toward God like a prayer, fervent and full of hope, and children's voices, penetrating and silvery, responded to that prayer like the far-off promises of heaven expressed by the organ of the angels. (Sand, *Lélia* 2: 18)

51 There is then no true association in love between the sexes; for the woman plays the role of the child, and the hour of emancipation never tolls for her. What, then, is this crime against nature of keeping one half of humankind in an eternal childhood? The stain of original sin weighs, according to the Judaic legend, upon the head of woman, and hence her bondage. (Sand, *Lélia* 1: 171)

English Translations to Pages 70–81

52 We are worth more than they in one sense [. . .]. They have let our minds sleep; but they have not perceived that in forcing the divine torch in us to be snuffed out, they concentrated in the depths of our hearts the immortal flame, whereas it went out in them. They have assured themselves possession of the least noble part of our love, and they do not perceive that they no longer possess us. By affecting to believe us incapable of keeping our promises, they have all the more assured themselves of legitimate heirs. They have children, but they do not have women. (Sand, *Lélia* 1: 171)

53 has to be brought out of the night, out of the shadow, out of the rock, out of her total paralysis by a social order that condemns itself even as it condemns her. (Irigaray, *ESD* 119)

54 Creon, who has forbidden burial for Polynices, who has suggested that Antigone keep quiet for ever about her relations with the gods, Creon who has had her closed up in a hole in the rock, leaving just a little food so that he cannot be guilty of her death, Creon has condemned society to a split in the order of a reason that leaves nature without gods, without grace; the family without any future other than work for the state; procreation without joy, love without ethics. (Irigaray, *ESD* 119)

55 To be man or woman already comes to not being the whole of the subject, nor of the community, nor of the spirit. (Irigaray, *I Love* 106)

56 . . . the court of love is not really an answer, because the woman is desired there corporally and not spiritually, energetically. (Irigaray, *I Love* 98)

57 The bodies of women assure—by their usage, by their consummation, by their circulation—the condition of possibility of sociality and of culture, but they remain an "infrastructure" misrecognized in their elaboration. The exploitation of woman-sexed matter is so constitutive of our socio-cultural horizon that it cannot find its interpretation inside of it. (Irigaray, *This Sex* 171)

58 This is why I did not want to take a place in their society. Could I not have seated myself among *their* women [. . .]? (Sand, *Lélia* 1: 171; emphasis added)

59 the exclusive valorization of the needs-desires of men, and the exchanges among them [. . .] where man engenders man as his likeness, and the woman, the girl, the sister, are valued only insofar as she serves as the possibility and the stake for relations between men. (Irigaray, *This Sex* 171)

60 with *Lélia* George Sand introduced, and in a radically new way, philosophy into the novel. Interrogations of the modalities and the

182

English Translations to Pages 82–84

deviations of the social tie were succeeded by an interrogation of the very foundation of society. (van Rossum-Guyon 82)

61 those exceptional souls, scattered over the face of a world where everything bruises them, repels them and forces them to retire within themselves, searched for each other and called to each other in vain. Their union would not be consecrated by human laws, or rather *their existence* would not be protected by the sympathy of other existences. So it is that any attempt at this ideal life has miserably failed among beings who had been able to identify with each other, under the eye of God, in a better world. (Sand, *Lélia* 1: 170; emphasis added)

62 I want to complete a book wherein I've put all the bitterness of my suffering, and wherein I want to put today the ray of hope that has appeared to me. (Sand, *Correspondance* 3: 595; also qtd. in *Lélia* 1: 11)

63 She would have pardoned heaven for having frustrated her out of every happiness if she could have read clearly in the destinies of a future humanity something better than what she herself had had a share in. (Sand, *Lélia* 2: 156)

64 For ten thousand years I have felt you [Truth] in my heart without being able to translate you to my mind. (Sand, *Lélia* 2: 159)

65 Names which are still imposed by consciousness to signify that outside-scene, that other scene, which for it [consciousness] is *cryptic*. Thereby indicating the place where consciousness no longer masters itself, that "dark night" but also those fires and flames in which it sinks abyssally to its extreme confusion. The place where "she"—or he, but through recourse to "her"—speaks of the dazzling by that source of light which is logically suppressed; of the effusion of the "subject" and of the Other in an embracing/burning that confounds them as terms; of the disdain of form as such; of the mistrust of that understanding which constitutes itself as an obstacle to persevering in jouissance; of the desolate dryness of reason . . . (Irigaray, *Speculum* 191)

66 not to be able to specify what she wants. Deficient in her words. Having the presentiment of a *yet to be said* that resists all words, that one could scarcely stammer out. (Irigaray, *Speculum* 193)

67 It is better, then, to refuse all speech, to be quiet or to hold fast to some clamor so little articulate as scarcely to form *a song*. (Irigaray, *Speculum* 193)

68 a jouissance so extreme, a love so incomprehensible, an illumination so excessive, that nescience becomes desire. (Irigaray, *Speculum* 194–95)

English Translations to Pages 85–104

69 Some have called you Satan, others crime: I call you desire. (Sand, *Lélia* 2: 158)

70 And for ten thousand years, as the only answer to my cries, the only assuagement of my agony, I have heard soaring above this accursed earth the despairing sob of impotent desire! [. . .] For ten thousand years I have cried out in the infinite: *Truth, truth!* For ten thousand years the infinite has answered me: *Desire, desire!* (Sand, *Lélia* 2: 159)

71 [She is the] prey of a nameless delirium, of a limitless despair. [She] float[s] in shadows and [her] tired arms embrace only deceitful shades. (Sand, *Lélia* 2: 158)

72 in this nocturnal vagabondage? If not further into the night until she becomes a transverberating ray, a luminous shadow? [. . .] For toward where can one head in that ignorance which can receive its knowledge only from a burning/embrace? (Irigaray, *Speculum* 193–94)

73 But how to continue to live in such a violence, however sweet it be? (Irigaray, *Speculum* 196)

Chapter Two
What Does a Woman Enjoy? Colette's *Le pur et l'impur*

74 With her short nose and her plump face, she resembled those favorite models of Renoir, those beauties of 1875, so much so that in spite of the olive green coat with its fox collar and the little hat in style about eighteen years ago, one could find in her something of the old fashioned. (Colette, *PI* 557)

75 free, fresh, still dark air [. . .] everyday desire for bright mornings, escapes to the fields and forests, or at least to the neighboring wood [the Bois de Boulogne]. (Colette, *PI* 557)

76 "You have no car?" said my companion. "Me neither. But at this hour one always finds taxis in this neighborhood . . ."
    As she was speaking, a taxi appeared, coming from the woods, slowed, stopped and my companion drew aside [*s'effaça*].
    "After you, Madame . . ." (Colette, *PI* 557)

77 in a calm rhythm at first, so harmoniously, so regularly accelerated that I was surprised to find myself following, with a shaking of the head, her cadence which was as perfect as her melody. (Colette, *PI* 556)

78 The charming sound of her voice, the raspy attack of certain syllables, a defeated and soft way of letting the end of her sentence

English Translations to Pages 105–08

fall into the low register... What seduction!... Through the open window on "Charlotte's" right, there blew towards me her rather banal perfume and a healthy, active odor of flesh that the stale tobacco smell spoiled. (Colette, *PI* 558)

79 "Someone that one loves is so wearing!..." she sighed. "I don't have much of a taste for lying."
"How do you mean, lying?... Why? Don't you love him?"
"Naturally, I love him."
"But then..."
She imposed on me a magnificent look of superior to inferior, which she then softened:
"Let's say I don't know anything about it," she said politely. (Colette, *PI* 561)

80 nightingale's lament, notes full, reiterated, identical, one by another prolonged, precipitated until the rupture of their trembling equilibrium at the summit of a torrential sob... (Colette, *PI* 561)

81 melodious and merciful lie [...] female genius [...] reassuring friend of men [...] a dupery maintained with ardor, an unrecognized valor that hopes for no recompense. (Colette, *PI* 561–62)

82 Seated with her legs extended, *she waited* idle, at my side, to take up again the task assigned to the one who loves best: daily deceit. (Colette, *PI* 562; emphasis added)

83 "A few more seconds," I thought, "a few seconds of awkward conversation, and I'll learn from Charlotte what she hides from the ferocious little lover..." (Colette, *PI* 562)

84 [E]verything pleased me in Charlotte [...] "little spouse," "naughty brat," "sweet sin," "little girl," [...] "my boy," adding to her ambiguous maternity a plain and forthright accent of authority. (Colette, *PI* 563)

85 Already, I wanted her to resemble in no way those thronging nuns that one runs into at every turn. I call nuns those predestined women who sigh between the sheets, but from resignation, who secretly love abnegation, sewing, housework, and sky-blue satin bedspreads, for lack of another altar to adorn with the virginal color... (Colette, *PI* 563)

86 Charlotte belonged, I assured myself silently, to another rule. Her easy idleness elevated her in my eyes; few women know, empty-handed, how to remain immobile and serene. I observed her feet, her hanging and unfolded fingers, all the signs revealing wisdom, self-control... (Colette, *PI* 563)

185

English Translations to Pages 109–12

87 "I thought so ... A novel?"
    And I despised him the more, for believing me incapable—as in fact I was—of enjoying this luxury: a tranquil pleasure, rather low, a pleasure inspired only by a certain kind of snobbery, a spirit of bravado, a curiosity more affected than real ... I had brought nothing with me but a well-hidden grief that gave me no rest, and a terrible stillness of the senses. (Colette, *PI* 554)

88 that no nude dancers would disturb the evening, that no danger of Americans, loaded up with alcohol, would threaten us, and that the *Columbia* [phonograph] itself would fall silent. (Colette, *PI* 555)

89 a female voice, downy, rough and sweet like a firm, velvety peach, began to sing, and was so pleasant to all of us that we kept ourselves from applauding, even by a murmur. (Colette, *PI* 554–55)

90 All sighing died up there. And the sages down below felt, all together, the cold of the winter dawn. I drew close and fastened my fur coat, a stretched-out neighbor pulled a flap of embroidered fabric over his shoulder and closed his eyes. In the back, near a silk lantern, the two sleeping women drew still nearer each other without waking, and the little flames of the oil lamps fluttered under the weight of the cold air that descended from the balcony. (Colette, *PI* 556)

91 "How well you must know how to wait, Madame Charlotte!" [. . .]
    "Pretty well, it's true. But now, as a retired doctor would say, I no longer practice." (Colette, *PI* 563)

92 "One always waits ... You just said: 'I expect him in a week ...'"
    "Ah! yes ... [. . .] It's true, I expect him ... But I expect nothing from him. There's a nuance ..." (Colette, *PI* 564)

93 It would be *too beautiful,* the love of such a young man, if I weren't forced to lie. (Colette, *PI* 564; emphasis added)

94 "Madame Charlotte, that which you 'truly' lack ... do you seek it out?"
    She smiled, her head thrown back, showing in the confused light the underside of her pretty, short nose, her slightly fat chin, a faultless arc of teeth:
    "I am not so naive, Madame, nor so shameless. That which I lack, I do without, and that's that, don't make a merit of it, no ... But one is never completely deprived of a thing one knows well for having in fact possessed it. That, no doubt, is the reason for my boy's great jealousy. Try as I might—and you have heard that I'm not unskilled—my poor boy, who has an instinct, flies into rages without cause, and shakes me as if he wanted at all cost to open me up ... It's laughable," she said. And indeed she laughed.

English Translations to Pages 115–20

"And . . . that which you lack . . . is it really out of reach?"

"Possibly not," she said haughtily. "But I'd be ashamed of the truth next to the lie. Look, Madame, imagine . . . Abandoning myself like an imbecile, simply no longer knowing what escapes you in gestures or words . . . Just the idea of it . . . Oh! I can't stand that idea."

And she must even have blushed, for her face looked darker to me. She turned her head from one side to the other on her white cushion, agitated, her mouth half-opened, like a woman whom pleasure threatens. (Colette, *PI* 565)

95 I succeeded only in rendering her quite cold and circumspect, such as I had seen her in the taxi. Little by little, she recovered herself, closed herself back up. In the space of a few words, she barred me from the mental domain that she seemed to disdain from so high, and that bears a red, visceral name: the heart; —she forbade me too the cavern of odors, of colors, the dumb asylum where, surely, there frolicked a powerful arabesque of flesh, a cipher of intermingled limbs, the symbolic monogram of the Inexorable . . . (Colette, *PI* 565)

96 How pleasant it is to know each other so little! We are speaking here of those things that don't get confided between friends. Women friends—if there are any—never dare to confide to each other what they truly lack. (Colette, *PI* 564)

97 My heart is completely devoted to this child. But what is the heart, Madame? It's worth less than its reputation. It's very accommodating, it accepts everything. One furnishes it with what one has, it makes so little fuss . . . But as for the body . . . Quite another thing! It has, as they say, a cultivated taste, it knows what it wants. A heart doesn't choose. One always ends up by loving. I'm certainly proof of that. (Colette, *PI* 564)

98 "Very well," I assured her promptly. "Madame Charlotte," I added with *involuntary warmth*, it is probable that I understand you better than anyone in the world."

She paid me with a smile that was entirely contained in her look:

"That's saying quite a bit." (Colette, *PI* 564; emphasis added)

99 We have also to find, to find anew, to invent the words, the sentences that speak the most archaic and most contemporary relationship to the body of the mother, to our body, the sentences that translate the tie between her body, ours and that of our daughters. We have to discover a language [*langage*] that does not substitute itself for the bodily encounter [*le corps-à-corps*], as paternal language [*langue*] attempts to do, but that accompanies it, words

English Translations to Pages 120–29

which do not bar the corporeal, but which speak corporeal. (Irigaray, *Irigaray Reader* 43)

100 And what would he have said had he met that one who, from magnanimity of soul, deceives man by simulating pleasure? But I can be at ease on that account: he *inevitably* [*fatalement*] met Charlotte, and perhaps more than once. (Colette, *PI* 586; emphasis added)

101 She poured out to him her broken vocalization, while she turned her head aside and her hair covered her forehead, her cheek, her half-closed eye, lucid and attentive to her master's pleasure . . . Charlottes almost always have long hair . . . (Colette, *PI* 586)

102 At a time when I was—or believed myself—insensible to Damien, I suggested to him that we could make, for a trip, a pair of companions, courteously selfish, comfortable, friends of long silences . . .
 "I only like to travel with women," he replied.
 The soft tone could have helped the brutal words to pass away . . . He was afraid he had angered me, and "fixed everything" with a worse remark:
 "You, a woman? Well, try as you might . . ." (Colette, *PI* 586)

103 If Damien's decretal remark angered me, it's because I then hoped to shed that ambiguity, its imperfections and its prerogatives, and to throw them warm at the feet of a man, to whom I offered a fine, truly female body and its vocation, perhaps fallacious, of servant. (Colette, *PI* 586)

Chapter Three
Nathalie Sarraute: After the Feminine Subject

104 So you see, I've given up, I am the whole universe, all virtualities, all possibles . . . the eye doesn't perceive it, it extends to the infinite . . . (Nathalie Sarraute, *Tu ne t'aimes pas*)

105 Angels, very rapid messengers who transgress, thanks to this speed, all enclosures [. . .]. They proclaim that this crossing is accessible to the body of man. And above all to the body of woman. They figure and tell of another incarnation, another parousia of the body. (Irigaray, *ESD* 16)

106 "[. . .] that's precisely one of our deficiencies . . . those images of ourselves that others send back to us, we don't manage to see ourselves in them . . . [. . .]"
 "[. . .] they slide over us, they don't adhere, everything that stirs in us moves them aside, they cannot fix themselves." (Sarraute, *Tu ne* 15)

English Translations to Pages 132–37

107 *Monique Wittig:* You started to write *Tropism[s]* in 1932?

Nathalie Sarraute: Yes. Up to then I hadn't found any form that could interest me in conveying what I felt. When I began to write, the novelistic forms which existed did not allow me to bring to light those elusive inner movements. Those movements could not be accommodated by any preexisting forms. When I wrote my first Tropism, I tried to convey an interior sensation, movement, for which the character, so to speak, was but the simple support, barely visible. (Wittig, "Le déambulatoire" 4)

108 In my last book, *Ici*, it seemed to me I was approaching nearer to what is "reality." [...] "Here," one doesn't know that one is in the *for intérieur*. That which appears occupies everything. And when it appears, one establishes partitions so that it might occupy precisely all the space that one reserves for it.

And behind, as in an ambulatory, words circulate, always standing at the ready to rise up, *whether one makes them come or pushes them away. There is in this a whole interaction* which interested me. *I had the illusion* again this time of approaching, *if this has any meaning,* "reality." (Wittig, "Le déambulatoire" 7–8; emphasis added)

109 But they said to you: You don't love yourself. You ... You who showed yourself to them, you who proposed yourself, you wanted to be of use ... you advanced toward them ... as if you were not only one of our possible incarnations, one of our virtualities ... you separated yourself from us, you put yourself forward as our unique representative ... you said "I". ... (Sarraute, *Tu ne* 9)

110 Each of us does that at every instant. How to do otherwise? Every time one of us shows himself outside, he designates himself by "I," by "me". ... as if he were alone, as if you all didn't exist ... (Sarraute, *Tu ne* 9)

111 It is not to all of us that this "we" applies ... We are never all present ... there are always some among us who are sleeping, lazing about, getting distracted, turning away ... this "we" can only designate those who were there when you made that sortie, those whom that kind of performance makes ill at ease, they feel struck ... (Sarraute, *Tu ne* 10)

112 The "for intérieur" from which these voices emanate evolves in a sort of anarchy but maintains relations with an external society that invests it, towards which one delegates "emissaries," "representatives" as different and interchangeable as the "faces" that every individual shows the society that surrounds her [...]. Over the years, Nathalie Sarraute has often alluded to the "inside-out glove." The metaphor applies perfectly to this "novel." All the

English Translations to Pages 138–41

voices of the world of her writings find their place here; but situated in the interior of the *terrain* of this fragmented ego. (Brée 42)

113   For this becoming, it is not enough to accede to the immediate needs or desires of a woman, nor simply to grant her help in obtaining the object she wishes for, even an intellectual object. [. . .] *It is mediations and means of distanciation that women need above all.* The immediate is their traditional task—associated with a purely abstract duty—but it resubmits them to the spiritual authority of men. Thus to grant to a woman that which she wants without teaching her the detour of mediation amounts to acting as patriarch, at fault with respect to her. (Irigaray, *I Love* 5; emphasis added)

114   "They truly love themselves? [. . .] But how do they do it then?"
"It's very simple. They feel that all the elements of which they are composed are indissolubly joined, all without distinction . . . the lovely and the ugly, the bad and the good, and this compact ensemble that they call 'I' or 'me' possesses the faculty of dividing itself into two, of looking at itself from the outside, and that which it sees, that 'I,' it loves.
"Exactly the way it happens to us when we look at others, those who are not us—and we love them . . . They love *themselves* as well." (Sarraute, *Tu ne* 14)

115   looks of love, of admiration . . . they saw themselves reflected in the eyes of others . . . and that image . . . (Sarraute, *Tu ne* 15)

116   "And us? Have there not been moments when we too . . ."
"Brief moments, rather of astonishment . . . Is that me, really? . . . But there came very quickly another and still another reflection . . . And then our looks, occupied elsewhere, hardly stopped to contemplate . . ." (Sarraute, *Tu ne* 20–21)

117   "Yes, but our hand too, when you think about it . . ."
"But precisely, we don't think about it." [. . .]
"[. . .] And yet in us as well two cigarettes . . . and even one sometimes . . . It must be a more frequent effect than one thinks . . ." [It's a question of the hand-man's comments about cigarettes and his digestive system.]
"But nothing like that slipped into us at that moment. [. . .]"
"And yet does it not seem that even at that moment, a brief memory . . . "
"Quickly pushed back . . . not worth the attention [. . .]"
"That recalls that we were not alone in looking at him, listening to him. Some persons were seated like us at that table . . . they were also contemplating him in silence . . ."

English Translations to Pages 142–44

"But then . . . those people, so attentive and silent, would they not be like us? Would they too, like us? . . ."
"Cease to exist in his presence?"
"They would not love themselves? We wouldn't be an exception?" (Sarraute, *Tu ne* 21–24)

118 "[. . .] I wanted to find that sensation one has when one lives in Happiness . . . I had it already . . . but your continual interruptions . . ."
"We were only trying to help . . ."
"Now I have to start all over . . . Where was I?" (Sarraute, *Tu ne* 63)

119 But remember . . . there are some even among us . . . [. . .] You recognize that you reached out towards Happiness . . . and with what nostalgia . . . you went there . . . (Sarraute, *Tu ne* 52)

120 "We were dragged . . . you know how easily influenced, how gullible we are . . . Well, all those advertisements, that continuous propaganda, those illustrious models on exhibit, that advice, those encouragements, those narratives about those who find themselves there . . . one couldn't resist . . . Anyway, you who are so strong, you who don't let yourself be taken in, you followed us . . ."
"Say rather that you pulled us along with you, aided by those from without, our near and dear, our relations, our friends . . . they wrapped us up in what was flowing from their looks, from their words . . ." (Sarraute, *Tu ne* 52)

121 the sky, of course, was blue, and the air seemed to be gently vibrating . . . and at that moment, it came . . . something unique . . . which will never again come back in that way [. . .] but what? what word can get hold of it? not the all-encompassing word "happiness," which is the first to come to mind, no, not that . . . (Sarraute, *Childhood* 56–57; translation modified)

122 It's already an advantage not to be obligated to plaster that name of Happiness onto every sensation still intact, living . . . to crush it . . . (Sarraute, *Tu ne* 64)

123 "And not to see spilled everywhere that glossy varnish, shining, gaudy . . . without a blemish, without a crack . . ."
"And that exhausting vigilance, that continual surveillance. A police regime. The least deviation, the least suspicion of freedom that might put Happiness in danger, and one is called back to order . . . brought back into Happiness bound hand and foot . . ." (Sarraute, *Tu ne* 65)

124 [W]e rushed out, we mounted the assault . . . "What Happiness? That's not happiness!" "Not Happiness?" We were seized,

191

English Translations to Pages 145–54

interrogated . . . "It is not a happiness to have children? Did yours by any chance not give you any?" (Sarraute, *Tu ne* 67)

125 "When something . . . how to evoke it? . . ."
"Was it a color, a line, a barely perceptible nuance, an intonation, a silence . . . but it does not let itself . . ."
"It never let itself be captured by any word . . ." [. . .]
"Wasn't it Cézanne who said about something else . . ."
"But was it really something else about which he said that 'it is entangled at the very roots of being . . . At the impalpable of feeling'?"
"Feeling, for its part, is over there where words circulate, alight, designate . . ."

"It was fun from time to time to make an excursion there . . ." (Sarraute, *Tu ne* 123)

126 Isn't he like the child who abruptly, in the middle of the game, leaves his friends, runs toward his mother, receives a kiss and returns reassured, fortified . . . (Sarraute, *Tu ne* 131)

127 "[A]mong us, we don't use those 'me's, those 'I's . . ."
"[. . .] [W]e saw ourselves, with more clearness than ever, disintegrated into a multitude of disparate 'I's . . . whom could one love in all that? [. . .]"
"And then those 'I's, those 'you's were erased . . ."
"[. . .] of themselves diluted into formless masses, into 'us'es, 'you all's . . . made up of numerous similar elements . . ." (Sarraute, *Tu ne* 86–87)

128 "there are two men in me, I am sometimes the one and sometimes the other, not both at once," [to which the narrator replies,] "two contradictory beings . . . [. . .] That's very few . . ." (Sarraute, *Tu ne* 17)

129 "How do they manage to feel so clear, so simple?"
"They must train for it very early . . ." [. . .]
"Once they've gotten this habit of feeling themselves the way they are seen, they keep it forever . . . at every stage of their life, they feel themselves to be women, men . . ."
"And nothing but that. 'Real' women, 'real' men . . . [. . .]"
"If they stopped feeling 'real,' how would they be? One would be perhaps very surprised . . ."
"There are many who feel like a mixture of man and woman . . . but always the most simple of mixtures . . ." (Sarraute, *Tu ne* 30–31)

130 "You rose up before them, chest thrown out, one hand over your breast . . . 'With me, it's pathological . . .'"

English Translations to Pages 154–56

"Nothing of the sort, you're making it up, we were turned in on ourselves, we said it as if we were talking to ourselves . . ." (Sarraute, *Tu ne* 207–08)

131 But even before they could make a move, you escaped [from one of their "cells" within which you were about to shut yourselves], running toward them, [. . .] Wait a second, don't close me in . . . not completely . . . I have split myself in two . . . an operation that you recommend, [. . .] I know how to look at myself from the outside, I can see myself, know myself . . . Know yourself, right? you prescribe that . . . I'm capable of it, you see, I come and place myself beside you, at the same distance you are at, and from there I look at myself with the same impartiality, the same pitiless clairvoyance . . . I have learned how to assimilate your teachings, I have retained your classifications, I am applying your regulations, [. . .] let's look together at what is there in me . . . ah yes, it's sad to say, but one cannot designate it otherwise: it's "pathological." (Sarraute, *Tu ne* 208–09)

132 "We didn't understand anything about it, we didn't seek to understand . . ."
"It was one of those strange phenomena about which one says that one couldn't believe one's eyes, nothing one knows would allow one to explain it . . ." (Sarraute, *Tu ne* 212)

133 "But now, after all that we have seen, can we not ask ourselves if what we made them feel when we rose up before them . . ."
"One sole block, locked, closed in on itself." [. . .]
"It unfurled over them, indifferent to their presence."
"It came who knows how and then who knows how it passed . . ."
"A blind force . . ."
"A hurricane that made them bend down . . ."
"Were they not a bit afraid?"
"Afraid?"
"Yes, why not? It's not impossible, it was so abrupt, so violent . . . they could have felt at first a slight, fleeting fright . . ." (Sarraute, *Tu ne* 212–13)

134 Our involuntary "sortie" had not provoked in them what one would have expected, not the slightest retort, or hint of a rebuff. And even . . . (Sarraute, *Tu ne* 212)

135 "so much firmness, strength, assurance, princely unconstraint, perfect liberty . . ." "fortified them . . ." "reassured them . . ." "raised them up . . ." "They felt themselves traversed by a beneficent wave . . ." (Sarraute, *Tu ne* 213)

136 If we listen to it now, that "You don't love yourself" that so surprised us, quite a long time ago now, we hear in it above all a reproach, a blame not only for the wrong we are doing to ourselves, but for what we make *them* undergo. (Sarraute, *Tu ne* 215)

137 it's so good, beneficent [...] They felt themselves traversed by a beneficent wave [...] [T]he one among all who is most gifted at loving oneself. (Sarraute, *Tu ne* 131, 213, 214)

138 The culture of this universal does not yet exist. The individual has been considered particular without sufficient interpretation of that universal which is in him or her: woman or man. (Irigaray, *I Love* 48)

139 Language itself remains generally at the level of needs, including the need to master nature, objects, others, notably by naming them [...] not only in the form of transfers of information, but of intersubjective exchanges. (Irigaray, *I Love* 43–44, 45)

140 It would be a question [...] of finding a new economy of existence and of being which is not that of mastery nor of slavery, but rather of *exchange without a constituted object, a vital, cultural exchange, of words, of gestures,* etc. (Irigaray, *I Love* 45)

141 Thus, between the hierarchical transmission of a language and a tongue, of an order and a law that would be there already, and the current exchange of a meaning between us, there is a difference of subjective economy. The first model of transmission of teaching is more parental, more genealogical, more hierarchical; the second is more horizontal and intersubjective. The first model risks being enslaved to the past, the second maintains a present for the construction of a future. (Irigaray, *I Love* 45–46)

142 "it would be good for everyone . . ." "If we could . . ." "We wouldn't ask for better . . ." "We wouldn't ask for better?" "No better? Really?" (Sarraute, *Tu ne* 215)

Conclusion: The Psyche of Feminism

143 I recognize that you are, that you exist, that you are becoming. In this recognition, I mark you, and I mark myself, with incompletion [...] Neither you nor I are the whole, nor the same, the principle of totalization. (Irigaray, *I Love* 105)

144 To remain at the level of affect in relations among women also risks robbing them of their liberty by means of a bait which exiles them from a return to themselves and removes them from the construction of a specific will and history. To endow women with their own conscience in private and public life, and with mediations that

English Translations to Page 170

permit them to exercise that conscience, often shows more esteem with respect to them than a sensible, immediate love in more than one way ensnaring, alienating, and utopian, in view of the lack of a culture of sexual difference. There is no need to hold out to women's hearts the prospect of some new evening promised to relations limited to the interior of their kind/gender! [...] Is not homo-sexuality that which has structured [the laws that govern patriarchal culture], consciously or not, for centuries? A parallel organization of the same type hardly questions these laws compared to what an alteration of the principles of their economy might do. (Irigaray, *I Love* 5)

Notes

Preface

1. Cf. Felman, *Literature and Psychoanalysis* 105.
2. Rochefort 183. She continues with an anecdote:

> I got some free analysis after my first book [*Le repos du guerrier*] was published. One journalist wrote that I probably was ugly and frustrated—till, meeting him at a cocktail party, I patted him on the shoulder saying: "Ho, sir, I'm the ugly, frustrated one." He ran away while the others laughed. He himself was a piece of fat.

Had her writing provided this reader with more or less unconscious insights into his own, sexed, position as a male reader and critic? And does Rochefort's sneering reaction tell us anything more about her—frustrated?—observation that her books are considered "a woman's" books?

3. Also cited in Holmes 27, 44. For the reader's convenience, I have provided page references to published English translations where possible. However, in most cases the translations themselves are my own, as I have preferred to give as literal a rendering as possible of the French. When I have used someone else's translation, I make note of this in the reference.

Introduction
Psychoanalytic Feminism: Sexual Difference and Another Love

1. Throughout this book, ellipses in citations will be placed in brackets unless they appear in the cited text. I have adopted this convention for the purpose of clarity, since many of the writers I will cite make extensive use of ellipses.

2. We can note, by way of example, that Irigaray has a stake in beginning *Speculum, de l'autre femme* with and from psychoanalysis: in this way, with the curved, sexed mirror of her "Speculum" (the book's middle section), she reads the history of philosophy as a history now inflected/reflected (and hence, transformed) by a specifically feminist psychoanalytic interrogation of sex(uality).

3. For a recent re-reading of Simone de Beauvoir's work, see Toril Moi's *Simone de Beauvoir: The Making of an Intellectual Woman*. And for a reading of de Beauvoir as anticipating a feminist psychoanalysis, see chapter 13 ("The Female Body and the Male Mind: Reconsidering Simone de Beauvoir") of Elaine Hoffman Baruch's *Women, Power, and Love*. Baruch claims that, although de Beauvoir rejected the centrality of the unconscious and herself spoke out against psychoanalysis, some

aspects of her thinking nevertheless find echoes in later feminist engagements with psychoanalysis (notably, the phallus/penis distinction, the importance of the pre-Oedipal, and the understanding of female sexual organs as their own referent, not as versions of masculine organs).

4. See Elizabeth Wright's introduction to her *Feminism and Psychoanalysis: A Critical Dictionary,* especially pp. xiv–xix.

5. For other examples of feminist refusals of psychoanalysis, see de Beauvoir's *Le deuxième sexe,* Millett's *Sexual Politics,* Friedan's *The Feminine Mystique,* and Nina Baym's "The Madwoman and Her Languages: Why I Don't Do Feminist Theory."

6. To name the most important examples where femininity was at issue, there is the series of works published by Freud and others ("the great debate") from the early 1920s into the 1930s. These include, by Freud, three papers that deal specifically with female sexuality: his 1925 "Some Psychical Consequences of the Anatomical Distinction between the Sexes," his 1931 "Female Sexuality," and the 1933 "Femininity"; and by others: Karl Abraham's 1922 "Manifestations of the Female Castration Complex"; Karen Horney's 1926 "The Flight from Womanhood"; Ernest Jones's 1927 "The Early Development of Female Sexuality"; Jean Lampl-de Groot's 1928 "The Evolution of the Oedipus Complex in Women"; Melanie Klein's 1928 "Early Stages of the Oedipus Complex"; Helene Deutsch's 1930 "The Significance of Masochism in the Mental Life of Women"; and Marie Bonaparte's 1935 "Passivity, Masochism, and Femininity."

7. See Freud, "Analysis Terminable and Interminable" (*SE* 23: 226n2).

8. Brennan sums up the "real riddle of femininity" for Freud thus:

> Why does femininity appear to afflict more women than men, yet why does it affect men at all? For that matter, why does it affect some women more than others, and why does its impact on both sexes vary and fluctuate? (216)

Such an understanding of the riddle hinges on Brennan's assertion that there is indeed a psychical condition (not necessarily equivalent to female development or neurosis) called femininity. "It does [exist], and inhibits both sexes" (216).

9. Thus for Irigaray, the question of sexual difference is an ontological question and an ethical one (see *EDS*). While I do not address Irigaray's relation to Heidegger here, it is necessary to note that, in her work on sexual difference, Irigaray is not only aware of Jean-Luc Nancy and Philippe Lacoue-Labarthe's critique of Lacan (*Le titre de la lettre*), but will also directly take up Heidegger. See Irigaray, *L'oubli de l'air chez Martin Heidegger.*

10. On Irigaray's refusal of egalitarianism, see Jean-Joseph Goux, "Irigaray Versus the Utopia of the Neutral Sex," especially pp. 180–86.

11. For a concise reading of Irigaray's account of the feminine as a constitutive exclusion, see Judith Butler, "Bodies That Matter" 141–73, especially the section entitled "Irigaray/Plato."

12. While Joan Copjec, in her essay "Sex and the Euthanasia of Reason" speaks against a general feminist hostility to Lacan, a hostility that often sees itself as following or drawing on an Irigarayan critique, Irigaray's name itself is conspicuously absent from Copjec's text. In fact, I will suggest that Copjec's analysis of sexual difference in Lacan heads in an Irigarayan direction—a direction that can be called the attempt to think toward an ethics of sexual difference.

13. Lacan, *XX* 61–71. Although I've provided the translations from this seminar used here, Bruce Fink's translation has recently been published, so that English-language readers now have access to a reliable, and thoroughly annotated, edition.

14. See "La signification du phallus" in Lacan, *Ecrits* 685–95, or "The Signification of the Phallus" in *Ecrits, a Selection* 281–91. Hereafter cited with French pagination first, followed by English.

15. See Moi, *Sexual/Textual Politics: Feminist Literary Theory* 139.

16. See for example Juliet Mitchell and Jacqueline Rose (*Feminine Sexuality: Jacques Lacan and the Ecole Freudienne*), Lisa Jardine ("The Politics of Impenetrability"), and Moi, the last of whom provides an oft-cited misreading of Irigaray (as essentialist) in her *Sexual/Textual Politics*. (For Irigaray's commentary on misreadings of her work, see the interview with her entitled "Je—Luce Irigaray" in *Hypatia*.)

17. See chapter 2, "Cogito and the Sexual Difference," of Slavoj Žižek's *Tarrying with the Negative: Kant, Hegel, and the Critique of Ideology*.

18. For a reading of Lacan's work as ruling out any such possibility for feminist thought, see Nancy Fraser, "The Uses and Abuses of French Discourse Theory for Feminist Politics." Fraser claims that Lacan's thinking of gendered subjectivity is but "an ironclad determinism":

> Phallocentrism, woman's disadvantaged place in the symbolic order, the encoding of cultural authority as masculine, the impossibility of describing a nonphallic sexuality, in short, any number of trappings of male dominance now appear as invariable features of the human condition. Women's subordination, then, is inscribed as the inevitable destiny of civilization. (88–89)

For a similar argument, see also Dorothy Leland, "Lacanian Psychoanalysis and French Feminism: Toward an Adequate Political Psychology."

19. Cf. Lacan's comment in *Le séminaire de Jacques Lacan, Livre XI, "Les quatre concepts fondamentaux de la psychanalyse"* 130: "repérer le sujet par rapport à la réalité, telle qu'on la suppose nous constituant, et non par rapport au signifiant, revient à tomber déjà dans la dégradation de la constitution psychologique du sujet" ("to locate the subject in

relation to reality—such that we suppose reality as constituting us—and not in relation to the signifier, amounts to falling already into the degradation of the psychological constitution of the subject").

20. Similarly, Irigaray writes: "L'amour en devient tragédie perpétuelle [. . . et] le désir s'en trouve [. . .] finissant dans l'ennui et le report du bonheur à l'au-delà" ("Love thus becomes a perpetual tragedy [. . . and] desire [. . .] ends up in boredom and the putting off of happiness until the beyond"; *EDS* 70, *ESD* 67). Thus she remarks the seemingly eternal link between love and death as needing to be rethought, such that the beyond of the living other and of the self is what will be addressed in love.

21. See Boothby 216, and Lacan, *Le séminaire de Jacques Lacan, Livre II, "Le moi dans la théorie de Freud et dans la technique de la psychanalyse."*

Chapter One
George Sand and the Impossible Woman

1. See also Sand, *Correspondance* 8: 391–92, and 8: 400–08, for letters in which Sand explains that she has no part in certain contemporary women's groups' efforts to gain the right for women to vote and to participate in the parliament.

2. Naomi Schor, *George Sand and Idealism;* Isabelle Hoog Naginski, *George Sand: Writing for Her Life.* See also Nicole Mozet, *George Sand: Écrivain des romans,* in particular chapter 4: "De l'égalité: La théorie sandienne du féminisme (de *Mauprat* à la "candidature impossible" de 1848)."

3. Schor's *George Sand and Idealism* includes a brief subchapter entitled "Sand, Feminism, and the Ideology of Gender: *Lettres à Marcie,*" where she argues for the work's importance as a "major document" from the perspective of current debates around sexual difference.

4. See Sand, *Correspondance* 3: 710–14, for the letter from Sand to l'Abbé Lamennais in which she politely protests the cutting up of her work without her authorization; and also for an extract from Marie d'Agoult's letter to Franz Liszt in which d'Agoult discusses this affair. D'Agoult writes: "A cela [Sand's letter] il [Lamennais] a répondu une lettre assez froide. Il ne veut pas du divorce; il lui demande de ces fleurs qui tombe de sa main, autrement dit des contes et des piffoëlades. De plus, on n'a pas inséré sa quatrième lettre; elle est mécontente . . ." ("To that [Sand's letter] he [Lamennais] responded with a rather cold letter. He wants nothing of divorce; he asks her for those flowers that fall from her hand, in other words fairy-tales and piffle. What's more, he has not published her fourth letter; she is displeased . . ."; 714n1).

It would seem that in stopping the *Lettres à Marcie,* Sand was making good (after continuing through to the sixth letter) on a threat. She had written to Lamennais: "Si vous me défendez d'aller plus avant, je terminerai les *lettres à Marcie* où elles en sont, et je ferai toute autre chose que vous me commanderez, car je puis me taire sur bien des points et ne me crois pas appelée à rénover le monde" ("If you forbid me to go further, I will stop the *lettres à Marcie* where they are, and I will do any other thing that you command, for I can be quiet on many points and do not believe myself called to renew the world"; 714).

5. Especially "the impossible" as it is thought by today's feminists. Irigaray, for example, qualifies her view of the future, and of utopia, thus: "Je suis donc une militante politique de l'impossible, ce qui n'est pas dire utopiste. Je veux plutôt ce qui n'est pas encore comme la seule possibilité d'un futur" ("I am then a political militant for the impossible, which is not to say a utopian. I want rather that which is not yet as the only possibility for a future"; *J'aime* 26, *I Love* 9).

6. Saint-Simonism's founder, Claude Henri, comte de Saint-Simon, was succeeded after his death in 1825 by Prosper Enfantin, with whom the movement was largely associated. As Leslie Rabine has pointed out, however, Enfantin excluded women from the movement (in accordance with the absence of the "ideal" Woman who was yet to be found, or rather, given birth to, by the movement itself), and many of the Saint-Simoniennes spoke and wrote critically of their erstwhile male comrades' theories. The Saint-Simoniennes founded the journal *Apostolât des Femmes* in 1832 (which changed its name the following year to *La Tribune des Femmes*). See Leslie Rabine, "Essentialism and Its Contexts: Saint-Simonian and Post-Structuralist Feminists."

7. See Sand, *Correspondance* 8: 400–08. This committee had recently included Sand's name in a list of candidates it would endorse, a candidacy that Sand calls "impossible, chose à laquelle je n'ai jamais songé" ("impossible, a thing I have never considered"; 400).

8. The entire passage reads: "Les femmes doivent-elles participer un jour à la vie politique? Oui, un jour, je le crois avec vous, mais ce jour est-il proche? Non, je ne le crois pas, et pour que la condition des femmes soit ainsi transformée, il faut que la société soit transformée radicalement" ("Should women participate one day in political life? Yes, one day, I believe this with you, but is this day near? No, I think not, and for the condition of women to be thus transformed, society must be transformed radically"; Sand, *Correspondance* 8: 401).

9. "Quel bizarre caprice vous pousse aux luttes parlementaires, vous qui ne pouvez pas seulement y apporter l'exercice de votre indépendance personnelle? Quoi, votre mari siégera sur ce banc, votre amant peut-être sur cet autre, et vous prétendrez représenter quelque chose, quand vous n'êtes pas seulement la représentation de vous-mêmes?" ("What bizarre caprice pushes you to parliamentary struggles, you who cannot even bring there the exercise of your personal independence? What, your husband will sit on this bench, your lover perhaps on this other, and you will claim to represent something, when you are not even the representation of yourselves?"; Sand, *Correspondance* 8: 407).

Notes to Pages 45–75

10. *Apostolât des Femmes* 2: 6, qtd. in Rabine at 116; Rabine's translation.
11. Cf. Lacan (*Ecrits* 813/311) on the imposture of the Legislator, discussed in the Introduction, pp. 27–28.
12. In French "le nom du père" is at least two phrases in one, as it is pronounced: the name of the father, and the no of the father (to, ultimately, the child's union with the mother).
13. The edition I shall refer to throughout is: George Sand, *Lélia*, ed. Béatrice Didier, 2 vols. (Paris: Editions de l'Aurore, 1987). This edition, introduced and annotated by Didier, is based on Sand's 1839 revision of the original 1833 version. Didier provides notes for all the 1833 variants.
14. Cf., for example, Lacan's account of the masculine misrecognition of the woman, who then comes to represent the object of desire (the phallus) either as virgin or as prostitute ("Signification du Phallus" 695/290; qtd. and discussed in the Introduction, pp. 13–15).
15. For two such examples, see Eileen Boyd Sivert, "Lélia and Feminism," and Pierrette Daly, "George Sand's *Lélia:* From *Belle Ténébreuse* to Annunziata."
16. We can add that such a critical analysis of woman's place, or lack thereof, hardly needs to wait for the second wave of feminism. Closer to Sand's time, in 1792, or about forty years before Sand wrote *Lélia*, Mary Wollstonecraft points out much the same predicament, in moral rather than anthropological terms:

> If there be but one criterion of morals, but one architype [*sic*] for man, women appear to be suspended by destiny [. . .]; they have neither the unerring instinct of brutes, nor are allowed to fix the eye of reason on a perfect model. They were made to be loved, and must not aim at respect, lest they should be hunted out of society as masculine. (119)

17. On the question of idealism and realism with regard to Sand, see Schor, *George Sand and Idealism*.
18. See, apart from Irigaray and as only one of many examples, Monique Wittig's essay "On the Social Contract," in her collection *The Straight Mind*, in which she interrogates Aristotle's discussion of woman, master, and slave in book one of his *Politics*.
19. Most readings of *Lélia* agree that her ideal is at least in part a maternal ideal of love. See especially Schor and Naginski. And on the maternal ideal in Sand's autobiographical writing, see Berger.
20. The edition I refer to is *The Complete Works of Aristotle: The Revised Oxford Translation*, ed. Jonathan Barnes, vol. 2 (Princeton: Princeton UP, 1984). Quotations from Aristotle will be by line number.
21. See the interview with Irigaray in *Hypatia*, in which she elaborates on the subtitle of *Speculum*.

Notes to Pages 86–92

22. Perhaps this is one of the things at stake in calling the modern era the era of psychosis, as Brennan does, reading Lacan.

Chapter Two
What Does a Woman Enjoy? Colette's *Le pur et l'impur*

1. Marie Bonaparte was Freud's analysand in 1925, and was thereafter his friend until his death in 1939. See Forrester 138, and Ernst Freud, letters 221, 288, 290, 305, 309, 313.

2. Qtd. in Jones, *Life and Work* 2: 421.
According to Shoshana Felman, who also cites Jones for this quotation, Freud wrote this in a letter to Marie Bonaparte. Jones, however, writes that Freud once *said* this to Bonaparte, and there is no extant letter from Freud to Bonaparte that includes this phrase. It seems, then, that the source for one of Freud's most well-known utterances is Ernest Jones's memory of Marie Bonaparte's memory of Freud's oral communication, made at some point thirty years or more into his career, which is to say at the earliest during their 1925 analysis, and more likely around the time of the "great debate" in the late twenties and early thirties. See Felman, *What Does a Woman Want?* 2.

3. Cf. "Female Sexuality" (Freud, *SE* 21: 234).

4. See Brennan, *Interpretation*.

5. For example, in her *Tender Geographies: Women and the Origins of the Novel in France*, DeJean argues that in France, "the novel was a feminist creation." "Without exception," she adds, "the strains of prose fiction that today's readers would identify with the novel were the creation of women writers" (5). DeJean's book discusses the development of the novel in France in the seventeenth and eighteenth centuries, and is an important source for readers of both canonical and lesser-known writers of the period. Writing with a different argument in mind, Alain Badiou makes a similar point: "[The] coupling of love and the novel is essential, and it will further be remarked that women have not only excelled in this art, but provided its decisive impetus: Madame de La Fayette, Jane Austen, Virginia Woolf, Katherine Mansfield, among many others. And before all these, in an eleventh century unimaginable for western barbarians, Dame Murazaki Shikubu composed *The Story of Gengi*, the greatest text in which what is sayable about love in its masculine dimension is deployed" (Badiou 7).

6. I will be referring to the Gallimard edition, in volume 3 of Colette's *Œuvres*, throughout, although there is an extant English edition of *Le pur et l'impur* (trans. Herma Briffault with an introduction by Janet Flanner). As a literary translation, Briffault's version necessarily loses some of the literal nuances important for my purposes. I provide my own, inelegantly literal, translations here.

7. Cf. Dupont 1508.

203

Notes to Pages 93–114

8. See also Apollon.

9. However, for a brief but clear gloss on the difference and relation between the subject and the ego in Lacan, see Jacques-Alain Miller, "An Introduction to Seminars I and II," especially 22–24. Miller relates Lacan's early definition of the ego to Sartre's in *The Transcendence of the Ego*, in that like Sartre, Lacan understands the ego as an object. The process of analysis thus turns on a constant back and forth between the inertia of the ego and the mobility of the subject.

10. The character "Charlotte" is the figure Colette deems best suited to occupy the opening of this book on pleasure: "La figure voilée d'une femme fine, désabusée, savante en tromperie, en délicatesse, convient au seuil de ce livre qui tristement parlera du plaisir" ("The veiled face of a refined, disabused woman, skillful in deception and delicacy, belongs at the threshold of this book, which will speak sadly of pleasure"; *PI* 566).

11. Colette also referred to *La maison de Claudine* as *La maison de "Sido."* See *Œuvres* 2: 1621.

12. Huffer's chapter on *Le pur et l'impur* is the most sophisticated and attentive reading of this work currently available. Other critical treatments include: Elaine Harris, especially 2–76; Sherry Dranch; Elaine Marks, *Colette;* Michel Tournier, "Colette ou le premier couvert" 239–51; Ann Cothran, "*The Pure and the Impure*: Codes and Constructs"; Ann Cothran and Diane Griffin Crowder; and Maryann De Julio.

13. For studies that address this association, see Huffer; Marks, *Colette,* especially 219; and Nancy K. Miller's discussion of Colette's narrative "I" in regard to the Sido-Colette relation, in N. Miller, "Anamnesis" 164–75.

14. Jerry Aline Flieger comments, "In Lacanian terms, one could say that Colette's identity as a writer, in spite of detours and transformations, is by way of the Name of the Father" (71).

15. See Colette, *La naissance du jour,* for the most prominent example, and also *La maison de Claudine* and *Sido.* Marks notes that both Sido and Colette "have an unusual gift of observation and a very keen sensitivity to flowers, animals and weather" (*Colette* 212).

16. For an apt contemporary representation of this phenomenon, one could point to the character Annie in Steven Soderberg's 1990 film *Sex, Lies, and Videotape*. Annie is in therapy, and in a loveless marriage with an unfaithful husband of whose infidelity (with her sister) she is ignorant. At one point, just before she discovers the evidence of his cheating (an earring), we are shown her fanatically cleaning house, fairly ripping off the chrome from sink fixtures, polishing a flawlessly clean table with tremendous energy, etc. In Soderberg's film, ironically, it is precisely her manic cleaning (she finds the tell-tale earring while vacuuming under the bed) that leads to a real confrontation with her husband, and hence with her own willful blindness.

17. I have in mind Irigaray's essay "Ethique de la différence sexuelle" in *EDS* 113–24, *ESD* 116–29.

18. See Dupont 1506. The book, under the title *Ces plaisirs* . . . , was first published serially in the weekly *La Gringoire* in 1931.
19. See Freud, "Femininity," *SE* 22: 112–35.
20. In Cixous, "Le rire de la Méduse" 42, "The Laugh of the Medusa" (in Marks and de Courtivron) 249. (The other two writers named are Marguerite Duras and Jean Genet.)

Chapter Three
Nathalie Sarraute: After the Feminine Subject

1. This is the title of the first essay in the middle section ("Speculum") of Irigaray's *Speculum* ("Toute théorie du 'sujet' aura toujours été appropriée au 'masculin,'" "Any Theory of the 'Subject' Has Always Been Appropriated by the 'Masculine'").
2. As mentioned in the previous chapter, in that essay, Cixous names Colette, Marguerite Duras, and Jean Genet as the only French writers of the twentieth century in whose work one can find "inscriptions of femininity" ("Le rire" 42, "Laugh" 249).
3. Also cited in Schor, *Bad Objects* 128.
4. In her most recent book, *Entre Orient et Occident*, Irigaray, for example, has attempted "to say how it is that the practice of respiration, of breaths, is not neutral, and how woman and man breathe and use their breath in specific ways: the one (she) keeping it more inside, especially for the purpose of parturition, the other using it almost exclusively to make, to construct outside of the self" ("j'ai tenté de dire en quoi la pratique de la respiration, des souffles, n'est pas neutre, et comment femme et homme respirent et utilisent leur souffle de manière spécifique: le gardant davantage en soi, notamment à fin de partage, pour l'une, l'employant presque exclusivement à faire, à construire à l'extérieur de soi, pour l'autre"; 21).
5. Irigaray and other feminist thinkers have much to say on the subject of touch as opposed to vision or the line of sight in relation to mastery. I merely wish to signal here that touch, for all the blurring it effects of limits that may look clear-cut to the eye, is of course an ambiguous sense. If one can caress with one's eyes, one can also wound with a mere touch. And further, the gentle caress of a touch may not (ever?) be devoid of an element of mastery: does not even the nurturing mother necessarily manipulate her infant even as she soothes it? Indeed, if she does not "master" her child in some fashion, will she not be failing her or him?
6. Scott is referring generally to feminist appeals to the experience of women, and specifically to historian Christine Stansell's "insistence that 'social practices' in all their 'immediacy and entirety' constitute a domain of 'sensuous experience' (a prediscursive reality directly felt, seen, and known"; 31). See, Stansell. As another example of the appeal to women's experience in feminist scholarship, also referred to by Scott, see Hawkesworth.

Notes to Pages 131–35

7. Indeed, in the first essay of *Bad Objects,* Schor cites Scott on just this point, discussing the problem of the universal. Schor writes,

> For, as Joan Scott notes [. . .], what is significant is not that particularity is puffed up into universality or even that universality depletes particularity; it is that what appears as a prior cause (i.e., particularity) is in fact a subsequent effect. (9)

And in her preface, Schor literally states that it is discourse, or the story, that makes experience: "My 'story,' which *makes my experience* both unique and typical [. . .]," she writes, indicating by her syntax, at least, the made, not the immediate, nature of experience (ix; emphasis added).

8. Scott concludes the above-cited passage, "Indeed, the possibility of politics is said to rest on, to follow from, a pre-existing women's experience" (31).

9. This is a fact whose importance has asserted itself more clearly within feminist thinking during the 1990s, in works by such scholars as Scott, Butler, and others. Perhaps it could not be so asserted earlier because of the widespread anxiety about undermining the validity of egalitarian feminism's subject: woman, and women, who are the ones *having* all the *experiences* that *authenticate* their claims against oppression and to *equality.* It seems that only once these basic assumptions (expressed in the keywords *having* [transitively], *experience, authentic,* and *equality*) have been both questioned and found inadequate, is feminism able to start thinking without their grounding. Only when equality is no longer prescribed or exalted, in other words, can one begin to imagine an ethics without its reigning guarantee.

10. *For intérieur* means conscience, or consciousness, and it is a term that lends itself to Sarraute's employment of multiple voices, since *for* comes from the Latin *forum.* As Brée notes, "'For,' according to the Littré, as everyone knows, is an allusion to the Roman 'forum,' a public tribunal; the 'for intérieur' is thus an intimate tribunal, but like the other one, endowed with several voices" (38).

11. Qtd. in Bell 16. Bell cites "a corrected version [of a discussion at the 1971 Cerisy colloquium on the new novel] supplied to me by Sarraute" as her source. See also Ricardou and van Rossum-Guyon.

12. Hewitt adds, "Because she strives to undermine notions of uniqueness, fixed identity, and unequivocal truth, the specificity of gender constitutes for Sarraute another firm categorization that the tropism unravels. Her wariness of the notion of feminine writing goes in tandem with her desire to avoid making women writers marginal, and her interest in the tropism transcends the content of gendered experience" (64).

Hewitt joins Schor in the interpretation of Sarraute's style as "veer[ing] away from androcentric conceptions of human representation. The privileged status of the unitary voice, of unique identity, is undermined" (67).

13. With respect to feminism, one could imagine the phrase "You don't love yourself" in a consciousness-raising context. It would represent, for example, the moment when a woman realizes that she has internalized masculinist thinking to such an extent that she fails to value herself "as a woman." In this sense, Sarraute's book could be read as a response to a certain strain within feminism that concerns itself with the affirmation and celebration of woman-ness and female selfhood. To the challenge, or revelation, "You don't love yourself," Sarraute responds with another challenge: *Who* doesn't love *whom?* What version of the subject are you presupposing, or even enforcing, in your rush to affirm what you are?

14. See Irigaray, *J'aime*.

15. Which brings to mind Irigaray's remark, à propos of any particular subject's inscription in a genealogy that transcends her or him: "En ce sens, il n'y a pas de subjectivité immédiate. Ce concept, cette notion ou cette expression sont erronées" ("In this sense, there is no immediate subjectivity. That concept, or that notion or expression, is erroneous"; *J'aime* 92, *I Love* 52).

16. Hewitt's reading of Sarraute's tropisms tends to continue this train of thought in gendered terms, focusing on the differing childhoods of boys and girls. She speculates that Sarraute's writing might be an example of Nancy Chodorow's theories of gendered psychological development. She writes, "Although Sarraute's tropisms are resistant to modern gender theory at the level of individual characters, they do seem to respond to the insights of feminist psychoanalytic theory at the level of textual creation and reception, that is, the way the text stresses relational configurations, rather than individualized identity. The theories of Nancy Chodorow on the dissymmetries between girls' and boys' early development and Judith Kegan Gardiner's use of those theories [. . .] stress that masculine identity is based on successful separation and individuation from the mother: to be a male is not to be a female like the mother; the boy's sense of self is rooted in the need for autonomy and independence. Women's identity, on the other hand, is traced more along relational lines. A girl's [. . .] ego boundaries tend to be more permeable, emphasizing contact and fusion with the other rather than differences. [. . .] In writing, this translates as a breakdown in traditional generic boundaries (autobiographies are novelistic, novels are autobiographical)" (Hewitt 68–69). I take such theories of development to be fundamentally flawed in that, in brief, they equate experience and subjectivity without interrogating the grounds of the former, which is then itself understood as the (causal) condition of possibility for the latter.

17. Wittig provides the exact reference in her own article: *Le mariage de Figaro*, from act V, scene 3: "Quel est ce moi dont je m'occupe, un assemblage informe de parties inconnues" ("What is this I with which I concern myself, an unformed assemblage of unknown parts"; Wittig, "Avatars" 109 and 116n2).

18. Also qtd. in Schor, *Bad Objects* 128.

19. Or again, such readings can lead the reader into hasty psychoanalytic generalities about the author herself. Ramsay strays into this realm in writing about Sarraute's resistance to being read as a woman writer and of her keeping gender difference at bay in her work, speculating that such refusals "may conceal anxieties of influence and self-image" (*The French New Autobiographies* 137), thereby overlooking the vital point Sarraute is pursuing about the very possibility of something like a self-image.

20. In the very technical sense that one could imagine, the author might not say no to the suggestion that the tropistic realities of the book have some kind of origin within her. Although one suspects that Sarraute herself would disagree even with this possibility. In 1994, speaking with Ramsay and reacting to her study of this book as a "new autobiography," Sarraute "insisted that *Tu ne t'aimes pas* was in no way autobiographical, that just as there was no relationship between Picasso's art and his life, there was no necessary connection between her life and her writing" (Ramsay, *The French New Autobiographies* 227n1).

21. Cf. Babcock 70, where he quotes Sarraute debating whether or not there is a "pre-language."

22. Also qtd. in Schor, *Bad Objects* 128.

23. Also qtd. in Hewitt 62.

Incidentally, I would suggest that this is the sexual difference that Woolf is talking about, too, when she notes that it is fatal for anyone writing to think about their sex, their "female" or "male" "condition." This is not the same thing as thinking about sexual difference in Irigaray's sense.

24. Especially in Derrida's *Spurs: Nietzsche's Styles* (*Epérons: Les styles de Nietzsche*).

25. This act of emerging and making a statement could be the same one that begins the book, described on the first page as an episode when "[tu] t'es montré à eux, toi qui t'es proposé" ("you showed yourself to them, you who proposed yourself to them"), a "performance" that makes others of us feel ill at ease. The main difference, at the end of the book, is that there is none of the regret or chagrin that accompanies the scene at the beginning ("Vous auriez dû me retenir . . ." ["You should have restrained me . . ."]), nor is there any longer a resistance to seeing that, in fact, we presented to them a form "d'une simplicité toute classique" ("of a classic simplicity"), a simplicity that becomes, in the final episode, that of a "bloc serré" ("tight block"), which, when we return from the sortie to ourselves, produces "aucun regret, aucun reproche" ("no regret, no reproach"; Sarraute, *Tu ne* 9–11; 212). By this point, it seems the subject has accepted the inevitability of what happens when it presents itself to others, and has recognized that even in this self-gathering, there is still a fundamental incompletion and openness that are a function of our relation to others. Thus, that which has prompted the book also concludes it, but transformed.

Notes to Pages 163–72

Conclusion: The Psyche of Feminism

1. See, for example, the exchanges in two issues of *Critical Inquiry:* Susan Gubar's "What Ails Feminist Criticism?"; Robyn Wiegman's "What Ails Feminist Criticism? A Second Opinion"; Susan Gubar's response, "Notations *in Medias Res*"; and two letters-to-the-editor, one by Carolyn Heilbrun and the other by Sandra M. Gilbert. Wiegman describes the current state of feminism in academe as a "tension . . . between one generation's critique of patriarchal masculinism and another's interest in a self-reflexive articulation of differences among women" (363). Heilbrun, saddened and angered by what she calls Wiegman's tone of rudeness, complains, "[T]he younger female generations fight the pioneers of feminism, while the men in power (and in most universities, trust me, they are still in power) watch us destroy each other" (399).

2. See especially pp. 137–39 and 158–59, above.

3. See Irigaray's essay "Ethique de la différence sexuelle" in *EDS* 113–24, *ESD* 116–29.

4. To take one example, in addition to the one briefly sketched out above concerning the thought of listening in *J'aime à toi*, Irigaray suggests that her notion of the incompletion of the subject (as, always, a gendered subject, never the whole of the subject) "est susceptible de servir de lieu d'interprétation de l'Œdipe de Freud. Nous n'avons pas à choisir, comme il se dit, entre l'interdit de l'inceste et la psychose. Il nous suffit de devenir notre genre pour sortir d'une relation indifférenciée avec la mère—si tant est que cette forme de relation ne soit pas déjà une fable masculine" ("is a possible site for an interpretation of Freud's Œdipus. We do not have to choose, as is claimed, between the prohibition of incest and psychosis. It is sufficient that we become our gender in order to exit from an undifferentiated relation with the mother—if in fact this form of relation is not already a male fable"; *J'aime* 167, *I Love* 106).

Bibliography

Abraham, Karl. "Manifestations of the Female Castration Complex." *International Journal of Psycho-Analysis* 3 (1922): 1–29.

Angelfors, Christina. *La double conscience: La prise de conscience féminine chez Colette, Simone de Beauvoir, et Marie Cardinal.* Lund, Sweden: Lund UP, 1989.

Apollon, Willy. "Nothing Works Anymore!" Trans. Tracy McNulty. *differences* 9.1 (Spring 1997): 1–13.

Aristotle. *Politics. The Complete Works of Aristotle: The Revised Oxford Translation.* Vol. 2. Ed. Jonathan Barnes. Princeton: Princeton UP, 1984.

Asso, Françoise. *Nathalie Sarraute: Une écriture de l'effraction.* Paris: PUF, 1995.

Babcock, Arthur E. *The New Novel in France: Theory and Practice of the Nouveau Roman.* New York: Twayne, 1997.

Badiou, Alain. "What Is Love?" *UMBR(a)* no. 1 (1996): 7–21.

Balint, Enid. *Before I Was I: Psychoanalysis and the Imagination.* Ed. Juliet Mitchell and Michael Parsons. New York and London: Guilford, 1993.

Barbour, Sarah. *Nathalie Sarraute and the Feminist Reader: Identities in Process.* Lewisburg, PA: Bucknell UP, 1993.

Barr, Marleen S., and Richard Feldstein, eds. *Discontented Discourses: Feminism/Textual Intervention/Psychoanalysis.* Urbana and Chicago: U of Illinois P, 1989.

Bartky, Sandra. *Femininity and Domination.* New York: Routledge, 1990.

Baruch, Elaine Hoffman. *Women, Love, and Power: Literary and Psychoanalytic Perspectives.* New York and London: New York UP, 1991.

Baruch, Elaine Hoffman, and Lucienne J. Serrano, eds. *Women Analyze Women: In France, England, and the United States.* New York: Harvester Wheatsheaf, 1988.

Baym, Nina. "The Madwoman and Her Languages: Why I Don't Do Feminist Theory." *Tulsa Studies in Women's Literature* 3 (1984): 153–57.

Beauvoir, Simone de. *Le deuxième sexe.* 2 vols. (1: *Les faits et les mythes;* 2: *L'expérience vécue.*) Paris: Gallimard, 1949. Trans. H. M. Parshley as *The Second Sex.* New York: Knopf, 1952.

Bell, Sheila M. *Nathalie Sarraute: "Portrait d'un inconnu" and "Vous les entendez?"* London: Grant, 1988.

Bibliography

Benjamin, Jessica. *The Bonds of Love: Psychoanalysis, Feminism, and the Problem of Domination.* New York: Pantheon, 1988.

Benmussa, Simone. *Nathalie Sarraute.* Qui êtes-vous? Ser. 21. Lyon: La Manufacture, 1987.

Berger, Anne. "Let's Go to the Fountain: On George Sand and Writing." Sellers 54–65.

Bernheimer, Charles, and Claire Kahane, eds. *In Dora's Case: Freud-Hysteria-Feminism.* New York: Columbia UP, 1985.

Berthu-Courtivron, Marie-Françoise. *Espace, demeure, écriture: La maison natale dans l'œuvre de Colette.* Paris: Nizet, 1992.

———. *Mère et fille: L'enjeu du pouvoir: Essai sur les écrits autobiographiques de Colette.* Genève: Droz, 1993.

Blanchot, Maurice. *L'attente l'oubli.* Paris: Gallimard, 1962.

———. *L'écriture du désastre.* Paris: Gallimard, 1980.

———. *L'espace littéraire.* Paris: Gallimard, 1955.

———. *Le pas au-delà.* Paris: Gallimard, 1973.

Bonaparte, Marie. *Female Sexuality.* London: Imago, 1951.

———. "Passivity, Masochism, and Femininity." *International Journal of Psycho-Analysis* 16 (1935): 325–33.

Boncenne, Pierre. "Nathalie Sarraute." Interview in *Lire* (June 1983): 87–92.

Boothby, Richard. *Death and Desire: Psychoanalytic Theory in Lacan's Return to Freud.* New York and London: Routledge, 1991.

Borch-Jacobsen, Mikkel. *The Freudian Subject.* Trans. Catherine Porter. Stanford, CA: Stanford UP, 1988.

Boustani, Carmen. *L'écriture-corps chez Colette.* Villenave-D'Ornon: Fus-Art, 1993.

Brée, Germaine. "Le 'for intérieur' et la traversée du siècle." *Esprit Créateur* 36.2 (Summer 1996): 37–43.

Brennan, Teresa, ed. *Between Feminism and Psychoanalysis.* London and New York: Routledge, 1989.

———. *History after Lacan.* London: Routledge, 1993.

———. *The Interpretation of the Flesh: Freud and Femininity.* London and New York: Routledge, 1992.

Brown, Terry. "Feminism and Psychoanalysis, a Family Affair?" Barr and Feldstein 29–40.

Burke, Carolyn. "Irigaray through the Looking Glass." Burke, Schor, and Whitford 37–56.

Bibliography

Burke, Carolyn, Naomi Schor, and Margaret Whitford, eds. *Engaging with Irigaray: Feminist Philosophy and Modern European Thought.* New York: Columbia UP, 1994.

Butler, Judith. "Bodies That Matter." Burke, Schor, and Whitford 141–73.

———. *Bodies That Matter: On the Discursive Limits of "Sex."* New York: Routledge, 1993.

———. *Gender Trouble: Feminism and the Subversion of Identity.* New York: Routledge, 1990.

Butler, Judith, and Joan W. Scott, eds. *Feminists Theorize the Political.* New York: Routledge, 1992.

Calle, Mireille, ed. *Du féminin.* Sainte-Foy, QC: Le Griffon d'argile, 1992. Trans. Catherine McGann as *On the Feminine.* Atlantic Highlands, NJ: Humanities, 1996.

Cheah, Pheng, and Elizabeth Grosz. "On Being-Two." Introduction. *Irigaray and the Political Future of Sexual Difference.* Ed. Cheah and Grosz. Spec. issue of *Diacritics* 28.1 (Spring 1998): 3–18.

Chodorow, Nancy. *Feminism and Psychoanalytic Theory.* London and New Haven, CT: Yale UP, 1989.

———. *The Reproduction of Mothering: Psychoanalysis and the Sociology of Gender.* Berkeley: U of California P, 1978.

Chisholm, Dianne. "Irigaray's Hysteria." Burke, Schor, and Whitford 263–83.

Cixous, Hélène. *Dedans.* Paris: Grasset, 1969.

———. "Le rire de la Méduse." *L'Arc* (1975): 39–54. Trans. Keith Cohen and Paula Cohen as "The Laugh of the Medusa." *Signs* (Summer 1976). Rpt. Marks and de Courtivron 245–64.

Cixous, Hélène, and Catherine Clément. *La jeune née.* Coll. 10/18. Paris: Union Générale d'Editions, 1975.

Clayton, Alan J. *Nathalie Sarraute ou le tremblement de l'écriture.* Archives des lettres modernes 238. Paris: Lettres modernes, 1989.

Clément, Catherine. *Les fils de Freud sont fatigués.* Coll. Figures. Paris: Grasset, 1978.

———. *Vies et légendes de Jacques Lacan.* Coll. Figures. Paris: Grasset, 1981.

Colette. *La maison de Claudine. Œuvres* 2: 965-1090.

———. *Œuvres.* 4 vols. Ed. Claude Pichois. Paris: Gallimard, 1984–91.

———. *Sido. Œuvres* 3: 495–549.

Colette. *Le pur et l'impur. Œuvres* 3: 553–653. Trans. as *The Pure and the Impure.* Trans. Herma Briffault. Introd. Janet Flanner. New York: Farrar, 1975

Conley, Verena Andermatt. *Hélène Cixous: Writing the Feminine.* Lincoln and London: U of Nebraska P, 1984.

Copjec, Joan. *Read My Desire: Lacan against the Historicists.* Cambridge: MIT P, 1995.

———. "Sex and the Euthanasia of Reason." *Supposing the Subject.* Ed. Copjec. S ser. 1. London and New York: Verso, 1994. 16–44.

Corbin, Laurie. *The Mother Mirror: Self-Representation and the Mother-Daughter Relation in Colette, Simone de Beauvoir, and Marguerite Duras.* New York: Lang, 1996.

Cothran, Ann. "*The Pure and the Impure:* Codes and Constructs." *Women's Studies* 8 (1981): 335–57.

Cothran, Ann, and Diane Griffin Crowder. "Image Structure, Codes and Recoding in Colette's *The Pure and the Impure.*" Eisinger and McCarty 176–84.

Daly, Pierrette. "George Sand's *Lélia:* From *Belle Ténébreuse* to Annunziata." *George Sand Studies* 8.1–2 (1986/87): 4–9.

Datlof, Natalie, et al., eds. *George Sand Papers: Conference Proceedings, 1976.* New York: AMS P, 1976.

de Certeau, Michel. *Heterologies: Discourse on the Other.* Trans. Marie-Rose Logan. Minneapolis: U of Minnesota P, 1986.

DeJean, Joan. *Tender Geographies: Women and the Origins of the Novel in France.* New York: Columbia UP, 1991.

De Julio, Maryann. "Writing Aloud: A Study of Voice in Colette's *Le pur et l'impur.*" *MMLA: The Journal of the Midwest Modern Language Association* 22.1 (Spring 1989): 36–42.

De Lauretis, Teresa. "The Essence of the Triangle or, Taking the Risk of Essentialism Seriously: Feminist Theory in Italy, the U.S., and Britain." Schor and Weed 1–39.

de Man, Paul. Rev. of *L'ère du soupçon. Monde Nouveau* 12.101 (June 1956): 57—61.

Derrida, Jacques. *La carte postale de Socrate à Freud et au-delà.* Paris: Aubier-Flammarion, 1980. Trans. Alan Bass as *The Postcard: From Socrates to Freud and Beyond.* Chicago and London: U of Chicago P, 1987.

———. "Choreographies." Interview with Christie V. McDonald. McDonald 163–85. Originally published in *Diacritics* 12 (1982): 66–76.

Bibliography

———. *Epérons: Les styles de Nietzsche.* Venezia: Corbo e Fiore (and Flammarion), 1976. Trans. Barbara Harlow as *Spurs: Nietzsche's Styles.* Chicago: U of Chicago P, 1979.

———. "*Geschlecht:* Différence sexuelle, différence ontologique." Haar 419–30. Trans. as "*Geschlecht*: Sexual Difference, Ontological Difference." *Research in Phenomenology* 13 (1983): 65–83.

———. "Women in the Beehive: A Seminar with Jacques Derrida." Jardine and Smith 189–203. Originally published in *Subjects/Objects* (Spring 1984).

Deutsch, Helen. *The Psychology of Women: The Psychoanalytic Interpretation.* 2 vols. New York: Grune, 1944–45.

———. "The Significance of Masochism in the Mental Life of Women." *International Journal of Psycho-Analysis* 9 (1930): 48–60.

Dranch, Sherry. "Reading through the Veiled Text: Colette's *The Pure and The Impure.*" *Contemporary Literature* 24.2 (1983): 176–89.

Dupont, Jacques. "*Le pur et l'impur:* Notice." Colette, *Œuvres* 3: 1501–11.

Duras, Marguerite, and Xavière Gauthier. *Les parleuses.* Paris: Minuit, 1974.

Eisinger, Erica Mendelson, and Mari Ward McCarty, eds. *Colette: The Woman, the Writer.* University Park: Pennsylvania State UP, 1981.

Eisenstein, Hester, and Alice Jardine, eds. *The Future of Difference.* Boston: Hall, 1980.

Evans, Martha Noel. *Masks of Tradition: Women and the Politics of Writing in Twentieth-Century France.* Ithaca, NY: Cornell UP, 1987.

Feder, Ellen K., Mary C. Rawlinson, and Emily Zakin, eds. *Derrida and Feminism.* New York and London: Routledge, 1997.

Feldstein, Richard, Bruce Fink, and Maire Jaanus, eds. *Reading Seminars I and II: Lacan's Return to Freud.* SUNY Ser. in Psychoanalysis and Culture. Albany, NY: SUNY P, 1996.

Feldstein, Richard, and Judith Roof, eds. *Feminism and Psychoanalysis.* Ithaca, NY: Cornell UP, 1989.

Felman, Shoshana. *Jacques Lacan and the Adventure of Insight: Psychoanalysis in Contemporary Culture.* Cambridge and London: Harvard UP, 1987.

———, ed. *Literature and Psychoanalysis: The Question of Reading: Otherwise.* Yale French Studies 55–56. New Haven, CT: Yale UP, 1977.

Bibliography

Felman, Shoshana. *What Does a Woman Want? Reading and Sexual Difference.* Baltimore and London: Johns Hopkins UP, 1993.

Fink, Bruce. *A Clinical Introduction to Lacanian Psychoanalysis: Theory and Technique.* Cambridge, MA: Harvard, UP, 1997.

Finzi, Silvia Vegetti. *Mothering: Toward a New Psychoanalytic Construction.* Trans. Kathrine Jason. New York and London: Guilford, 1996.

Flax, Jane. "Psychoanalysis as Deconstruction and Myth: On Gender, Narcissism and Modernity's Discontents." Lenz and Shell 320–51.

———. "Re-membering the Selves: Is the Repressed Gendered?" *Michigan Quarterly Review* 26 (1987): 92–110.

———. *Thinking Fragments: Psychoanalysis, Feminism and Postmodernism in the Contemporary West.* Berkeley: California UP, 1990.

Flieger, Jerry Aline. *Colette and the Fantom Subject of Autobiography.* Ithaca, NY: Cornell UP, 1992.

Forrester, John. "Freud's Female Patients/Female Analysts." *Feminism and Psychoanalysis: A Critical Dictionary.* Ed. Elizabeth Wright. Cambridge, MA: Blackwell, 1992.

Fraser, Nancy. "The Uses and Abuses of French Discourse Theories for Feminist Politics." *boundary 2* 17. 2 (1990): 82–101.

Fraser, Nancy, and Sandra Bartky, eds. *Revaluing French Feminism.* Bloomington: Indiana UP, 1992.

Freud, Ernst, ed. *Letters of Sigmund Freud.* New York: Basic, 1960.

Freud, Sigmund. *The Standard Edition of the Complete Psychological Works of Sigmund Freud* [*SE*]. Ed. and trans. James Strachey, in collaboration with Anna Freud, assisted by Alix Strachey and Alan Tyson. 24 vols. London: Hogarth and the Institute of Psychoanalysis, 1953–74.

———. "Analysis Terminal and Interminable." *SE.* Vol. 23. 1937. 209–54.

———. *Beyond the Pleasure Principle. SE.* Vol. 18. 1920. 3–66.

———. "Female Sexuality." *SE.* Vol. 21. 1931. 221–43.

———. "Femininity." *SE.* Vol. 22. 1933. 112–35.

———. *Fragment of an Analysis of a Case of Hysteria. SE.* Vol. 7. 1905. 3–122.

———. "Some Psychical Consequences of the Anatomical Distinction between the Sexes." *SE.* Vol. 19. 1925. 248–58.

Bibliography

———. *Three Essays on the Theory of Sexuality* ("The Sexual Aberrations," "Infantile Sexuality," and "The Transformations of Puberty"). *SE*. Vol. 7. 1905. 125–245.

Friedan, Betty. *The Feminine Mystique*. New York: Dell, 1963.

Fuss, Diana. *Essentially Speaking: Feminism, Nature, and Difference*. New York: Routledge, 1989.

———. "Reading like a Feminist." Schor and Weed 98–115.

Gallop, Jane. *The Daughter's Seduction*. Ithaca, NY: Cornell UP, 1982.

———. "Moving Backwards or Forwards." Brennan, *Between Feminism and Psychoanalysis* 27–39.

———. *Reading Lacan*. Ithaca, NY: Cornell UP, 1985.

———. *Thinking through the Body*. New York: Columbia UP, 1988.

Garner, Shirley Nelson, Claire Kahane, and Madelon Sprengnether, eds. *The (M)other Tongue: Essays in Feminist Psychoanalytic Interpretation*. Ithaca, NY: Cornell UP, 1985.

Gilbert, Sandra M. Letter to the Editor. *Critical Inquiry* 25 (Winter 1999).

Gilligan, Carol. *In a Different Voice*. Cambridge, MA: Harvard UP, 1982.

Giry, Jacqueline. *Colette et l'art du discours intérieur*. Paris: Pensée universelle, 1980.

Goux, Jean-Joseph. "Irigaray Versus the Utopia of the Neutral Sex." Burke, Schor, and Whitford 175–90.

Grosz, Elizabeth. "The Hertero and the Homo: The Sexual Ethics of Luce Irigaray." Burke, Schor, and Whitford 335–50.

———. "Sexual Difference and the Problem of Essentialism." Schor and Weed 82–97.

Gubar, Susan. "Notations *in Medias Res*." *Critical Inquiry* 25 (Winter 1999): 380–96.

———. "What Ails Feminist Criticism?" *Critical Inquiry* 24 (Summer 1998): 87–92.

Haar, Michel, ed. *Martin Heidegger*. Paris: L'Herne, 1983.

Harris, Elaine. *L'approfondissement de la sensualité dans l'œuvre romanesque de Colette*. Paris: Nizet, 1973.

Hawkesworth, Mary. "Knowers, Knowing, Known: Feminist Theory and Claims of Truth." *Signs* 14.3 (Spring 1989): 533–57.

Heilbrun, Carolyn. Letter to the Editor. *Critical Inquiry* 25 (Winter 1999).

Bibliography

Hewitt, Leah. *Autobiographical Tightropes: Simone de Beauvoir, Nathalie Sarraute, Marguerite Duras, Monique Wittig, and Maryse Condé.* Lincoln and London: Nebraska UP, 1990.

Hirsh, Elizabeth. "Back in Analysis: How to Do Things with Irigaray." Burke, Schor, and Whitford 285–315.

Hirsch, Marianne. *The Mother-Daughter Plot: Narrative, Psychoanalysis, Feminism.* Bloomington: Indiana UP, 1989.

Hirsch, Marianne, and Evelyn Fox Keller, eds. *Conflicts in Feminism.* New York: Routledge, 1990.

Holmes, Diana. "Monstrous Women: Rachilde's Erotic Fiction." Hughes and Ince 27–48.

Horney, Karen. "The Denial of the Vagina." *International Journal of Psycho-Analysis* 14 (1933): 57–70.

——. "The Dread of Woman." *International Journal of Psycho-Analysis* 13 (1932): 348–60.

——. *Feminine Psychology.* London: Routledge, 1967.

——. "The Flight from Womanhood." *International Journal of Psycho-Analysis* 7 (1926): 324–39.

——. "On the Genesis of the Castration Complex in Women." *International Journal of Psycho-Analysis* 5 (1924): 50–65.

Huffer, Lynne. *Another Colette: The Question of Gendered Writing.* Ann Arbor: U of Michigan P, 1992.

Hughes, Alex, and Kate Ince, eds. *French Erotic Fiction: Women's Desiring Writing, 1880–1990.* Oxford and Washington, DC: Berg, 1996.

Irigaray, Luce. *Ce sexe qui n'en est pas un.* Coll. Critique. Paris: Minuit, 1977. Trans. Catherine Porter and Carolyn Burke as *This Sex Which Is Not One.* Ithaca, NY: Cornell UP, 1985.

——. *Entre Orient et Occident: De la singularité à la communauté.* Paris: Grasset, 1999.

——. *Ethique de la différence sexuelle.* Coll. Critique. Paris: Minuit, 1984. Trans. Carolyn Burke and Gillian C. Gill as *An Ethics of Sexual Difference.* Ithaca, NY: Cornell UP, 1993.

——. *Etre deux.* Paris: Grasset, 1997.

——. *The Irigaray Reader.* Oxford and Cambridge, MA: Blackwell, 1991.

——. *J'aime à toi: Esquisse d'une félicité dans l'histoire.* Paris: Grasset, 1992. Trans. Alison Martin as *I Love to You: Sketch of a Possible Felicity in History.* Ithaca, NY: Cornell UP, 1996.

Bibliography

———. "'Je—Luce Irigaray': A Meeting with Luce Irigaray." Interview conducted by Elizabeth Hirsh and Gary Olson. *Hypatia* 10.2 (Spring 1995): 92–114.

———. *L'oubli de l'air chez Martin Heidegger.* Coll. Critique. Paris: Minuit, 1983. Trans. Mary Beth Mader as *The Forgetting of Air in Martin Heidegger.* Austin: U of Texas P, 1999.

———. *Parler n'est jamais neutre.* Coll. Critique. Paris: Minuit, 1985.

———. *Sexes et parentés.* Paris: Minuit, 1987.

———. *Speculum, de l'autre femme.* Coll. Critique. Paris: Minuit, 1974. Trans. Gillian C. Gill as *Speculum of the Other Woman.* Ithaca, NY: Cornell UP, 1985.

Jardine, Alice. *Gynesis: Configurations of Woman and Modernity.* Ithaca, NY: Cornell UP, 1985.

Jardine, Alice A., and Anne M. Menke, eds. *Shifting Scenes: Interviews on Women, Writing, and Politics in Post-68 France.* New York: Columbia UP, 1991.

Jardine, Alice, and Paul Smith, eds. *Men in Feminism.* London: Methuen, 1987.

Jardine, Lisa. "The Politics of Impenetrability." Brennan, *Between Feminism and Psychoanalysis* 63–72.

Jefferson, Ann. "Nathalie Sarraute—Criticism and the 'Terrible Desire to Establish Contact.'" *Esprit Créateur* 36.2 (Summer 1996): 44–62.

Jones, Ernest. "The Early Development of Female Sexuality." *International Journal of Psycho-Analysis* 8 (1927): 459–72.

———. *The Life and Work of Sigmund Freud.* 3 vols. New York: Basic, 1955.

Kamuf, Peggy. "The Sacrifice of Sarah: Woman before Death (or: 'Apprendre, à vivre, à mourir')." Delivered as a plenary lecture at the conference "French Feminism across the Disciplines," Texas Tech U, 30 Jan. 1997.

Klein, Melanie. "Early Stages of the Oedipus Complex." *International Journal of Psycho-Analysis* 11 (1928): 167–80.

———. *The Writings of Melanie Klein.* 4 vols. London: Hogarth and the Institute of Psychoanalysis, 1985.

Kofman, Sarah. *L'énigme de la femme: La femme dans les textes de Freud.* Paris: Galilée, 1980.

Kristeva, Julia. *Au commencement était l'amour: psychanalyse et foi.* Coll. Textes du XXe Siècle. Paris: Hachette, 1985.

Bibliography

Kristeva, Julia. *Histoires d'amour.* Paris: Denoël, 1983. Trans. Leon Roudiez as *Tales of Love.* New York: Columbia UP, 1987.

———. Interview. *Women Analyze Women.* Ed. Elaine Hoffman Baruch and Lucienne J. Serrano. New York: New York UP, 1988.

———. *Pouvoirs de l'horreur: Essai sur l'abjection.* Coll. Tel Quel. Paris: Seuil, 1980. Trans. Leon S. Roudiez as *Powers of Horror: Essays on Abjection.* New York: Columbia UP, 1982.

———. *Soleil noir: Dépression et mélancholie.* Paris: Gallimard, 1987. Trans. Leon S. Roudiez as *Black Sun: Depression and Melancholia.* New York: Columbia UP, 1989.

Lacan, Jacques. *Ecrits.* Paris: Seuil, 1966. Partially trans. Alan Sheridan as *Ecrits, a Selection.* New York and London: Norton, 1977.

———. "On Freud's 'Trieb' and the Psychoanalyst's Desire." Trans. Bruce Fink. Feldstein, Fink, and Jaanus 417–21.

———. *Le séminaire de Jacques Lacan, Livre II, "Le moi dans la théorie de Freud et dans la technique de la psychanalyse."* Paris: Seuil, 1978.

———. *Le séminaire de Jacques Lacan, Livre XI, "Les quatre concepts fondamentaux de la psychanalyse."* Paris: Seuil, 1973.

———. *Le séminaire de Jacques Lacan, Livre XX, "Encore."* Paris: Seuil, 1975. Trans. Bruce Fink as *The Seminar of Jacques Lacan, Book XX: Encore.* New York: Norton, 1998.

———. "La signification du phallus." Lacan, *Ecrits* 685–95. Trans. Alan Sheridan as "The Signification of the Phallus." *Ecrits, a Selection.* New York and London: Norton, 1977. 281–91.

Lampl-de Groot, Jeanne. "The Evolution of the Oedipus Complex in Women." *International Journal of Psycho-Analysis* 9 (1928): 332–45.

———. "Problems of Femininity in Women." *Psychoanalytic Quarterly* 12 (1933): 489–518.

Leland, Dorothy. "Lacanian Psychoanalysis and French Feminism: Toward an Adequate Political Psychology." *Hypatia* 3.3 (1989): 81–103.

Lenz, Gunter H., and Kurt L. Shell. *Crisis of Modernity: Recent Critical Theories of Culture and Society in the United States and West Germany.* Boulder, CO: Westview, 1986.

Lyotard, Jean-François. "One of the Things at Stake in Women's Struggles." *Sub-Stance* 20 (1978): 9–17.

MacCallum-Schwartz, Lucy. "Sensibilité et sensualité: Rapports sexuels dans les premiers romans de George Sand (1831–43)." *Vierne* 171–77.

Bibliography

McDonald, Christie, ed. *The Ear of the Other: Otobiography, Transference, Translation.* Lincoln and London: Nebraska UP, 1988.

Marks, Elaine. *Colette.* New Brunswick, NJ: Rutgers UP, 1960.

Marks, Elaine, and Isabelle de Courtivron, eds. *New French Feminisms: An Anthology.* New York: Schocken, 1981.

Meyers, Diana Tietjens. *Subjection and Subjectivity: Psychoanalytic Feminism and Moral Philosophy.* Thinking Gender 17. New York and London: Routledge, 1994.

―――. "The Subversion of Women's Agency in Psychoanalytic Feminism: Chodorow, Flax, Kristeva." Fraser and Bartky 136–61.

Miller, Jacques-Alain. "Commentary on Lacan's Text." Trans. Bruce Fink. Feldstein, Fink, and Jaanus 422–27.

―――. "An Introduction to Seminars I and II: Lacan's Orientation Prior to 1953." Feldstein, Fink, and Jaanus 15–25.

Miller, Nancy K. "The Anamnesis of a Female 'I': In the Margins of Self-Portrayal." Eisenger and McCarty 164–75.

―――, ed. *The Poetics of Gender.* New York: Columbia UP, 1986.

―――. "Writing from the Pavilion: George Sand and the Novel of Female Pastoral." *Subject to Change: Reading Feminist Writing.* Ed. Miller. New York: Columbia UP, 1988.

Millett, Kate. *Sexual Politics.* New York: Avon, 1969.

Minogue, Valérie. *Nathalie Sarraute and the War of the Words: A Study of Five Novels.* Edinburgh: Edinburgh UP, 1981.

Minogue, Valérie, and Sabine Raffy, eds. *Autour de Nathalie Sarraute: Actes du colloque international de Cerisy-la-Salle des 9 au 19 juillet 1989.* Paris: Diffusion les Belles Lettres, 1995.

Mitchell, Juliet. "Looking at the Notion of 'On Being Empty of Oneself.'" Lecture delivered at Cornell U, March, 1998.

―――. *Psychoanalysis and Feminism.* New York: Random, 1974.

―――. *Women, the Longest Revolution: On Feminism, Literature and Psychoanalysis.* New York: Pantheon, 1984.

Mitchell, Juliet, and Jacqueline Rose, eds. *Feminine Sexuality: Jacques Lacan and the Ecole Freudienne.* New York and London: Norton, 1982.

Mitchell, Juliet, and Michael Parsons, eds. *Before I Was I: Psychoanalysis and the Imagination.* By Enid Balint. New York and London: Guilford, 1993.

Moi, Toril. *Sexual/Textual Politics: Feminist Literary Theory.* London and New York: Routledge, 1985.

Bibliography

Moi, Toril. *Simone de Beauvoir: The Making of an Intellectual Woman.* Oxford and Cambridge, MA: Blackwell, 1994.

Mozet, Nicole. *George Sand: Ecrivain des romans.* Saint-Cyr-sur-Loire: Pirot, 1997.

Naginski, Isabelle Hoog. *George Sand: Writing for Her Life.* New Brunswick: Rutgers UP, 1991.

Nancy, Jean-Luc, and Philippe Lacoue-Labarthe. *Le titre de la lettre.* Paris: Galilée, 1973.

Newman, Anthony. "Le sentiment de culpabilité: Domaine tropismique par excellence?" *Esprit Créateur* 36.2 (Summer 1996): 89–102.

Penrod, Lynn Kettler. "Héléne Cixous: Lectures initiatiques, lectures centrifuges." Calle, *Du féminin* 83–95. Trans. Catherine McGann as "Hélène Cixous: Initiatory Readings, Centrifugal Readings." Calle, *On the Feminine* 57–65.

Phillips, John. *Nathalie Sarraute: Metaphor, Fairy-tale and the Feminine of the Text.* New York: Lang, 1994.

Rabine, Leslie Wahl. "Essentialism and Its Contexts: Saint-Simonian and Poststructuralist Feminists." *differences: A Journal of Feminist Cultural Studies* 1.2 (1988): 105–23. (This article appears also in Schor and Weed 130–50.)

Rachilde. *Monsieur Vénus.* Paris: Flammarion, 1977.

Ragland, Ellie. "Dora and the Name-of-the-Father: The Structure of Hysteria." Barr and Feldstein 208–40.

———. *Essays on the Pleasures of Death: From Freud to Lacan.* New York and London: Routledge, 1995.

———. *Jacques Lacan and the Philosophy of Psychoanalysis.* Chicago: U of Chicago P, 1985.

———. "Seeking the Third Term: Desire, the Phallus and the Materiality of Language." Feldstein and Roof 40–64.

Ramsay, Raylene L. *The French New Autobiographies: Sarraute, Duras, and Robbe-Grillet.* Gainesville: UP of Florida, 1996.

———. "The Unself-Loving Woman in Nathalie Sarraute's *Tu ne t'aimes pas.*" *French Review* 67.5 (1994): 793–804.

Ricardou, Jean, and Françoise Rossum-Guyon, eds. *Nouveau roman: Hier, aujourd'hui.* Paris: Union Générale d'Editions, 1972.

Rochefort, Christiane. "Are Women Writers Still Monsters?" Marks and de Courtivron 183–86.

Rose, Jacqueline. *Sexuality in the Field of Vision.* London: Verso, 1986.

Bibliography

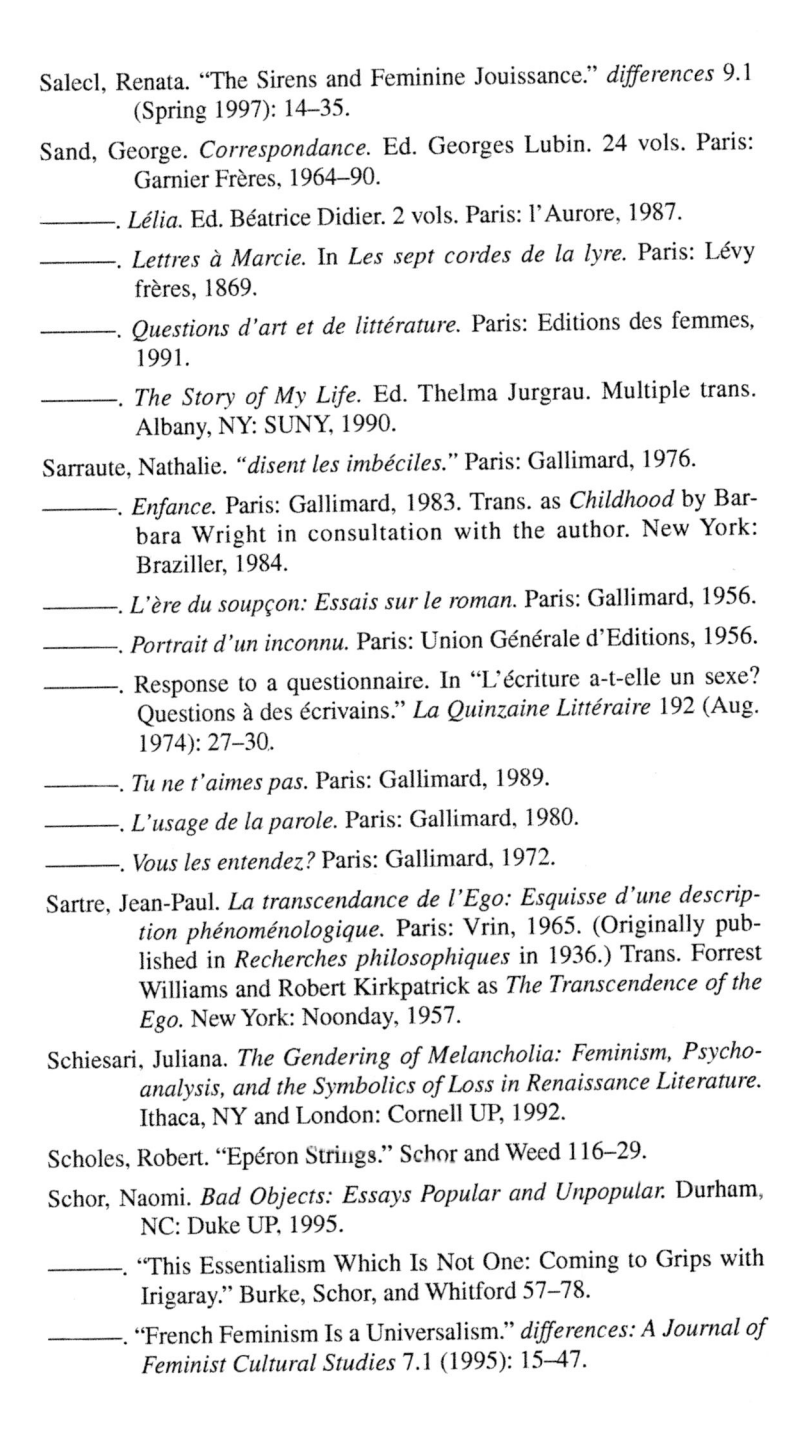

Salecl, Renata. "The Sirens and Feminine Jouissance." *differences* 9.1 (Spring 1997): 14–35.

Sand, George. *Correspondance*. Ed. Georges Lubin. 24 vols. Paris: Garnier Frères, 1964–90.

———. *Lélia*. Ed. Béatrice Didier. 2 vols. Paris: l'Aurore, 1987.

———. *Lettres à Marcie*. In *Les sept cordes de la lyre*. Paris: Lévy frères, 1869.

———. *Questions d'art et de littérature*. Paris: Editions des femmes, 1991.

———. *The Story of My Life*. Ed. Thelma Jurgrau. Multiple trans. Albany, NY: SUNY, 1990.

Sarraute, Nathalie. *"disent les imbéciles."* Paris: Gallimard, 1976.

———. *Enfance*. Paris: Gallimard, 1983. Trans. as *Childhood* by Barbara Wright in consultation with the author. New York: Braziller, 1984.

———. *L'ère du soupçon: Essais sur le roman*. Paris: Gallimard, 1956.

———. *Portrait d'un inconnu*. Paris: Union Générale d'Editions, 1956.

———. Response to a questionnaire. In "L'écriture a-t-elle un sexe? Questions à des écrivains." *La Quinzaine Littéraire* 192 (Aug. 1974): 27–30.

———. *Tu ne t'aimes pas*. Paris: Gallimard, 1989.

———. *L'usage de la parole*. Paris: Gallimard, 1980.

———. *Vous les entendez?* Paris: Gallimard, 1972.

Sartre, Jean-Paul. *La transcendance de l'Ego: Esquisse d'une description phénoménologique*. Paris: Vrin, 1965. (Originally published in *Recherches philosophiques* in 1936.) Trans. Forrest Williams and Robert Kirkpatrick as *The Transcendence of the Ego*. New York: Noonday, 1957.

Schiesari, Juliana. *The Gendering of Melancholia: Feminism, Psychoanalysis, and the Symbolics of Loss in Renaissance Literature*. Ithaca, NY and London: Cornell UP, 1992.

Scholes, Robert. "Epéron Strings." Schor and Weed 116–29.

Schor, Naomi. *Bad Objects: Essays Popular and Unpopular*. Durham, NC: Duke UP, 1995.

———. "This Essentialism Which Is Not One: Coming to Grips with Irigaray." Burke, Schor, and Whitford 57–78.

———. "French Feminism Is a Universalism." *differences: A Journal of Feminist Cultural Studies* 7.1 (1995): 15–47.

Bibliography

Schor, Naomi. *George Sand and Idealism*. New York: Columbia UP, 1993.

———. "*Lélia* and the Failures of Allegory." *Esprit Créateur* 29.3 (1989): 76–83.

Schor, Naomi, and Elizabeth Weed, eds. *The Essential Difference*. Books from differences ser. Bloomington: Indiana UP, 1994.

Scott, Joan. "'Experience.'" Butler and Scott 22–40.

Sellers, Susan, ed. *Writing Differences: Readings from the Seminar of Hélène Cixous*. New York: St. Martin's, 1988.

Sivert, Eileen Boyd. "Lélia and Feminism." *Yale French Studies* 62 (1981): 45–66.

Smith, Joseph Carman, and Carla J. Ferstman. *The Castration of Oedipus: Feminism, Psychoanalysis, and the Will to Power*. New York: New York UP, 1996.

Soderberg, Steven. *Sex, Lies, and Videotape*. Miramax Pictures, 1990.

Spivak, Gayatri. "Feminism and Deconstruction, Again." Brennan, *Between Feminism and Psychoanalysis* 206–23.

Sprengnether, Madelon. *The Spectral Mother: Freud, Feminism, and Psychoanalysis*. Ithaca, NY: Cornell UP, 1990.

Stansell, Christine. "Response." *International Labor and Working Class History* 31 (Spring 1987): 24–29.

Stanton, Domna C. "Difference on Trial: A Critique of the Maternal Metaphor in Cixous, Irigaray, and Kristeva." N. K. Miller, *Poetics* 157–82.

Suleiman, Susan Rubin. "Writing and Motherhood." Garner, Kahane, and Sprengnether 352–57.

Tournier, Michel. "Colette ou le premier couvert." *Le vol du vampire: Notes de lecture*. Paris: Mercure de France, 1981. 239–51.

———. *Le coq de cruyère*. Paris: Gallimard, 1978.

van Rossum-Guyon, Françoise. "Puissances du roman: George Sand." *Romantisme* 24 (1994): 79–92.

Vareille, Kristina Wingard. *Socialité, sexualité et les impasses de l'histoire: L'évolution de la thématique sandienne d' "Indiana" (1832) à "Mauprat" (1837)*. Uppsala, Sweden: Acta Universitatis Upsaliensis, 1987.

Vierne, Simone, ed. *George Sand: Colloque de Cerisy*. Paris: SEDES, 1983.

Waller, Margaret. "Toward a Feminist Mal du Siècle: Sand's *Lélia*." *The Male Malady: Fictions of Impotence in the French Romantic Novel*. Ed. Waller. New Brunswick, NJ: Rutgers UP, 1993.

Bibliography

Weed, Elizabeth. "The Question of Style." Burke, Schor, and Whitford 79–109.

Whitford, Margaret. "Irigaray, Utopia, and the Death Drive." Burke, Schor, and Whitford 379–400.

———, ed. *The Irigaray Reader.* Oxford and Cambridge, MA: Blackwell, 1991.

Wiegman, Robyn. "What Ails Feminist Criticism? A Second Opinion." *Critical Inquiry* 25 (Winter 1999): 362–79.

Wittig, Monique. "Avatars." *Nathalie Sarraute ou le texte du for intérieur.* Spec. issue of *Esprit Créateur* 36.2 (Summer 1996): 109–16.

———. "Le déambulatoire: Entretien avec Nathalie Sarraute." *Nathalie Sarraute ou le texte du for intérieur.* Spec. issue of *Esprit Créateur* 36.2 (Summer 1996): 3–8.

———. *The Straight Mind and Other Essays.* Boston: Beacon, 1992.

Wollheim, Richard. "Psychoanalysis and Feminism." *New Left Review* 93 (1975): 61–69.

Wollstonecraft, Mary. *A Vindication of the Rights of Woman.* New York and London: Penguin, 1992.

Woolf, Virginia. *A Room of One's Own.* London: Harcourt, 1929.

Wright, Elizabeth, ed. *Feminism and Psychoanalysis: A Critical Dictionary.* Oxford: Blackwell, 1992.

———. "Introduction." Wright, *Feminism and Psychoanalysis* xiii–xix.

Young-Bruehl, Elizabeth, ed. *Freud on Women: A Reader.* New York: Norton, 1990.

Žižek, Slavoj. *Tarrying with the Negative: Kant, Hegel, and the Critique of Ideology.* Durham, NC: Duke UP, 1993.

Index

Age of Suspicion, The (Sarraute).
See Sarraute, Nathalie:
works: *ère du soupçon, L'*
"Analysis Terminable and
Interminable" (Freud).
See under Freud,
Sigmund: works
Antigone (Sophocles), 75, 114,
170–72
Aristotle, 66–69, 202nn18 and 20

Babcock, Arthur, 133–34, 208n21
Balint, Enid, 112–14, 118
Beauvoir, Simone de, *xiii*, 10,
126–27, 197–98Intro n3
Berger, Anne, 202n19
Between East and West (Irigaray).
See Irigaray, Luce:
works: *Entre Orient et
Occident*
Bible, the, 69–70
Bonaparte, Marie, 87, 198n6,
203n1
Boothby, Richard, 31, 200n21
Brée, Germaine, 137, 206n10
Brennan, Teresa, 1, 6–7, 89,
198n8, 203n22
Butler, Judith, 199n11, 206n9

Ce sexe qui n'en est pas un
(Irigaray). See under
Irigaray, Luce: works
Ces plaisirs . . . (Colette). See
Colette: works: *pur et
l'impur, Le*
Cheah, Pheng, and Elizabeth
Grosz, 147, 158
Childhood (Sarraute). See
Sarraute, Nathalie:
works: *Enfance*
Cixous, Hélène, *xiii–xiv*, 52, 90,
125, 127, 158, 205n20,
205n2

Colette [pseud. for Sidonie
Gabrielle Colette], 30,
86, 205n2
and androgyny (bisexuality,
hermaphrodism), 91–92,
121–25
compared with Sand, 91, 99
and maternity, 97–98, 101–25
and mortality, 112–14,
119–25
and narrative voice, 90–91,
104, 118–19, 123–25
on sexual identity, 91–92
and sexual pleasure, 102, 104–
06, 110–12, 115–22
works
maison de Claudine, La,
204nn11 and 15
naissance du jour, La,
204n15
pur et l'impur, Le, 90–125,
164, 203n6
Sido, 204n15
*Consuelo, La Comtesse de
Rudolstadt* (Sand). See
under Sand, George:
works
*Consuelo, The Countess of
Rudolstadt* (Sand). See
Sand, George: works:
*Consuelo, La Comtesse
de Rudolstadt*
Copjec, Joan, 12, 16–20, 199n12

death drive, 31–32, 123–25, 164
de Man, Paul, 135
Derrida, Jacques, 153, 167,
208n24
Dupin, Amandine Aurore Lucie,
baronne Dudevant. See
Sand, George
Duras, Marguerite, 205n2
and Xavière Gauthier, 58–59

227

Index

Huffer, Lynne, 97–99, 204nn12 and 13

I Love to You (Irigaray). *See* Irigaray, Luce: *works: J'aime à toi*
Irigaray, Luce, 93, 126, 135, 205n5, 208n23
and "hom(m)osexuality," 71–78
and multiplicity as opposed to "being two," 147–48, 158–62, 166
and psychoanalysis, 3, 6, 10, 13–16, 31
and "taking the negative upon ourselves," 12, 20–21, 29–30, 75, 114–15
works
  Ce sexe qui n'en est pas un, 2, 6, 8, 9, 13, 71, 79–80
  Entre Orient et Occident, 205n4
  Ethique de la différence sexuelle, 20–21, 27, 73–75, 127, 200n20, 204n17, 209n3
  J'aime à toi, 21, 30, 31, 75, 137, 138–39, 151, 158–60, 168–71, 201n5, 207n15, 209n4
  oubli de l'air chez Martin Heidegger, L', 198n9
  Sexes et parentés, 119–20
  Speculum de l'autre femme, 2, 8, 10, 11, 83–85, 197Intro n2, 202n21, 205n1

J'aime à toi (Irigaray). *See under* Irigaray, Luce: *works*
jouissance, 2, 57–58, 86, 120–25
  and desire, 92–97
  feminine, 22–32, 95–96, 123–25, 165–66
  and knowledge, 19, 28–29
  and love, 11–30
  and pleasure, 92–97

Kamuf, Peggy, 31

Lacan, Jacques, 2, 37, 54, 75, 79, 80, 86, 139
and the father-figure as impostor, 27
and graph of sexual difference, 17
on love, 23–30
and the paternal metaphor, 47–50
and the subject of the unconscious, 92–95, 204n9
and "There is no Woman ... ," 16–20, 164
works
  Ecrits, 12–15, 27, 93–94, 199n14, 202nn11 and 14
  "On Freud's 'Trieb,'" 94–95
  séminaire, Livre II, "Le moi dans la théorie de Freud et dans la technique de la psychanalyse," Le, 200n21
  séminaire, Livre XI, "Les quatre concepts fondamentaux de la psychanalyse," Le, 199–200n19
  séminaire, Livre XX, "Encore," Le, 12, 16–30, 199n13
Lamennais, Félicité Robert de (l'Abbé), 34, 35, 200n4
Lélia (Sand). *See under* Sand, George: *works*
lesbianism, 62–63, 71–77
Letters to Marcie (Sand). *See* Sand, George: *works: Lettres à Marcie*
Lettres à Marcie (Sand). *See under* Sand, George: *works*

229

Index

Ecrits (Lacan). *See under* Lacan, Jacques: *works*
egalitarianism (equality), 89, 153, 163, 166–68, 206n9
 as non-emancipatory, 10–11, 198n10
Enfance (Sarraute). *See under* Sarraute, Nathalie: *works*
Entre Orient et Occident (Irigaray). *See under* Irigaray, Luce: *works*
ère du soupçon, L' (Sarraute). *See under* Sarraute, Nathalie: *works*
Ethics of Sexual Difference, An (Irigaray). *See* Irigaray, Luce: *works: Ethique de la différence sexuelle*
Ethique de la différence sexuelle (Irigaray). *See under* Irigaray, Luce: *works*
experience (as prediscursive or immediate)
 and representation, 129–37, 143–47, 152, 205n6, 206n9

Felman, Shoshana, ix, x, 89–90, 99–100, 197Pref n1, 203n2
"Female Sexuality" (Freud). *See under* Freud, Sigmund: *works*
femininity (the feminine), 104–25
 "the great debate" about, 198n6
 as inscribed in writing, 125, 205n2
 and masquerade, 13
 as pathological, 15, 53, 89, 106–25
 "riddle" of, 6–7, 87–90, 198n8
"Femininity" (Freud). *See under* Freud, Sigmund: *works*
Ferstman, Carla J., and J. C. Smith, 1

Fink, Bruce, 45–49, 199n13
Forgetting of Air in Martin Heidegger, The (Irigaray). *See* Irigaray, Luce: *works: oubli de l'air chez Martin Heidegger, L'*
Fragment of an Analysis of a Case of Hysteria (Freud). *See under* Freud, Sigmund
Freud, Sigmund, 25, 26, 87–89, 92–93, 100, 123, 171, 209n4
 alleged misogyny of, 3–7
 and exposure of cultural norms, 4–5
 on "housewife psychosis," 107–08, 118
 and "What does a woman want?" 87–90, 97, 138, 203n2
 works
  "Analysis Terminable and Interminable," 5–6, 198n7
  "Female Sexuality," 4, 198n6, 203n3
  "Femininity," 11, 87–88, 122, 198n6, 205n19
  Fragment of an Analysis of a Case of Hysteria (the Dora Case), 107–08
  "Some Psychical Consequences of the Anatomical Distinction between the Sexes," 198n6

Gauthier, Xavière, and Marguerite Duras, 58–59
Grosz, Elizabeth, 9–10,
 and Pheng Cheah, 147, 158

Heidegger, Martin
 and Irigaray, 198n9
Hewitt, Leah, 135, 206n12, 207n16, 208n23

228

Index

love
    impossibility of, 52, 55, 56, 60–62, 86
    and jouissance, 2, 11–30
    and the novel, 203n5
    as two becoming one, 23–30, 139, 156
Lyotard, Jean-François, 126–27

maison de Claudine, La (Colette). See *under* Colette: *works*
Marks, Elaine, 97, 100–01, 204nn12 and 13 and 15
masculinity, 17–18, 25, 209n4
    as imposture, 15, 86
maternity, 64–65, 97–98, 101–25, 145–46, 162, 165
Meyers, Diana Tietjens, 3–6
Miller, Jacques-Alain, 95, 204n9
Mitchell, Juliet, 2–3, 7–9, 113–14, 121
Moi, Toril, 14, 197Intro n3, 199nn15 and 16
My Mother's House (Colette). See Colette: *works: maison de Claudine, La*

Naginski, Isabelle Hoog, 33, 59, 200n2, 202n19
naissance du jour, La (Colette). See *under* Colette: *works*

"On Freud's 'Trieb'" (Lacan). See *under* Lacan, Jacques: *works*
oubli de l'air chez Martin Heidegger, L' (Irigaray). See *under* Irigaray, Luce: *works*

penis envy, 3–4, 7, 88
phallus (phallic function), 12–20
psychoanalytic feminism, 31–32, 89–90, 99–100, 163–72

definition of, 1–7
    feminism as hostile to psychoanalysis, 3–8, 198n5, 199n18
    feminism and psychoanalysis as mutually necessary, 1–3, 49–50
    history of, 1–10
    as turning psychoanalysis in on itself, 9
Pure and the Impure, The (Colette). See Colette: *works: pur et l'impur, Le*
pur et l'impur, Le (Colette). See *under* Colette: *works*

Ramsay, Raylene, 149–50, 208nn19 and 20

Saint-Simonism, 37–39, 44–46, 49–50, 201n6
    compared with contemporary feminisms, 45–46
Salecl, Renata, 92–94
Sand, George [pseud. for Amandine Aurore Lucie Dupin, baronne Dudevant]
    on desire, 54–55, 57–58, 64, 84–86, 167
    on the divine, 55, 65–66, 74, 78–86
    and female sexuality, 40, 52, 61–66
    feminist thinking compared with Irigaray's, 36, 43–45, 52–54, 78–80, 83–84
    on marriage and divorce, 33, 34, 37–39, 42–48, 200–01n4
    and narrative form, 59–60
    on nonexistence of male-female relationship, 61, 74, 79–80
    on woman as artist, 39–41

Index

on women in the public
  sphere, 33, 37–44,
  201nn8 and 9
on women as slaves, 52, 60–
  61, 64, 66–70
works
  *Consuelo, La Comtesse de
    Rudolstadt,* 39
  Correspondance, 41, 42–
    43, 82, 200n1, 201n7
  Lélia, ix, 33, 51–86, 131,
    164, 167, 202nn13 and
    19
  Lettres à Marcie, 33–51,
    164
Sarraute, Nathalie [pseud. for
  Natasha Tcherniak]
  and author's relation to work,
    150–51, 208n20
  and the *for intérieur,* 133, 137,
    206n10
  and form, 132, 135
  and "happiness," 140–45
  and language, 133–34, 138,
    143–47, 159–62
  and the neutral, 32, 126, 128,
    135, 165
  and sexual difference,
    rejection of, 126, 128,
    149–53
  and the subject, plasticity
    (plurality) of, 127–29,
    135–37, 139–42, 153–
    62, 166
  works
    Enfance, 143, 149
    ère du soupçon, L', 135
    Tropismes, 126
    Tu ne t'aimes pas, 126–62
Schor, Naomi, 33, 200n2, 205n3,
  207n18, 208n22
  on Sand and frustration, 52
  on Sand and iconoclasm, 59
  on Sand and the invisible
    woman, 36

on Sand and the maternal ideal
  of love, 202n19
on Sand and sexual difference,
  71, 200n3
on Sand's idealism, 36, 81,
  202n17
on Sarraute and experience,
  133, 206n7
on Sarraute and the rejection
  of sexual difference,
  128–30, 149, 161,
  202n12
Scott, Joan, 130–32, 152, 205n6,
  206nn7–9
*séminaire, Livre II, "Le moi dans
  la théorie de Freud et
  dans la technique de la
  psychanalyse," Le*
  (Lacan). *See under*
  Lacan, Jacques: *works*
*séminaire, Livre XI, "Les quatre
  concepts fondamentaux
  de la psychanalyse," Le*
  (Lacan). *See under*
  Lacan, Jacques: *works*
séminaire, Livre XX, "Encore," Le
  (Lacan). *See under*
  Lacan, Jacques: *works*

Sexes and Genealogies (Irigaray).
  See Irigaray, Luce:
  works: Sexes et parentés
Sexes et parentés (Irigaray). *See
  under* Irigaray, Luce:
  works
sexual difference
  and androgyny, 127
  and Being, 10–11, 18–19, 58,
    158–59
  and ethics, 14–16, 71–81
  and the failure of reason, 17
  Lacan's account of, 16–21
  and misrecognition, 13–16, 54,
    202n14
  as opposed to equality, 10–11, 89

231

Index

sexual difference *(continued)*
  writing (literature) and,
    xi–xiv
Sido (Colette). *See under* Colette:
    works
Smith, J. C., and Carla J.
  Ferstman, 1
"Some Psychical Consequences
  of the Anatomical
  Distinction between the
  Sexes" (Freud). *See
  under* Freud, Sigmund:
  works
Speculum de l'autre femme
  (Irigaray). *See under*
  Irigaray, Luce: *works*
Speculum of the Other Woman
  (Irigaray). *See* Irigaray,
  Luce: *works: Speculum
  de l'autre femme*
Spivak, Gayatri, 152–53

Tcherniak, Natasha. *See* Sarraute,
  Nathalie
This Sex Which Is Not One
  (Irigaray). *See* Irigaray,
  Luce: *works: Ce sexe
  qui n'en est pas un*

Tournier, Michel, 55–56, 204n12
Tropismes (Sarraute). *See under*
  Sarraute, Nathalie:
  works
Tropisms (Sarraute). *See* Sarraute,
  Nathalie: *works:
  Tropismes*

Weed, Elizabeth, 21, 26
Wittig, Monique, *x–xi,* 45, 68,
  71–78, 80, 132–33, 148,
  202n18, 207n17
Wollstonecraft, Mary, 202n16
women
  as slaves, 52, 60–61, 64,
    66–70
women's studies, 166–72, 209n1
Woolf, Virginia, 126–27, 131,
  208n23
Wright, Elizabeth, 2, 198n4

You Don't Love Yourself (Sarraute).
  See Sarraute, Nathalie:
  works: Tu ne t'aimes pas

Žižek, Slavoj, 17, 199n17